The Power of Virtual Reality Cinema for Healthcare Training

The Power of Virtual Reality Cinema for Healthcare Training

A Collaborative Guide for Medical Experts and Media Professionals

Edited by

John Bowditch and Eric R. Williams
with illustrations by Adonis Durado
and Foreword by Bob Fine

Routledge
Taylor & Francis Group

A PRODUCTIVITY PRESS BOOK

First published 2022
by Routledge
600 Broken Sound Parkway #300, Boca Raton FL, 33487

and by Routledge
2 Park Square, Milton Park, Abingdon, Oxon, OX14 4RN

Routledge is an imprint of the Taylor & Francis Group, an informa business

Library of Congress Cataloging-in-Publication Data
A catalog record for this title has been requested

ISBN: 978-0-367-76823-2 (hbk)
ISBN: 978-0-367-76822-5 (pbk)
ISBN: 978-1-003-16868-3 (ebk)

DOI: 10.4324/9781003168683

Typeset in Garamond
by KnowledgeWorks Global Ltd.

I would like to dedicate this book to my wife and best friend, Catherine. From the very beginning, she has supported the GRID Lab through the highs and lows. Why she loves an easily distracted, stoic, *Star Wars* geek will be one of the last great mysteries of the universe. Thank you for being an indefatigable mother to Spud and Luke! – John

Contents

SECTION III

SECTION IV

List of Figures and Photographs

Illustrations

All illustrations created by Adonis Durado.

Photographs

Foreword

When John and Eric asked me to write the foreword for this groundbreaking collaborative guide, I was of course quite flattered. But very honestly, when I first met them and their team back in early 2017, at only our second annual conference at Harvard Medical School, I didn't have the appreciation then for the early work they were presenting and the foundations that they were building for the medical and media production communities.

An important question you should be asking on this opening page is why is this book even important or necessary?

First, it's key to understand today that we're seeing the convergence of a number of new technologies that will come into maturity all or about at the same time during this current decade of 2020–2030, of which were only in year two. Besides immersive, there's the advent of 5G and the Internet of Things. All of these platforms will be dependent on each other both for effective performance, but also for ubiquity. It's going to be a decade of rapid change and impact, and I think when we look back at the year 2020 from 2030, much of our everyday life will look radically different (and not just because of COVID-19). But it's likely to be 2025 at the earliest before we really see the impact of this convergence on daily living, as the deployment and usage of 5G is going to take longer than some expect.

Further, the next ten years, specifically for healthcare and virtual reality contain a few important points that the reader should understand. The healthcare industry is notoriously slow to change and adapt to new technology, no matter how shiny or innovative the technology may be. We've seen this time and time again for the last thirty years. Telemedicine had been a buzzword for decades, and it's only now being considered and used as a viable platform since 2020 (because of COVID-19). So, we're only now *finally* seeing the very early dissemination of healthcare through our smartphones, tablets, PCs, and virtual reality headsets, but we're still in the infancy stage.

And that's why this book is important. Reading it could make the difference between a team of healthcare and media professionals building a new teaching module in virtual reality in three months, instead of three years. The contributing practitioners throughout the book have spent countless hours in the last five years figuring out just how to build this module efficiently and effectively. They've gone through all the various scenarios and permutations of filming a particular scene this way, that way, and the other way around. I will not be surprised when you find a nugget of information in one of these chapters that makes you go: "Oh! That's how you do that!" But you're not going to just find one nugget, you're going to find many.

Knowledge in and of itself is great. But collected and organized knowledge is really powerful, and that's what Eric and John have done with this book in collaboration with their contributors.

They're providing you a best of recipe book for building and distributing informational healthcare knowledge that can be absorbed and learned in a very efficient manner (through virtual reality). Very soon, you'll be referring to this as your favorite recipe book.

Robert Fine
Founder and Executive Director
IVRHA (International Virtual Reality and Healthcare Association)

Acknowledgments

The editors wish to thank the numerous Ohio University scholars, video specialists, audio producers, cinematographers, editors, developers, digital artists, graphic designers, writers, actors, set designers, lighters, grips, animators, technicians, nurses, physicians, and healthcare professionals, whose efforts made this book possible.

This book reflects the work of over 250 faculty, students, and staff from the past five years (as of this writing). The accumulation of projects completed has created one of the most expansive, multidisciplinary initiatives in our university's extensive history.

To the Game Research and Immersive Design (GRID) Lab's staff, we thank you for your long hours and even tempers. Matt Love, Anthony Zoccola, Jeff Kuhn, and Carrie Love are immeasurably gifted individuals who are always willing to take a risk.

We salute our faculty and staff colleagues in the J. Warren McClure School of Emerging Communication Technologies. They have supported our cine-VR initiative from its earliest experiments. Thanks, Julio Arauz, Charles "Chip" Linscott, Hans Kruse, Brandon Saunders, Doug Bowie, and Barb Moran.

To Scott Titsworth, our dean of the Scripps College Communication, thank you for your leadership, guidance, and overall support of the troublemaker factory known as the GRID Lab. You continue to push us when we feel like a square peg in a round hole, and we will always be grateful for that. We apologize for any headaches or indigestion we've caused.

Thanks to Roxanne Male'-Brune, Joe Shields, and Mike Boyle, whose belief in us funded the very foundation of what made this book possible. None of these projects would have gotten off the ground without you.

Without our collaborators, our productions would continue to be over-the-top Hollywood-esque attempts at faking healthcare expertise. A heartfelt thank you to Liz Beverly from the Heritage College of Osteopathic Medicine and Dean John McCarthy, Debby Henderson, Sherleena Buchman, Char Miller, Kerri Shaw, Mel Brandau, and Judi Rioch, from the College of Health and Science Professionals. Thanks to our favorite bootstrappers, Dean Patti McSteen of the Division of Student Affairs and detective Rick Sargent of the Ohio University Police Department. Cheers to Merri Biechler and Shelley Delaney from our Theater Department and Adonis Durado, Becky Sell, and Juan Thomassie from our School of Visual Communication.

We are grateful for our partners at the University of California San Francisco's Better Lab: Amanda Sammann and Devika Patel, as well as Petra Williams at Rasmussen University and the work she did with us while she was at Northern Arizona University.

The GRID Lab would not exist without the hundreds of undergraduate and graduate student employees we've had the pleasure of working with. You truly make the GRID Lab a place of boundless energy and creativity. Many of these students have gone on to work at notable companies and universities, shaping the future of VR and media production.

Note on a Key Contributor

The book's illustrator, Adonis Durado, spent a significant part of his career working as a visual journalist in the Middle East. He also operates as a newspaper design consultant with clients in Africa, Asia, and Europe. His work received highest honors from the Society for News Design, Society of Publication Designers, Type Directors Club, Society of Illustrators, Malofiej Infographics Awards, and WAN-IFRA Media Awards. Adonis is an assistant professor in the Scripps College of Communication at Ohio University.

Editor Biographies

John Bowditch is an award-winning game and virtual reality developer. He is the director and co-founder of Ohio University's Game Research and Immersive Design (GRID) Lab and is an Associate Professor in the J. Warren McClure School of Emerging Communication Technologies, teaching VR and game development and themed immersive experiences courses. John is the GRID Lab's lead developer and has led research projects funded by the United States Department of Education, Department of Energy, Department of Labor, Department of Homeland Security, National Institutes of Health, and the Ohio Colleges of Medicine Resource Center.

Eric R. Williams, co-creator of the Immersive Media Initiative at Ohio University, is a professor in the McClure School of Emerging Communication Technologies. Williams recently co-authored the book *Virtual Reality Cinema: Narrative Tips and Techniques.* His cine-VR projects have screened internationally in film festivals and academic conferences, and his innovative approach to this new medium has been highlighted in the books *Storytelling for Virtual Reality* and *What is Virtual Reality? Exclusive Interviews with Leaders of the VR Industry.* Since 2016, Williams has played a central role in over two dozen funded projects at the GRID Lab, where he oversees the cine-VR department.

Author Biographies

Elizabeth A. Beverly, PhD, is an Associate Professor in the Department of Primary Care at the Ohio University Heritage College of Osteopathic Medicine and recipient of the Heritage Faculty Endowed Fellowship in Behavioral Diabetes, Osteopathic Heritage Foundation Ralph S. Licklider, D.O., Research Endowment. Dr. Beverly graduated from The Pennsylvania State University with a PhD in Biobehavioral Health in 2008. She completed a five-year postdoctoral fellowship in diabetes at Harvard Medical School with the Joslin Diabetes Center in 2013. Her research examines diabetes through a psychosocial lens, employing mixed methodology to examine the complex challenges to diabetes management in Appalachian, Ohio.

John Bowditch is an award-winning game and virtual reality developer. He is the director and co-founder of Ohio University's Game Research and Immersive Design (GRID) Lab and is an Associate Professor in the J. Warren McClure School of Emerging Communication Technologies, teaching VR and game development and themed immersive experiences courses. John is the GRID Lab's lead developer and has led research projects funded by the United States Department of Education, Department of Energy, Department of Labor, Department of Homeland Security, National Institutes of Health, and the Ohio Colleges of Medicine Resource Center.

Melvina Brandau, PhD, RN, is an Assistant Professor of Nursing at Ohio University in Athens, Ohio. Dr. Brandau has twenty-one years of nursing experience in medical-surgical settings, telemetry, and urgent and emergent care. Dr. Brandau has been a nursing educator for more than fifteen years and has taught at all levels of nursing, in the didactic, clinical, and laboratory settings, in-person and online. Dr. Brandau's research foci have primarily included online aggression and cyberbullying among youth, recently adding the inclusion of workplace violence, with a move toward implementation studies and the use of technology and virtual reality.

Rebecca Bryant, DNP, APRN, CNP-BC, is an Associate Professor at Ohio University School of Nursing over eight years using traditional, blended, and online delivery to graduate nursing students. Rebecca completed her MSN in 2000 and DNP in 2013. She is board certified as a family nurse practitioner for twenty years. In addition to her academic appointment, she is owner and nurse practitioner of a house call practice that provides chronic disease management and palliative care to older adults. Rebecca's research focus is on self-care and optimal health outcomes in older adults with chronic disease.

Sherleena Buchman, PhD, MSN, RN, is an Assistant Professor at Ohio University's School of Nursing in Athens, Ohio. Dr. Buchman has been a nurse for over twenty years and an educator for the past fifteen years. Her nursing practice includes a background in geriatrics, psychological conditions, medical/surgical and she currently maintains clinical practice in a per diem role as a nursing supervisor at a rural acute care facility. Dr. Buchman has a research focus on curriculum and design, with a specialty in technology, simulation, and virtual reality. Dr. Buchman's current focus of research is around the development of educational interventions surrounding the opioid crisis.

Ashley Crow, PT, DPT, has been a physical therapist since 2009 and worked primarily in inpatient settings. She is currently an assistant clinical professor in physical therapy at Ohio University, where she teaches acute care and cardiopulmonary content. Additionally, she works as an inpatient therapist at a local hospital. As an instructor both in the classroom and clinic, her research interests have centered around creating innovative ways to bridge the gap between classroom learning and clinical practice. Most recently, she is examining the impact of immersive media technology as a teaching tool in the preparation of physical therapy students for acute care practice.

Adonis Durado, MFA, is an Assistant Professor at the School of Visual Communication at Ohio University. In 2020, he was part of the inaugural graduating cohorts of Ohio University's Master of Fine Arts in Communication Media Arts, where he studied infographics and immersive media. Before coming to the U.S., he spent more than a decade working in the Middle East as an art director in advertising agencies and news media companies. As a visual journalist, his work received more than 200 international awards, including the highest honors from the Malofiej Awards, the Society for News Design, and the Society of Publication Designers.

Deborah Henderson, PhD, RN, CNE, is a Professor of Nursing at Ohio University. She has taught in undergraduate and graduate nursing programs. Scholarly interests include virtual reality learning, interprofessional education, simulation, nursing and behavioral health workforce development, online education innovations, population health and curriculum and instruction. Deborah has been funded on several federal and state grants with publications and presentations on interprofessional and nursing education, workforce, virtual reality, simulation, and nursing curriculum and instruction. Deborah has participated on several national and international nursing education and curriculum projects.

Charles P. ("Chip") Linscott, PhD, is Assistant Professor in the McClure School of Emerging Communication Technologies (ECT) at Ohio University, where he designed and teaches a series of classes on virtual reality theory, history, criticism, and production. He is Audio Director at the GRID Lab and has been exploring audio production and sound design since the late 1980s. Chip's writing has appeared in *ASAP/J, Black Camera, Cinema Journal, In Media Res, liquid blackness,* and the anthology *At the Crossroads.* He is on the editorial board of *liquid blackness* journal, and his chapter on XR appears in the textbook *Now Media* (Medoff and Kaye, 2021).

Carrie Love, MFA, MA, is an award-winning independent filmmaker with a BA in Biology Education from Southeastern University, MA in Educational Leadership from Oakland University and MFA in Film from Ohio University. After serving for a decade as Country Coordinator and Media Manager for ChildHope, an educational NGO in 21 countries across Latin America, she stepped into the role of Program Manager for Film and Video Production at Hocking College, where she is currently training a new generation of filmmakers. Carrie has produced and directed several projects in coordination with the GRID Lab, including multimillion-dollar cine-VR narrative productions.

Matt Love, MFA, is a Cinematographer whose work has contributed to several award-winning films. His work in photography and filmmaking has taken him to more than a dozen countries and has been featured in magazines and television. Matt earned his MFA in film from Ohio University before accepting his current position as Cinematographer and Project Manager for the GRID Lab at Ohio University. Matt applies his technical and cross-cultural skills toward the development of new methods in teaching and training that leverage emerging communication technologies, pushing the boundaries of what is possible to enhance immersion and create compelling and engaging content.

Patricia McSteen, PhD, currently serves as interim senior associate vice president for Student Affairs and dean of students at Ohio University. Her duties include oversight of the administrative operation of: Campus Involvement Center, Well-Being and Recreation, Community Standards and Student Responsibility, Counseling & Psychological Services, Sorority and Fraternity Life, and the Survivor Advocacy Program. Dr. McSteen created and chairs Ohio University's behavioral intervention team and leads response to student crisis. In addition, Dr. McSteen created and served as the director of the Margaret Boyd Scholars Program. She received her BFA in Art Therapy, MEd in College Student Personnel, and her PhD in Counselor Education.

Char L. Miller DNP, APRN, CNP, CNE, is an Associate Professor of Nursing at Ohio University with over sixteen years experience in nursing education, including traditional, blended, and online course delivery models, and is recognized by the National League for Nursing (NLN) as a Certified Nurse Educator (CNE). Dr. Miller has been a board-certified Nurse Practitioner for eighteen years, maintaining an active clinical practice in palliative care/geriatrics in addition to her academic appointment. Dr. Miller's research interests include situated learning for skill acquisition, simulation, and health outcomes in older adults.

Devika Patel, MS, is the Design Director at The Better Lab, where she oversees the application of the human-centered design process across a variety of projects addressing vexing healthcare challenges. She is also a Lecturer at San Francisco State University, where she teaches research and writing methods in design. Devika received her BS in Engineering, Product Design from Stanford University with Honors in Education and her Masters in Community Health and Prevention Research from Stanford University School of Medicine.

Amanda Sammann, MD, MPH, is an Assistant Professor in Residence in the Department of Surgery at the University of California, San Francisco. She works at Zuckerberg San Francisco General Hospital and Trauma Center where she practices as a trauma and emergency general surgeon and a critical care physician. Dr. Sammann is the Founder and Executive Director of The Better Lab, a multidisciplinary research laboratory dedicated to improving quality, efficiency, access and experience in health care. Dr. Sammann received a Masters in Public Health from Columbia University and a Medical Degree from UCSF. She completed her surgical training at UCSF and her critical care fellowship at Oregon Health & Sciences University.

Detective Rick Sargent is presently a state-certified police officer in the Criminal Investigations Unit at the Ohio University Police Department in Athens, Ohio. Rick is a veteran, Field Training Officer, and specializes in forensic accounting investigation, threat assessment, and fraud cases. He is involved in the officer selection process and conducts awareness and training programs for community and student groups. He has provided training and consultation in behavioral intervention to educators and has developed workplace violence training and safety protocols for Fortune 500 companies. Rick and his wife Sam have two daughters and live with their dogs in Lancaster, Ohio.

Kerri A. Shaw, MSW, LISW-S, is a Licensed Independent Social Worker and the Field Director in the Ohio University Department of Social Work. She is also the director of a successful Community Health Worker Training Program. Shaw has practiced social work in rural Appalachia for twenty years as a school social worker, program coordinator, and private practitioner. In 2014, Shaw was awarded Athens Foundation Woman of the Year for her work with women and children in the region. A proud two-time graduate from Ohio University with a Master's and Bachelor's degree in Social Work, she lives outside of Athens, Ohio, with her family.

Eric R. Williams, co-creator of the Immersive Media Initiative at Ohio University, is a professor in the McClure School of Emerging Communication Technologies. Williams recently co-authored the book *Virtual Reality Cinema: Narrative Tips and Techniques.* His cine-VR projects have screened internationally in film festivals and academic conferences. Williams' innovative approach to this new medium has been highlighted in the books *Storytelling for Virtual Reality* and *What is Virtual Reality? Exclusive Interviews with Leaders of the VR Industry.* Since 2016, Williams has played a central role in over two dozen funded projects at the GRID Lab, where he oversees the cine-VR department.

Petra Williams, PT, PhD, NCS, is a new faculty member at Rasmussen University, developing their forthcoming competency-based hybrid DPT program. Formerly an Associate Professor for the Program in Physical Therapy at Northern Arizona University, where she taught courses in neuroscience, pathophysiology, neurologic clinical practice, and foundations of PT practice. Dr. Williams is passionate about teaching and using evidence-based strategies to enhance student success and learning in the classroom and clinic. Her research involves using virtual reality to prepare PT students for clinical practice. Dr. Williams is a board-certified neurologic clinical specialist and has been a PT since 1994 and a DPT educator since 2003.

Introduction

John Bowditch

Our team loves to work with new technologies. We always have high expectations, even though much of this new tech isn't ready for practical use. As a result, we have several "shelves of shame" populated with technology that fell short. Even so, we're always eager to check out the next new thing.

One big reason for this: We want to use new technologies as storytelling engines, telling stories in compelling ways we would never have imagined.

At Ohio University's Game Research and Immersive Design (GRID) Lab, all of our projects revolve around telling stories. We look for new ways to tell better stories. We use many media types, including games, films, music, virtual reality, augmented reality, mixed reality, and other interactive simulations. Our selection of which media to use is dependent on what we find to be the best way to tell a particular story. Films, for example, are great for presenting emotionally rich stories. Games are perfect if you want your audience to interact with the story. All of these media engines have advantages and disadvantages; selecting the suitable medium is worth careful consideration.

Every once in a while, a new technology comes along that is genuinely transformative. It transforms the way we do research, teach our classes, and collaborate with others. It generates new methods for telling stories. Such innovation is not destined for our shelf of shame; instead, it becomes a primary tool for our creations. For us, working with 360° video, or what we call cine-VR, has been transformative. Cine-VR, with its 360° views, provides an immersive, you-are-there experience for the viewer. Along with video game development, cine-VR has become one of our go-to methods for storytelling.

Identifying the best production method is only half the equation and is almost always the latter half. Above all, the GRID Lab wants to tell compelling stories. We have found that partnering with others from all backgrounds and disciplines helps identify stories worth telling. Sometimes these stories are designed to be educational, journalistic, or purely entertaining. We work with experts from many fields, including education, business, and most notably, healthcare. Combining our media production skills with experts in healthcare subjects has created innovative techniques and practical, meaningful research. This book is a reflection of those collaborations and the best production practices we have learned.

How Did We Get Here?

Founded with a grant from the Appalachian Regional Commission, Ohio University's GRID Lab opened in 2005. Ohio University has a rich history as the oldest university west of the Allegheny Mountains[1] and the first university chartered by an Act of Congress.[2]

Our university is located in Athens County, Ohio, one of thirty-two Appalachian counties in the state. It is also the state's poorest county. The contrast of a world-class university surrounded by a significant portion of the community living below the poverty line cannot be ignored.

The GRID Lab was formed with the hope of creating new, innovative opportunities utilizing gaming technology in a region that desperately needed them. Our initial mandate was to research and educate with a focus on creating or drawing companies to our area using interactive technologies. Over the past fifteen years, we've developed video games to teach nutrition, developed technologies for first responders better to navigate critical infrastructure for the Department of Homeland Security, created space-themed piloting games for kids with ADHD, and most recently, produced more than a dozen virtual reality healthcare experiences. VR healthcare projects have become one of the hallmarks of our program.

This occurred through many pivots, failures, exciting partnerships, wild requests for money, more pivots, more requests for funds, and back-of-napkin drawings at our favorite Athens bar, Jackie O's. After all, many significant innovations begin at pubs near universities.

Personally, it all clicked for me over brainstorming sessions with my colleague, professor Eric Williams. At the time, Eric and I taught in our School of Media Arts and Studies but worked in different disciplines. I'm a game developer happiest when creating digital worlds, and Eric is an award-winning screenwriter and filmmaker who once (in a "different life") worked in the media department of a large medical center. We noodled out an idea on the back of a napkin how we might combine game design concepts with narrative storytelling to meet the needs of healthcare providers. Our collaboration started in 2014, and we've since worked on nearly a dozen funded projects.

Our research collaboration was made possible by a significant improvement in quality and affordability of VR headsets. In early 2013, with the release of the first Oculus Rift headset, the technology behind VR finally caught up with the dreams of its potential. Virtual reality became our common denominator, and it has led to the most fruitful academic collaboration of my career.

The Dream of Virtual Reality

VR dates back to the 1960s, but this new Rift headset from Oculus, a company no one had ever heard of, started by a recent college grad that favored sandals and Hawaiian shirts, would soon reignite a dormant industry. The funds for the Oculus Rift came from a Kickstarter crowdsourcing campaign. The goal was to manufacture a high-resolution, consumer-priced VR system to be used extensively by the masses. Consumer-grade VR headsets were not a new concept, but no other company had ever produced a successful commercial product. Rightfully, many colleagues believed this idea was farfetched. For a Kickstarter campaign pledge of $335, by the end of 2013 you would receive a pre-order of the Oculus Rift headset developer kit (DK-1), a copy of the game DOOM BFG, a poster, and a t-shirt.[3]

Kickstarter campaigns have no guarantee of successful fulfillment. A 2015 study by Ethan R. Mollick of the University of Pennsylvania found that nearly one-in-ten Kickstarter campaigns fail to follow through on promises.[4] But Oculus seemed worth the risk – to me anyway. I wanted a future full of virtual realities, and I believed this could be the vessel that kicks it off. Oculus had a unique prototype and seemed to have a good "plan," so I pledged. That was my first support of a company that would become an international brand. Within eighteen months of formation, Facebook acquired Oculus for $2 billion.[5] Surprisingly, there was no commercial Rift headset available at the time of acquisition. Facebook gambled $2 billion on an idea - the product would come later.

The Oculus Rift was not my first exposure to virtual reality. My first VR experience was as a preteen in my hometown Columbus, Ohio, in the mid-1990s. My sister and I would often visit Wyandot Lake waterpark (now known as Zoombezi Bay) to beat the summer heat and humidity. The park's wave pool had the closest "waves" within 500 miles, so this place was peak summer excitement in central Ohio. In addition to the wave pool, the park also had an arcade called Sea Dogs Arcade. As an ultra-pale Midwestern kid, this arcade was a perfect place for me to escape from the brutal sun, and I have fond memories of burning through my allowances there.

One summer in 1993, Sea Dogs acquired a new virtual reality gaming system. This installation was no mere arcade game. For one thing, it required several dollars to play instead of a quarter or two. The machine looked like a tank's cockpit, and the arcade games surrounding it aged a decade instantly. The new gaming platform was large, bright yellow, louder than any other game, had a headset dangling from an extended arm, and required a staff member to get you safely in and out. It was a vessel to the metaverse.

The game I played was a forgettable vehicle shooter, maybe even a tank-based match, but not remarkable enough to remember. It was Sea Dogs' marquee experience, and you had to pay a premium to enjoy it. My father was nice enough to cover the cost, but I quickly regretted my decision to try it. The experience was awful, and I spent the rest of the day hiding under my beach towel, managing nausea and dizziness. The graphics were underwhelming, and the audio mix overwhelming.

Though I hated the Sea Dogs' VR experience, something about it made me excited about its future potential, especially for video games. Unlike every other game that you played on a flat-screen, you did feel like you were "in" the game – disconnected from reality and transported to endless possibilities. Like Flynn from the movie *Tron* battling and gaming in a <u>fully</u> immersive metaverse, you could easily imagine yourself spending countless hours in future higher-quality VR experiences.

Twenty years after that landmark summer, Oculus released their long-awaited headset to the initial Kickstarter backers. With the DK1, I was able to transport myself to a Mediterranean villa from my office. There were wires everywhere, and the software was clunky, but it was a sneak peek at what I suspected this industry would rapidly become. The technology was finally catching up with the dream.

When the next iteration, the DK2, was released, we convinced our dean, Dr. Scott Titsworth, to buy several kits for the GRID Lab. He either saw the potential in this technology or simply gave in due to our stubbornness. Either way, the dean funded six development kits for faculty and student use, and in the following years we created several innovative games for these headsets.

One of our more prominent games was an undergraduate student-produced game called High Transit (see Figure 0.1). The objective of the game is to jump between passing high-speed trains miles above the ground. If you jumped and missed a passing training, you would fall into the abyss. It was pretty thrilling and heavily played at the GRID Lab.

Another early VR project was a car racing game with loops, twists, and over-the-top wrecking. While enjoyable, this game tended to be more vomit-inducing than thrilling. Regardless, our students and faculty fell in love with this platform, and we were eager to explore what else was possible. The Oculus DK2 was also the first platform where we were able to get 360° video to play in a headset. This breakthrough was our start in cine-VR production, and it quickly expanded as we demonstrated the potential.

Figure 0.1 "High Transit" created by Taylor Henning, Alexandra Higgins, Courtney Irby, Marc Nie, Ben Roberts, and Todd Thornley. Ohio University, 2015

Ohio University recognized this potential and awarded the GRID Lab with nearly one million dollars of internal funding from its Innovation Strategy Funds – funds that helped build a foundation for our future VR initiatives. Since then, we have received more than four million dollars of grants and contracts related to virtual reality. Their gamble, and ours, has paid off.

Additionally, these funds paved the way for a new school at the university. In 2019, Eric and I became faculty of the J. Warren McClure School of Emerging Communication Technologies, with one of our other GRID Lab colleagues: Dr. Chip Linscott. Together we teach both undergraduate and graduate courses. Our school shares a Master of Fine Arts program with two other Scripps College of Communication departments. Nearly half of the students in our Communication Media Arts graduate program focus on various VR research problems, with cine-VR research currently the most popular.

Who This Book Is for

This book focuses on cine-VR for healthcare training and education. This text guides healthcare workers, researchers, faculty, and students interested in using cine-VR to augment their work or education. The book consists of twenty-one chapters divided into four sections, outlined below. Some chapters focus on production considerations and the technologies that made these projects feasible, but the focus of the book is more of a study on the critical nature of multidisciplinary partnerships and recommended approaches to consider if you hope to create your own successful cine-VR content. We wished for a book like this when we started working our healthcare collaborations. But, like many things at the GRID Lab, instead of finding what we needed, we created it.

It is remarkable to reflect on how far this technology has evolved in the past five years. Our first cine-VR experience was challenging to put together. We created our camera setup with a 3D-printed holder for six GoPro cameras and patched together several different software tools to stitch and render the videos. Back then, our first footage was of Eric flying down a zipline in the Hocking Hills region of southeast Ohio. It took us nearly a month to get the zipline footage to play correctly in a headset. Thankfully today, due to advances in the hardware and software used to develop cine-VR productions, it is fast and relatively pain free to build elementary 360° video experiences. We found the potential of telling a story in 360° of space incredible – we hope you will too.

What This Book Is Not

This book is not a step-by-step guide on how to produce content. If you want to dive deeper into the production process, check out the GRID Lab's book *Virtual Reality Cinema: Narratives and Techniques* by Eric R. Williams, Carrie Love, and Matt Love (Routledge, 2021).

Instead, this book looks at healthcare-focused virtual reality experiences created with 360° video. We do not delve into other virtual reality experiences such as digitally created games or animated films.

Sections

This book is divided into four sections. Each section includes chapters on specific healthcare cine-VR projects the GRID Lab produced. All of these projects required multidisciplinary involvement, but not all of them were initially successful. Many production approaches were unsuccessful, and we discuss why. We have learned a lot along the way, and we would like to share with you our best practices.

Chapters help you dive deeper into our production methods and technological considerations. These sections are brief introductions to concepts that may influence how you create cine-VR.

You can quickly reference commonly used terms in our glossary at the end of the book.

Section Overviews

Section 1 – We start by introducing you to the basics of 360° video in producing virtual healthcare experiences. You will learn terminology and get a better sense of the production process. If you are new to media production, we cover the basics of video and audio production techniques.

Section 2 – This section focuses on using cine-VR for prepping individuals working in complex environments. We refer to this as PRE-ality, a term coined in 2016 by the GRID Lab as a portmanteau word combining "preparation" and "reality." The goal is to get individuals comfortable with an actual space's functioning (such as a trauma bay) before ever stepping foot inside the actual place. We have created PRE-ality experiences for medical residents and physical therapy students. We also cover best practices for working within a live medical facility.

Section 3 – There are many layers of media to balance when producing cine-VR experiences. Examples covered include audio production, graphical overlays, and practical solutions for creating emotion. This section focuses on three projects developed in collaboration with Ohio University's School of Nursing. Topics include Narcan delivery outside medical centers, treating patients with Parkinson's Disease, and reacting to workplace violence in an emergency room. Information about choosing the best cameras and VR headsets is included as well.

Section 4 – The most creative projects we've produced are a result of unique partnerships. The combination of subject experts with media producers created several accurate yet compelling cine-VR stories. You will meet two of our beloved fictional characters, Lula Mae and Destiny, and learn how they helped us address systemic biases in diabetes and opioid healthcare. We created a training tool for university police and dormitory resident advisors dealing with a person experiencing emotional distress. Additional topics include guided simulation, advanced production methods, distribution options, and guidelines for maintaining medical accuracy on set.

By the end of this book, we hope that you are able to see the potential for this relatively new medium. Many in the healthcare profession are amazed by the possibilities of interactive virtual reality – from the interactivity to the expanding digital worlds – and we are too. But we are equally as excited by cine-VR, and we feel that this is a medium that is currently being ignored. We hope that we can convince you of cine-VR's potential because it is just now coming to the fore.

Notes

1. Ohio University, History and Traditions, https://www.ohio.edu/student-affairs/students/history-traditions
2. Burke, Thomas Aquinas (September 1996). Ohio Lands: A Short History (8th ed.). Ohio Auditor of State. "Ohio Lands – A Short History" March 27, 2011. Archived http://freepages.rootsweb.com/~maggie/history/ohio-lands/ohl5.html
3. Oculus Rift Kickstarter Campaign, https://www.kickstarter.com/projects/1523379957/oculus-rift-step-into-the-game/, 2013.
4. Mollick, Ethan R., Delivery Rates on Kickstarter (December 4, 2015). https://ssrn.com/abstract=2699251 or http://dx.doi.org/10.2139/ssrn.2699251
5. Facebook, Facebook to acquire Oculus, https://about.fb.com/news/2014/03/facebook-to-acquire-oculus/

SECTION I

In the world of entertainment, 360° video has seen a sharp rise and fall. Writers and producers, distributors and advertisers – and especially audiences – don't know what to do with this technology as a form of entertainment. Seemingly very few people want to come home from work, throw on a headset, and watch a cinematic virtual reality (cine-VR) experience. Some might attribute this start and stop embrace to the Gartner Hype Cycle[1] – a peak of inflated expectations for 360° video in the 2010s, followed by a current "trough of disillusionment" about the technology. We see it differently.

While many people call the technology "360° video," we call it "cine-VR." Cine-VR, short for "cinematic virtual reality," is the moniker we use at Ohio University's GRID Lab to refer to 360° video treated with a feature film's creative approach (with actors, lights, sound design, etc.). That's not to say that all cine-VR looks cinematic. In fact, some cine-VR work intentionally appears more "raw" or "realistic." Yet, lighting, sound design, blocking, camera placement, and "actors" are all well considered in a cine-VR experience.

More importantly, though, each experience's intention is considered – as well as the specific audience and educational outcomes. This approach is where 360° video for entertainment differs from cine-VR for healthcare. In entertainment, you have to convince the audience to watch cine-VR instead of playing a video game, watching a movie, reading a book, or going to the theater or a concert. In healthcare, you simply need to demonstrate that you have chosen the best tool for the task at hand. For many healthcare, education, and training tasks, cine-VR is by far the best tool because it is a tool with new and unique capabilities.

DOI: 10.4324/9781003168683-1

Chapter 1

Cine-VR for Healthcare (not: 360° Video)

Deborah Henderson, Eric R. Williams, and John Bowditch

Contents

The cine-VR healthcare audience does not choose which educational tool they will be using. The educational facilitator selects the tool. The audience simply participates and then, hopefully, evaluates whether the tool was effective. This is why we have found cine-VR to be so potent: used for healthcare education, cine-VR continuously impresses its audience, especially when combined with other media and messaging.

Cine-VR brings a new set of tools and a new set of ideas to healthcare education. The equipment may differ, yet it shares similarities with traditional film and video production (see Chapter 2 for equipment details). It is not the equipment that sets this new medium apart from its predecessors. Instead, we believe an intellectual triptych needs to be created for 360° healthcare projects to be successful, a triptych based on vision, experience, and expertise (see Figure 1.1).

DOI: 10.4324/9781003168683-2

3

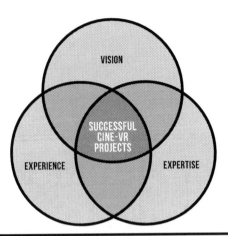

Figure 1.1   Intellectual tryptic for successful cine-VR projects

Vision

In 2015, GRID Lab director John Bowditch had the foresight to realize that VR was primed to make another pass across the consciousness of the human race. To be sure, visionaries of the past had tried to introduce this concept at least twice before[2]. Now, Bowditch believed, might just be the right time. He began recruiting a cross-disciplinary team to compete for Ohio University's Innovation Strategy Award, designed to bring cutting-edge ideas into the university. Bowditch's vision of how game design, VR, and immersive design would expand and fuse in the latter half of the 2010s was truly innovative. More importantly, it proved to be true.

To understand the potential of 360° videos, there needs to be a member of the team that can look past the traditional uses of standard video and film. There needs to be a team member that can look past the conventional uses of video games, simulations, and role-playing. There needs to be a member (or many team members) who are willing to imagine revolutionary approaches to common and newly arising problems. Without such vision, the 360° cameras and microphones are nothing more than modern versions of conventional devices.

Experience

One part of the initial team that Bowditch created included media practitioners – specialists in video and audio production, screenwriting, animation, design, et cetera. He was not building a team of immersive media specialists "from scratch." Instead, he was building an experienced team, albeit a team experienced in other media. This team was able to pivot on their strength to adapt to the new medium. And they were able to ask the right questions, such as:

- We understand video game interactivity, but how would that differ in 360° video?
- We know how to light a theatrical set, but how do we light a 360° set?
- We know how to design sound for two-dimensional images, but how do we design sound in the round?
- We understand design principles for a 2D object, but how do those concepts apply when our audience can look in any direction?

- We know how to edit a montage in video, but what does a 360° montage look like?
- We know how to write for film, but how do we write differently for 360°?

A member of Bowditch's newly assembled team, professor Eric R. Williams had worked as a film director and cameraman. He'd written screenplays for Universal Studios, developed television programs for American Movie Classics, and won awards for his interactive storytelling work. He'd also worked for several years in the field of healthcare education. Williams followed Bowditch's vision and focused a portion of it towards 360° video and healthcare education. In collaboration with other experienced professionals such as cinematographer/editor Matt Love, audio expert Chip Linscott, actor/director Merri Biechler, playwright Inna Tsyrlin, graphic designer Adonis Durado, director Josh Crook, sound designer Jordan Herron, and producer/director Carrie Love the GRID lab was able to develop the unique attributes of the medium into something new and exciting: into cine-VR.

A productive cine-VR team will incorporate expertise from a wide variety of areas. To do otherwise is detrimental to utilizing this new medium to its full potential. Beware of considering 360° video to be "film on steroids," or "a recorded version of theater in the round," or "videotape meets video game." A singular, misguided vision will quickly derail the cine-VR experience.

Expertise

An equally important part of the team is a set of open-minded content experts with a creative bent. Bowditch sought production people for his team. He sought subject matter specialists because it doesn't matter how good your communication team is if you don't have excellent content to communicate. Suppose your cine-VR experience is the house you're building. The content is the foundation upon which the house is built as well as the furnishings and the interior design.

Dr. Deborah Henderson, director of Ohio University's School of Nursing, was a team member from the start. She also understood Bowditch's vision and could see how this technology could help her school better educate hundreds of on-campus (and thousands of online) students. Other content experts joined the team from colleges across the university. However, the interest from the medical school and the College of Health Sciences and Professions (where the School of Nursing is located) lead the way in our cine-VR projects – the results of which are the foundations of this book.

The experts required for cine-VR projects need to be "open-minded," on two levels. First, the experts must be interested in using creative media to teach, which is not a ubiquitous interest. Second, they must be willing to use a new medium in new ways. An expert familiar with using video, an interactive website, or live simulations to teach must be ready to reconfigure their expectations for cine-VR.

Third, the content expert must realize that cine-VR is still in its infancy. We're still trying to figure out what works and why. There is still a good amount of experimentation happening in the process. The creative "experts" (quite frankly) don't always know exactly what they're doing. If a subject expert hired a crew to make an educational video, and they walked onto the set on the first day only to find the director and cinematographer wondering where to put the camera... well, they might just fire them on the spot and hire someone who "knows what they're doing." In cine-VR these days, the opposite might be true: a director pretending to know the perfect spot for a cine-VR camera most likely doesn't know what s/he's doing.

Henderson, and her medical colleagues across the university, were able to roll with the creative uncertainty and, in turn, offer their own imaginative insights into their projects. Without open-minded, fully engaged content experts, most cine-VR projects will get mired in rote decision-making that runs contrary to the vision and collaborative ingenuity found in the cine-VR team members.

Embracing Cine-VR

It takes a long time for a healthcare professional to develop experience and competence. The immersive medium of cine-VR on a headset is arguably the best alternative to actual experiences. With all complementary technologies leveraged, cine-VR can digitally transport the learner to nearly anywhere, while still providing consistency in exposure and experience. Transformative learning is difficult to provide through traditional means of the classroom and "luck of the draw" clinical experience based on the patients who happen to be there at the time of learning.

Further, cine-VR improves the authenticity of experience on a headset and therefore enhances the application of knowledge, skills, and attitudes to complement a healthcare professional or student's authentic expertise in ways that didactic lecture, skills lab with mannequins, and standardized patients cannot. Cine-VR provides a superior form of dynamic simulation learning for a specific health discipline or interprofessional team.

Embracing cine-VR's use for healthcare education allows for robust learning with many advantages over traditional learning and traditional simulation. Conventional learning techniques do not expose healthcare professionals and students to the reality of being immersed within a situation. It does not allow the user to authentically experience what patients or practitioners may be experiencing based on their symptoms, perceptions, or experiences.

VR is not new. Early VR was fraught with many issues, including bulky and costly equipment, software and internet limitations, and hardware sophistication – all of which held back development for healthcare education and training.

Today's learners are no longer hindered by such roadblocks, and their expectations are pushing the use of both VR and cine-VR forward. Learners who have grown up with smartphones and gaming consoles are naturally more comfortable with immersive experiences like cine-VR. The value of further expanding cine-VR approaches and combining associated complementary technologies is not only preferred but becomes the desired functionality of any VR experience for today's learners.

Another reason cine-VR is increasing is that learners, and healthcare professionals are no longer location-bound on campus. They do not have to be present in a physical healthcare setting to have meaningful learning experiences. While cine-VR costs can be substantial, the experiences are available to an unlimited number of learners or professionals once produced.

What Can Cine-VR Offer?

Cine-VR provides an enhanced, immersive simulation experience that improves the learning, skill acquisition, and attitude development of healthcare students and professionals. We have found seven key aspects of cine-VR that we tend to leverage into every new healthcare project:

> **Consistency.** Due to its linearly recorded nature, cine-VR provides routine consistency even though the audience may choose to view the experiences differently. For instance, one learner may choose to look at a monitor while another learner may choose to watch the

patient instead. The experience that each learner has is different, even though the experience itself is consistent. This unique factor invites nearly unlimited re-watchability and a multitude of educational opportunities.

Cost-effectiveness. The initial investment of cine-VR content needs careful planning to ensure the production of appropriate content capable of staying relevant for some time. Once high-quality cine-VR content is created, the per experience cost is simply determined by the distribution model. An experience designed for thirty students can just as easily accommodate 3,000 students.

Efficiency. Content used effectively in this format can be utilized repeatedly with varying groups of healthcare professionals and students. In comparison, faculty or trainers will still be involved in setting the stage for learning and providing reflection and debriefing. Preparation time goes down significantly for the facilitators with continuing use of the cine-VR.

Engagement. While cine-VR experiences are designed to be interesting to the audience, in many ways, someone in a headset has no other choice but to engage. A student can't randomly check for texts, phone a friend, or even just stare out the window (unless there is a window in the experience).

Flexibility. Learners are aware of how and when their educational experiences are available. Ideally, cine-VR training could be available to students twenty-four hours per day, seven days a week via personalized headsets and ubiquitous content availability.

Safety. Reminiscent of the "see one, do one" approach that has been a longstanding tradition in many healthcare disciplines, cine-VR can produce high-risk situations ideal for less experienced healthcare professionals to observe and revisit in real-time. For example, cine-VR can help less experienced professionals mentally rehearse the process of safely de-escalating aggressive behavior in a crowded emergency room.

Timeliness. Real-world experiences are difficult to schedule. If we learned anything from the COVID-19 pandemic of 2020, we learned that students need to continue learning. During that time, healthcare professionals and students had limited access to clinical settings and educational environments. Cine-VR can be used to strengthen real-world observational experiences in preparation for clinical experience.

With these seven aspects in mind, conversations about cine-VR don't simply manifest into current projects. Our minds race to projects into the future. We often ask, how might cine-VR expand? And what can we be doing now to ensure that direction in the future?

Expansion of Cine-VR

Expansion of cine-VR becomes more meaningful and cost-effective as synergy with other technologies grows. Educators work in tandem with those who possess the technical expertise to create cine-VR. While research needs to substantiate the value of cine-VR-based learning beyond our early research investigating how learners feel about cine-VR experiences, we have begun to explore how cine-VR can continue to expand. Picture this future for cine-VR:

A learner wears a VR headset with integrated audio and uses their virtual personal assistant and eye gaze to quickly convey their learning needs based on their statement of the learning objective and their healthcare discipline. Artificial Intelligence (AI) curates the cine-VR experience from a vast repository and tailors it for each individual. The learning objectives are synthesized from their specific healthcare discipline's perspective, combined with an intelligent system understanding of other relevant healthcare disciplines involved. The AI system curates the best cine-VR experience available from a global repository. Following the curation, the material automatically downloads on the learner's VR headset with automated troubleshooting for a seamless experience.

If you can imagine this type of cine-VR learning, you can see why we are so excited to be pioneering the steps that will make such a future possible. Instead of using the hype cycle to explain why this new technology isn't catching on unilaterally, we choose to look at the Roger's Innovation Curve,[3] theorizing that only 2.5% of the population ("Innovators") adopt new technology early. Following shortly after that are the "Early Adopters" (13.5%) who use and evaluate technology to reduce their own uncertainty about an innovation. We are the early adopters of cine-VR for healthcare, and we hope you'll follow our lead and embrace this technology for your own healthcare needs.

Become an Early Adopter

One of this book's central tenets is to inspire and encourage exciting new projects in this space. Just as we see ourselves as early adopters of cine-VR for healthcare, we invite you to join us. Be an early adopter yourself. To that end, we'd like to present you with at least fifteen areas where we expect to see cine-VR grow:

- **Competency development of discipline-specific techniques.**
  Example: A disaster situation as it unfolds, including specific hospital area set up.
- **Rare clinical situations.**
  Example: A healthcare professional deals with stabilizing an impaled object while awaiting a surgery team.
- **Situations for an entire healthcare team.**
  Example: How does the "rapid response team" function in the midst of rapidly changing patient conditions?
- **Foundational experiences that assess the ability to use the discipline knowledge.**
  Example: How can a care provider recognize and discuss trauma in a person's past?
- **Dangerous situations where mitigating potential harm is crucial.**
  Example: Observing proper technique to help a patient transfer from chair to bed.
- **Rare patient presentations requiring recognition of signs or symptoms.**
  Example: Assess a pregnant female presenting with an OB emergency.
- **Prevent "Never events."**
  Example: Steps taken by a healthcare team to avoid surgery on the wrong leg.
- **Discipline-specific routine care and "need to know" care.**
  Example: When a physician intubates a patient, what do registered nurses do during the procedure? What is the role of a respiratory therapist when intubation is occurring?
- **Situations requiring great attention across interprofessional teams.**
  Example: Recognizing signs of substance abuse and appropriate responses, including preparing and giving the antidote to reverse an illegal drug overdose.
- **Scenarios that will endure and includes vast intervention.**
  Example: Pre-hospital emergency personnel figuring out the best way to extricate someone from a vehicle after an accident.

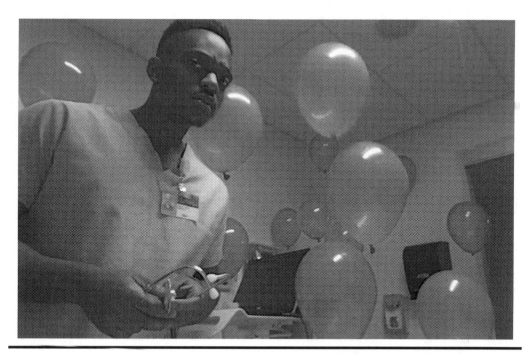

Photo 1.1   Partial screen grab from cine-VR project illustrating patient hallucinations

- **Soft skills development**.
  Example: Empathy training, identifying and eliminating implicit biases in caregivers, applying trauma-informed care concepts in a situation, or talking to someone who is grieving a loss.
- **Situations that do not change significantly over time**.
  Example: How to make a home safer for someone who will be using a walker at home.
- **Tricky situations**.
  Example: Four patients present during a catastrophic event, and the learner must prioritize the patients' life or death needs.
- **High-risk situation identification and practice**.
  Example: A patient on a ventilator with the alarms going off.
- **Understanding the patient experience**.
  Example: Demonstrate what a patient suffering from hallucination might see (see Photo 1.1).

Preparing for a Successful Cine-VR Project

Any successful cine-VR project starts with a good idea, followed by a straightforward question: "Why would this project benefit from cine-VR?" If the project can be done better with live simulation, use live simulation. If traditional video is just as effective, use traditional video. These seven key aspects of a cine-VR project should be used to answer that question:

1. Consistency
2. Cost-effectiveness
3. Efficiency

4. Engagement
5. Flexibility
6. Safety
7. Timeliness

Once you've decided on a cine-VR project, determine how you'll build the required intellectual triptych to ensure success: vision, experience, and expertise. Each one is vital to success – as you'll see throughout this book.

Viewing

To view and download cine-VR examples mentioned in this chapter, please visit: https://vimeo.com/channels/cinevr4healthcare/ (***password:*** *cineVR4health*).

Notes

1. Jackie Fenn & Mark Raskino (2008). *Mastering the Hype Cycle: How to Choose the Right Innovation at the Right Time.* Harvard Business Press. ISBN 978-1-4221-2110-8.
2. Lanier, Jaron. *Dawn of the New Everything: Encounters with Reality and Virtual Reality.* New York, NY: Henry Holt and Company, 2017.
3. Singer, Leif. *On the Diffusion of Innovations: How New Ideas Spread.* Dr. Leif Singer, November 9, 2020. https://leif.me/on-the-diffusion-of-innovations-how-new-ideas-spread/.

Chapter 2

Cine-VR Production Overview

Matt Love and Charles P. ("Chip") Linscott

Contents

Camera Basics

At a fundamental level, capturing cine-VR imagery is very similar to capturing other types of digital images. Light travels through a lens and lands on a sensor where the image is captured. In reality, traditional cinema cameras can actually be used to create cine-VR content. The camera can be panned to predetermined positions using wide-angle lenses and specialized tripod heads, allowing the 360° sphere to be captured in slices – usually in 30°/45°/60°/90°parts. These slices are later stitched together in specialized software to create the 360° sphere.

Dedicated 360° cameras are housings that hold multiple sensors and lens combinations to capture disparate slices simultaneously (see Figure 2.1).

While this removes the need for third-party software, the images still need to be stitched together. Some cameras offer an option to have this stitching compute inside the camera before

DOI: 10.4324/9781003168683-3

TWO LENS CAMERA   MULTI-DIRECTION CAMERA RIG   SPHERICAL CAMERA

Figure 2.1   Example of 360° cameras with various numbers of sensor/lens combinations

the image is saved to the memory card, which can be beneficial. However, there are reasons why you may still want to have the camera record each individual slice for stitching together in post-production. We'll explore different camera options and how to choose the best camera for your project in Chapter 7.

Image Basics

Regardless of which method was used to capture the video slices, it is the stitching software's job to orient them so that the images' overlapping portions align to create the final 360° sphere. The goal is to have stitch-lines blend into the video as much as possible. Visible stitch-lines that are noticed by the users signal poor production quality. This sphere, when depicted on a computer monitor, is most commonly displayed in an equirectangular format (see Figure 2.2).

Think of taking a globe and flattening it out. The portions at the poles would become distorted, which is what you see in the equirectangular image. The area where the slices meet is called the stitch-line. As a result of the parallax differences (a displacement or difference in the apparent position of an object viewed along two different lines of sight) between the sensor positions when each image is captured, the portions of the image at the stitch-line will never line up perfectly. We

FRONT LENS   ✚   BACK LENS   ＝   EQUIRECTANGULAR IMAGE

Figure 2.2   Example of how two images from a 360° camera are stitched together to make a single equirectangular image

can make them almost disappear with software options that offer additional features to help blend the splices together. Depending on the camera and software, stitch-lines can be imperceptible, or they can be poorly configured, causing distraction. We'll discuss how to increase your odds of success in later portions of this chapter.

Stereoscopic Imaging

Up to this point, we've discussed the capture of cine-VR content which would result in a monoscopic viewing experience, meaning a single flat image projected as a sphere for viewing. There is another type of cine-VR viewing experience that creates a 3D effect known as stereoscopic imaging. This technique leverages the parallax difference between multiple lenses to achieve the illusion of depth. Some viewers report being less likely to feel motion sickness with stereoscopic content. Provided that your camera can capture stereoscopic imagery, the postproduction process is similar, apart from the fact that you will have a separate image for each eye, requiring you to apply your edits, and effects to each. Stereoscopic content is generally contained within one media file with the images stacked above and below each other or in a side-by side-fashion. A headset will be needed to view the content, and settings will be configured for the file type.

Monitoring

We've introduced the basics of cine-VR capture systems, so let's discuss the process of capturing images. With our 360° camera in place, we want to remotely monitor the video to ensure the content is captured correctly. By nature, a 360° camera captures the entire 360° sphere surrounding itself, which is why you don't see many 360° cameras with built-in monitors. If you were standing next to the camera as you would with a traditional camera, you and your crew would end up in the shot! There is no delineation between "in front of" and "behind" the camera. This fact is often learned the hard way in cine-VR shoots.

For this reason, many 360° cameras have companion apps to stream a live feed of what the camera is seeing to a smartphone or tablet. This allows the director or camera operator to hide out of sight while still monitoring a video feed. In fact, some cameras allow for an HDMI or ethernet connection routed into a computer with a head-mounted display attached, allowing someone to observe the performance within a headset – note: these cables may end up in your captured footage.

Placement

With our monitoring plan in place, we can determine where to place the camera. Where and how we position the camera can significantly impact the way our end viewer perceives the content. Our work at the GRID Lab has shown us that camera placement in cine-VR should be carefully considered. Projects have had to be reshot because the camera position didn't work. Think about how a viewer will take the space in. Will their eye be drawn to a particular part of the room? Does this setting reward the viewer who looks around? How will the characters move about the space, interact with it? These are essential questions that inform the decision of where to place the camera.

How we generally determine camera placement:

1. We analyze the script. Who and what are essential to capture in the scene? Should any actor or props be closer or farther away to emphasize or minimize their importance?
2. We analyze the space. How will the characters move throughout the area, and what options are available to alter those movements in ways that enhance our story?
3. We analyze camera support options. What options are available to securely mount the camera in a way that would allow us to achieve our desired goals and minimize work in post-production?

We have found that placing the camera lens slightly lower than the primary actor's eye height you want your audience to connect with will serve you well. There are, of course, instances where you will want to place your camera lower or higher. Setting the camera low can suggest a child or pet's perspective, while placing the camera high can offer an unsettling experience if desired. We once rigged a camera to a ceiling fan to give the viewer a "God's eye view" of a scene and found that while the shot was powerful, the clip needed to be relatively short to avoid disorienting the audience. You should experiment with camera height to gain a feel for how it affects the viewing experience. Shoot test footage ahead of your primary production to make sure the placements meet your requirements. For a more in-depth look at camera placement, see Chapter 20.

Lighting

A critical component of what sets cine-VR apart from standard 360° video is that it is produced in cinematic fashion. While you may question what place cinematic lighting has in training content for healthcare, the reality is that lighting can play a crucial role in achieving desired outcomes. Lighting not only affords a more professional and polished look to your work, but it can also serve to call attention to elements in the scene, set a tone, and more. Starting with the end in mind, consider what type of emotional response would benefit your content and leverage your lighting as one of the available tools to create that response.

If the viewer can see all around in cine-VR, where do we put the lights? Generally, the methods fall into three categories.

1. **Practicals.** The easiest way to hide a light is in plain sight. Using table lamps, floor lamps, and overheads are a beautiful way to light a scene. Dimming and color temperature shifting bulbs are available to control the quantity and quality of light. Diffusion or black wrap (black aluminum foil) can be used to modify the light from light bulbs, and provided they'll be covered by window dressings, heavy black trash bags can be used to block sunlight coming through windows.
2. **Hidden.** Another option is to leverage thin, flexible LED lights in creatively concealed ways. Stand where you plan to place the camera and observe the space. Cupboards, doors, and around corners are examples of areas where lights can be hidden, allowing you to shape your environment.
3. **Removed.** Placing the light out in the open and then removing it in post-production can be a compelling way to light your scenes. Imagine you take an interior space and divide it in two. The action in the scene will take place on only one of those two sides for each take. On the other side, you can place the lights, the director, the sound recordist, etc. After recording

the scene, you "flip" the two sides and record the other half of the scene, compositing the two images in post. Removing lights involves working with plates, which is a technique with a variety of uses. While powerful, this process can be complicated and requires a lot of planning and practice before production. An explanation of how to work with plates can be found in Chapter 20.

Audio Production Considerations

Images are, of course, roughly half of cine-VR, but don't forget about audio. Two broad questions help clarify the particular uses of audio in cine-VR production:

1. What sort of audio is used in cine-VR?
2. How is that audio used?

Before exploring the answers to these questions, it is helpful to first recall that immersion and presence are central concerns in VR healthcare applications and many other VR training types. Users of virtual reality healthcare applications (and most other types of VR) should feel that they are "inside" the simulation and experiencing whatever is being simulated. This feeling of presence makes training more realistic and impactful. Immersion has objective components that can be advanced by technical considerations like image quality, sound quality, plot/story, and the like. Presence – the feeling of truly "being inside" the virtual world – is affected by individual users' subjective variations but is aided by the technical aspects that foster immersion.[1]

While video provides a more photorealistic user experience, current technology makes it difficult to move about in video and interact with recorded, real-world objects. In some ways, cine-VR is a trade-off, as fully computer-generated VR looks less realistic than cine-VR but is more interactive.[2] Computer-generated VR is also, not incidentally, much costlier and more time-consuming to produce than cine-VR. Therefore, the fundamental ethos for cine-VR audio is this: it should enhance the user's sense of presence.

Audio in cine-VR should work with images to make the virtual experience more dynamic, more memorable, more believable, more educational, and more effective. VR audio does not need to correlate with real-world sound, just as film, television, or video game audio is not, per se, precisely like sound as heard in the real world. The "realism" of cine-VR audio is found in its ability to make users feel as though they are in the simulated environment (healthcare or otherwise). This realism can be achieved in many ways, as detailed below and more thoroughly in Chapter 12.[3]

There are *a lot* of different types of audio that may be used in cine-VR, but some types of sound recording and playback are more critical than others. This half of the chapter defines audio types most commonly used in cine-VR while assuming very little audio production knowledge from the reader. Later in the book, Chapter 12 goes into detail about the audio practices widely employed in the GRID Lab's cinematic virtual reality projects.

One way of understanding the history of recorded sound is to trace the development of the technologies used to capture sounds and replay them. When media production professionals use the term "audio," they generally mean recorded sound. There are numerous historical and contemporary methods for recording sound (or "producing audio"). Similarly, methods for replaying or broadcasting audio are also myriad. Etched wax cylinders, grooved celluloid discs, eight-track tapes, compact discs (CDs), MP3s, and many other technologies have all played essential roles in capturing and distributing sounds at various historical junctures. In addition to the apparent fact that many audio recording and transmission formats are altogether outdated (not just for VR use, but for others as well), many modern playback systems are nevertheless ill-suited for VR and cine-VR distribution. Therefore, despite the popularity, utility, and unique properties of many audio distribution formats, cine-VR essentially requires digital production and distribution.

But the prevalence of digital production, post-production, and distribution is only the beginning of the unique audio requirements of cine-VR. While Chapter 12 digs deeply into many of the precise practices, possibilities, and problems posed by cine-VR audio production, a significant amount of background and historical context is necessary to proceed further.

DMEE

For most of our productions at the GRID Lab, we get our audio from four sources: dialogue, music, (sound) effects, and the environment (or DMEE, for short). Dialogue, music, and effects are common across audiovisual production, but quality VR requires that users feel present in a spherical or 360° space with sounds moving all around them. This means that we capture or create *environmental* sounds; these ambient and environmental sounds add to the realism of the audio half of cine-VR production. In healthcare scenarios, these environmental sounds might come from an operating room, a waiting room, a pharmacy, an ambulance, a patient/client home, and so on. Still, the central production consideration rests in creating environmental sounds that will make the user *feel* as though they are present in the simulated scenario. The DMEE sounds may be captured and played back in a variety of formats. Still, Ambisonic audio is vital to VR production due to its capacity to allow sounds to be affected by user input – to change as a user moves, just as in the real world – and present a spherical sound field. Thus, Ambisonic audio is becoming increasingly popular due to its efficacy for VR, but more common audio formats are also regularly employed.

Mono

In monophonic (or just "mono") sound, the exact same audio is played out of each channel – each ear gets the same sound. If a listener played mono sound using headphones or a car stereo with six speakers or a surround sound system with nine speakers, the same audio would still come out of each speaker equally (see Figure 2.3). There is no difference in mono sound between the left and right channels, a center channel, etc. Mono sound is mainly unsuitable for cine-VR because most humans hear things with both ears – essentially having a "stereo" experience of sound in real-life because of two ears being situated in two different places on the human head. (See Chapter 12 for more on this.) There is *one crucial exception* to this rule; the dialogue is chiefly recorded in mono, even in VR audio productions. Recording a single actor's stereo dialogue often results in unusual and confounding effects because one voice will be playing differently on two different channels. For example, imagine speaking to a doctor and having two slightly different-sounding versions of her voice (delayed or out of phase), one playing in each ear. This is confusing and disorienting for listeners and would really only be desirable when some sort of special effect was called for. It would also deter some of the aforementioned "realism" that is usually desired in clinical and training cine-VR scenarios. Thus, monophonic audio recording and playback are principally used for dialogue and voiceover narration in cine-VR production.

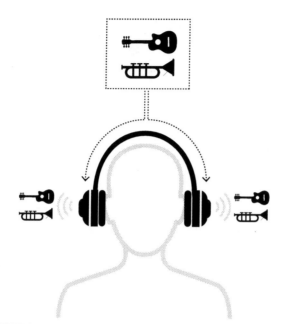

Figure 2.3   If a listener plays mono sound, the same audio will come out of each speaker equally

Stereo

In contrast to mono audio, stereophonic sound (or simply "stereo") has two distinct channels: usually left and right. Out of each of these channels, a different but often related sound is played. This means that recording occurs in a stereo format. This production can be achieved by manipulating two mono tracks on different channels to make them sound divergent or, much more commonly, by recording with two or more microphones or a stereo microphone. Imagine listening through a pair of headphones, and a flying bird chirps around your head, flitting from left to right and then back again. This stereo effect cannot be achieved with monophonic sound. Thus, it renders stereophonic sound as arguably the most basic type of "spatial" audio, a foundational part of cine-VR and VR broadly. Spatial audio is recorded and transmitted sound that makes the listener feel as though they are surrounded by sounds in space – similarly to how most humans hear sounds in real life. Sounds generally hit the pinnae (outer ear) and funnel into the auditory canal at slightly different times – a differential process that can be nearly imperceptible yet is nevertheless registered cognitively. This audible variation occurs because of the various locations of sound-generating objects in the world, the different areas of ears on human heads, the listener's position, the proximity of the sounds to our ears, and the medium through which sounds are traveling. Two-channel audio that strives to recreate such naturalistic human listening experiences is called *binaural audio*, which is different from stereo audio due to its emphasis on replicating human auditory functioning during capture and playback.

Stereo is almost always used for scores/soundtrack music or environmental sounds/sound effects that would not emanate from a precise direction (for example, leaves rustling all around a listener or rain falling in every direction at once). Stereo and mono sounds are principally used for audio cues that *should not* shift as the user moves. These sounds are known as "headlocked" audio because the motion tracking associated with headset movement will not affect how the sounds are heard. While mixing techniques and effects like panning and reverberation can be employed

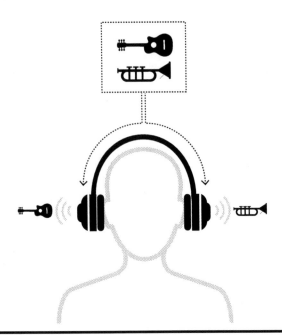

Figure 2.4   If a listener plays stereo sound, each track will be permanently fixed to the left and right channels in which it was initially mixed

to make VR feel spatially naturalistic, a stereo track will permanently be fixed to the left and right channels in which it was initially mixed, even if it is sent out to more than two speakers (see Figure 2.4).

Surround Sound

You are probably familiar with some form of surround sound audio since it is employed in most commercial movie theaters and has been popular in home theater setups for several decades. Such systems are another form of spatial audio similar to stereo but with more than two channels. Systems like 5.1 surround, 7.1 surround, and 9.1 surround disperse sounds throughout diverse arrays of speakers in front, beside, and behind the listener (with five, seven, or nine speakers, respectively, and the ".1" indicating a subwoofer). Cutting-edge systems like Dolby Atmos may employ even more speaker channels, with overhead arrays and multiple low-frequency effects generated by several subwoofers (22.2 surround is one such system).

Surround sound systems are like stereophonic systems on steroids. These systems use panning, effects, and channel separation to convey the appearance that the sources of sounds are moving around the listener. Such systems can be beneficial for gaming, immersive cine-VR experiences, amusement parks, and VR. Still, they generally do not allow for motion tracking or 360° sound fields in the same way that Ambisonic audio does. To allow for motion tracking in VR and enable user input and movement to affect sounds in a spherical, 360° field, Ambisonic audio production is commonly employed. Ambisonic audio can be output to surround systems, but speakers above and below the listener are needed for authentic spherical sound. Due to the focus on cinematic VR viewed through HMDs, Chapter 12 deals principally with binaural playback in headphones (most Ambisonic audio in VR is "decoded" for binaural playback via headphones). This type of spatial audio is usually created by Ambisonic audio production. Still, you should be aware that game engines like Unity and Unreal can spatialize sounds for computer-generated VR and cine-VR in other ways as well.

Ambisonic Audio

If you need sounds to move with a motion-tracked headset or be sent to an infinite array of output channels, you want Ambisonic audio. An Ambisonic recording is exponentially more powerful than stereo because of its capacity to enable the user to change the audio through movement and input. Furthermore, recording Ambisonically allows for sounds to be played back both above and below listeners and horizontally, creating a complete 360°, spherical soundfield that is uniquely suited to VR and has become a popular production method (see Figure 2.5). Ambisonic recording is agnostic of both the number and placement of speakers used for playback. Sound recorded in this way can be sent to an infinite number of speaker outputs in an endless set of configurations and does not require separate mixes to do so. Ambisonic productions can thus be conceptualized spatially rather than in terms of left-right stereo, 5.1, etc.

As an example of Ambisonic sounds, consider that a cine-VR simulation assumes a young medical resident's perspective in a trauma ward. Sounds such as the clanking of surgical tools, the opening and slamming of doors, cries of injured patients, and dialogue from orderlies or nurses can be placed anywhere around the resident's point-of-view, with precise heights, angles, distances, and so on. With HMD motion-tracking capabilities and the power of Ambisonic production, these sounds will change as the resident/user turns, looks around, and glances up or down. This is a compelling effect if you need to draw your audience's attention in a specific direction. If there is a fire behind you, you want the sound of a fire alarm blaring behind you to draw your attention.

Figure 2.5 With HMD motion-tracking capabilities and the power of Ambisonic production, sounds change as the user turns, looks around, and glances up or down

Other Production Aspects

In addition to capturing superb sounds and images, there are other considerations that impact the quality of a production. As the maxim goes, the devil is in the details. Communicating to all involved what time to arrive, where to park, where to store personal belongings on set, where to stage gear that isn't in use, where and when to get lunch, and more takes a lot of coordination. Producers and assistant directors handle many of these details on our sets, and such work is invaluable. Similarly, it is helpful to set up a craft services area for talent and crew, to have production assistants who can run errands, and to post signage to inform and direct passersby. See *Virtual Reality Cinema, Narrative Tips & Techniques* (Routledge 2021) for a deeper dive into producing.

Conclusion

This chapter has explored the foundations of both image and sound production in cinematic virtual reality. Numerous decisions must be made for your team to create believable and compelling cine-VR. There is a great deal more to cover, and later chapters are dedicated to the advanced aspects of each production area. While capturing and playing back virtual reality images and sounds can be divergent in practice, the two fields ultimately work together to create a unified project that situates users within the world of the healthcare environment.

Notes

1. For more on immersion and presence, see chapter 4 of Jason Jerald, *The VR Book: Human-Centered Design for Virtual Reality*, (Vermont: ACM Books, 2016).
2. Again, see Jerald, chapter 4.
3. For an excellent exploration of some of these issues of VR audio and realism, see Stephan Schütze and Anna Irwin-Schütze, *New Realities in Audio: A Practical Guide to VR, AR, MR and 360 Video* (London: CRC Press, 2018).

SECTION II

PREality is a term coined by the GRID Lab in 2016. It's a portmanteau word combining "preparation" and "reality." In essence, PREality uses cine-VR to *prepare* the viewer for a *reality* that they will experience in the near future. PREality.

We designed our first PREality experience for Grant Medical Center in Columbus, Ohio. Working with trauma surgeon Thanh Nguyen, we analyzed the training protocol for incoming medical residents. Dr. Nguyen, the program director of GMC's surgery education program, had noticed that it took residents quite a bit of time to acclimate to working in the emergency room – in some cases, up to three or four weeks. We hypothesized that this was due to three factors:

1. Residents had limited opportunities to attend a trauma; there were typically half-a-dozen residents in rotation at any given time and only room for one or two to observe in an active trauma bay.
2. Trauma bays are intense, highly active locations. There is a lot of information to soak in and not a lot of time for asking questions or seeking clarification in the moment.
3. Additional observation options were suboptimal. They were either too far away (observing from the next bay) or emotionally remote (observing via "security" cameras in the ceiling).

Dr. Nguyen did not want his residents to simply observe; he wanted them trained to participate. Training included direct observation of how the trauma team interacted with each other and with the patient. He expected awareness of processes and procedures and understanding the physical proximity of monitors and machinery. In Dr. Nguyen's opinion, "you have to be standing in our trauma bay to understand how our trauma bay works." We agreed.

In the summer of 2016, after nearly a year of preparation (logistical and legal), the GRID Lab began using 360° cameras to record live traumas in GMC's emergency room. By rigging cameras from the ceiling, we were able to keep the floor clear of tripods and wires. We dropped three small cine-VR cameras and microphones around the patient treatment area *(one at the head of the patient, one to the left of the patient, and one to the right)*. The cameras were lowered to a lens height of approximately 5'10". We recorded every patient that came through that particular trauma bay for an entire weekend, using all three cameras. We received permission to use the patients' images afterward. If we were unable to gain consent, we immediately deleted the footage.

Subsequently, we installed a closed-system VR viewing system (an HTC Vive) in Dr. Nguyen's office; "closed system" meaning that once the VR headset was configured, the HTC Vive was

DOI: 10.4324/9781003168683-4

disconnected from the internet (as per HIPAA protocol). The GRID Lab then loaded a small library of cine-VR patient experiences in the ER onto the Vives for Dr. Nguyen's residents to observe.

When placed in the headset, the residents felt they were standing shoulder-to-shoulder with the medical team in the trauma bay. They now had direct observation of how the trauma team interacted with each other and with the patient; they could see the exact processes and procedures used by the trauma team from their point of view; thus, they could directly experience physical proximity to the monitors and machinery.

More importantly, this library provided other distinct advantages to Dr. Nguyen's residential training protocol:

1. Every resident could now observe the same set of traumas, allowing the training program to build questions and prompts as part of their education.
2. These experiences were available for residents to view at any time, day or night.
3. The residents could pause and re-watch any aspect of the trauma. In such an active environment it is easy to miss details – especially in 360°. We recommended residents rewind, re-watch, and revisit scenarios multiple times.

GMC residents were now able to observe hours-upon-hours of real-world interaction in the GMC trauma bay. In Dr. Nguyen's words, the residents could now "experience patient care in our trauma bay with our team." Anecdotal evidence suggested that PREality reduced GMC residents' acclimation times from 4–5 weeks to 2–3 weeks. US News and World Report[1] and the Huffington Post[2] reported on the project.

Unfortunately, six months later, GMC began a major renovation of their trauma bays, and the project halted. Why? Because PREality has a particular effect on the audience. In essence, PREality is creating a "forced sense of déjà vu" for the viewer. When a resident walks into the trauma bay, you want them not only to be comfortable with trauma bays *in general*, you want them to have a familiarity with your specific trauma bay *in particular*. Our cine-VR experiences prepared the residents for a specific reality: the reality of the GMC trauma bay. When GMC renovated their ER, the PREality experience was negated. This trauma bay revamp turned our PREality library from an active training tool into a historical archive.

Basic Tenets of a PREality Experience

PREality, by its nature, only works if the recording takes place in the same environment that the audience is preparing to visit in real life since cine-VR prepares the audience for that particular reality. When the GMC trauma bays renovation occurred, the video libraries were less useful because the location was different, and the healthcare providers behaved differently in this new environment. Their proximity to monitors and machines was different, and simple changes (such as the location of doorways) affected the team's workflow.

Nevertheless, the experience solidified six tenets of PREality still in practice today.

1. **Site specificity:** PREality experiences must be site-specific to the location the audience is preparing to visit.

It is impossible to create a forced sense of déjà vu unless the audience experiences the exact location at two different times: (at least) once in cine-VR to **pre**pare, and then later in **reality**. Hence: PREality.

2. **Personnel specificity:** PREality experiences should include the actual people (or people in similar roles) that the audience will meet in the actual location.

In PREality, the people in an environment are as important as the environment itself. If you are trying to prepare the audience to engage in team dynamics, it would be necessary for the real people to be involved. For instance, it was important for the GMC residents to observe the actual anesthesiologists, head nurses, and surgeons they would be working with during their rotation.

However, it doesn't always need to be the same people. For instance, if PREality is familiarizing a student with patient care in the intensive care unit, the patient in each example may be unique because the experience isn't necessarily specific *to the patient*. Instead, it was particular *to the process and the location*.

3. **Procedural use:** PREality works best as part of a larger context. It helps if the audience discuss, debrief, and process the experience with a group leader, an instructor, a professor, and others going through the PREality training.

4. **Point of View:** Position the cine-VR cameras to approximate the human experience as accurately as possible (height, distance from camera, and proximity to other objects and actors).

It is vital that the audience feel as if they are standing invisibly amid the action (and not somewhere on the sidelines or floating above the experience). The closer the camera is placed to the action, the more imitate the experience feels, and the more likely it is to create that forced sense of déjà vu.

5. **Repetitive Engagement:** PREality experiences should not be a singular event. Repetition is vital. Audiences should be encouraged to rewind, re-watch, and revisit scenarios – as well as watch new experiences from the same vantage point.

Repetitive engagement increases the sense of PREality. We found that the use of cine-VR libraries significantly enhances the likelihood of a PREality experience. Additionally, the use of multiple camera angles of the same event (left of bed v. right of bed) allows for more detailed observations through repetitive viewing.

6. **Viewing Options:** PREality experiences *must* be viewed in a headset with headphones.

While it is possible to view cine-VR without a headset (via a computer screen or handheld devices), the sense of immersion significantly decreases when utilizing the audience's peripheral vision and aural spatiality. If the audience feels that they are "watching" the scenario rather than "experiencing" the scenario, then the likelihood of experiencing PREality is zero.

The Effects of PREality

The following three chapters will discuss the project-specific effects of PREality. We have noticed that PREality produces the following results regardless of audience or topic area:

1. Purposeful reflection,
2. Stronger soft skills,
3. Accelerated transition times.

Purposeful Reflection

On-going studies suggest that PREality increases observational awareness in the audience, specifically as it relates to the environment and to human interactions. This observational awareness subsequently creates a more meaningful and purposeful reflection about the location, the participants, and the process being observed. We have found that when a group experiences the same PREality scenario, each member observes something different. Through reflection and discussion, the group as a whole learns from the observations of others. To maximize the educational impact, we recommend reflection after each PREality experience. Additionally, repeating the experience allows for a more in-depth reflections.

Stronger Soft Skills

We have found PREality especially useful for interprofessional team training. Surprisingly so, when the GRID Lab initially demonstrated the trauma bay footage for Grant Medical Center personnel, the response was overwhelming. Not only did Dr. Nguyen's team show interest, but the rest of the medical education team began commenting on how the same footage could train nurses and x-ray technicians as well. Even the custodial staff director requested to use the footage to better understand how fluids might find their way to unexpected locations.

In a 360° video, each viewer has agency – they can choose where to look and when. They can choose who to follow and where to place their attention. If you want to observe the nurse's actions, you – as the audience – have the agency to do so. Someone else, however, may choose to watch the patient the entire time. Therefore, each cine-VR experience is unique to the individual even though the video recording itself is identical.

Accelerated Transition Times

Fiscal demands have limited the exposure to high-pressure medical environments. So have scheduling conflicts, unpredictability, and – quite simply – space for people to stand. Nevertheless, there is a need to acclimate incoming medical professionals to these new environments quickly. PREality has been shown to reduce anxiety in students entering high-pressure environments. Reduced stress subsequently leads to accelerated transition times – whether familiarizing people to an environment, educating them to patient care within that environment, or introducing them to the team who helps provide that care.

Conclusion

In closing, by consuming the audience's awareness both visually and aurally, cine-VR can immerse the audience in a new environment in a way that is similar to a shadow experience, where you might be able to peek over the shoulder of a professional. Yet, unlike a shadow experience, the PREality approach provides the educator with a relatively low-cost digital experience that allows the audience to pause and revisit every aspect of a "live event."

As you'll see in the following three chapters, PREality can play a crucial role in reducing fear for those entering medical professions. Whether experiencing a stressful environment, the time pressures associated with accurate patient assessment, or trying to fit seamlessly into a new team in a high-pressure situation, repetition and familiarization can help alleviate such trepidation.

Notes

1. Viviano, Joanne. "Ohio Doctors Employ Virtual Reality to Train for Trauma Care." *U.S. News & World Report*, March 26, 2017. http://www.usnews.com/news/best-states/ohio/articles/2017-03-26/ohio-doctors-employ-virtual-reality-to-train-for-trauma-care.
2. Williams, Eric R. "Virtual Reality: An Emerging Game Changer in Healthcare." The Huffington Post. TheHuffingtonPost.com, December 7, 2017. http://www.huffingtonpost.com/advertising-week/virtual-reality-an-emergi_b_13343112.html.

Chapter 3

Teaching Students to Read a Patient's Room

Ashley Crow

Contents

Simulation in Acute Care Education

Most physical therapy programs prepare students for practice in the acute medical environment with lectures and labs. Classroom application activities are often presented in patient cases and may accompany media sources such as photos or videos. Laboratory application activities attempt to recreate the hospital setting; however, they often lack environmental and patient authenticity.

DOI: 10.4324/9781003168683-5

The highest degree of specificity that an academic program could provide would be through the use of a simulation laboratory with high-fidelity human and mannequin simulation.

One of the significant benefits of using high-fidelity simulation in teaching is the sense of realness. These experiences require the student to interface with and regulate stress while making clinical decisions and maintaining patient safety. Many unfamiliar students with the hospital environment are unaware of their own emotions when faced with high patient acuity. The seriousness of the potential implication of harming patients renders some frozen with anxiety and unable to do their job. In contrast, a seasoned physical therapist practicing in acute care understands that this particular setting is where medical acuity meets physical activity and, through experience and exposure to various situations, have developed an ability to remain calm and clear. While not often the primary objective, high-fidelity simulation provides the structure to address the affective domain of learning. The degree to which a simulation can address the affective domain of learning depends on the degree of fidelity that a simulation provides.

Unfortunately, there are many barriers to high-fidelity simulations. Costs, material resources, and required faculty effort can make this option unfeasible.[1,2,3,4,5]

Challenges with Instruction

Designing a simulation that targets the cognitive, psychomotor, and affective domains of learning is challenging. The challenges are genuine when one considers that acute care's very nature is complex and highly variable. The interdependence of each variable in this setting contributes to the complexity. Implementation using a whole-practice approach better captures this interdependence. When using whole-practice, practice a skill in its entirety, from start to finish. Many of the barriers mentioned above create situations where instructors (myself included) have to resort to a part-practice approach. A task is broken down into its subcomponents and practiced in isolation of the whole task. This approach has value but loses effectiveness if not intentionally integrated back into the original task.

As a classroom and clinical instructor, I observed a disconnect in student performance between the classroom and the clinic. The paper cases, photos, and videos were not enough to provide the students with a realistic understanding of the acute care environment and what it takes to provide safe care to patients with medical instability. I needed a way to bring the dynamic, fast-paced, and stressful hospital environment into the classroom meaningful to students' current generation. Furthermore, do it in a way that created a safe and conducive environment for learning. At one point, I remembered thinking how much my students could learn if only they were a fly on the wall observing various scenarios they might encounter. Later I questioned, why watch from the wall when you could be in my shoes – to see what I see from my perspective. As I learned more about cine-VR, I realized that this could soon be a reality or, rather, PREality.

Requirements in Tool Design

Innovation is often a product of necessity. As the only acute care content expert in my department, I often found myself limited by a lack of time and personnel. My students needed practice in varied situations with the opportunity to fail, reflect, and grow safely. I also needed them to do it without me physically there all the time. These factors served as the driving force in designing a new teaching tool using cine-VR. The following elements outline the essential considerations in tool design.

- **Realism:** Space and equipment used in the scenario had to look authentic enough to simulate a hospital environment. Authenticity is crucial when high-fidelity human or mannequin simulation is not available or when academic programs cannot secure acute care clinical experiences.
- **Cost-effective:** The expense associated with building the tool itself had to be economical. Other savings through a reduction of resource utilization may replace a high-fidelity mannequin or human simulation. Cine-VR is easier to setup and distribute widely.
- **Facilitate critical thinking:** Students have the opportunity to observe the environment with critical reflection of the space and its potential limitations, patient status and precautions, synthesis of information from the medical and surgical equipment, and management of lines before formulating a mobility plan.[6,7] When used in conjunction with didactic work, students can improve nontechnical skills such as clinical judgment, communication, and independent thought before feedback.
- **Active engagement:** When using a VR headset, students can filter out the surrounding world to improve learning engagement. Studies have demonstrated that a fully immersive VR environment allows students to be more engaged and respond realistically. More of their senses are devoted to the VR simulation over other distractions.[8,9,10,11,12]
- **Improve confidence:** Increased exposure to equipment typically seen in the acute care setting and increased familiarity with the setting before their clinical internship can improve overall confidence in the setting.[13] Students can digest the clinical situation at their own pace and acclimate to any emotional responses experienced without the appearance of ignorance or insensitivity. Cine-VR experiences can be the right places for students to make mistakes.
- **Standardize assessment:** Every student can have the same cine-VR experience, which allows for the potential to standardize assessment by instructors. It can also be useful for remote/virtual learning environments.
- **Efficiency:** Produce the scenarios once, and there is no need to recreate them. Faculty will save time with set up and implementation. Supply students with space and the equipment, and they can use the scenario as a blueprint to independently set up unique simulations and develop the technical skills needed to work in this environment.
- **Accessible:** Students can access the library as often as they need and can be off-campus. Scenarios can be accessed anywhere and can be paused and replayed as often as needed.

The Cine-VR Library

The library consists of forty cine-VR acute care scenarios based in realistic hospital rooms with mock patients. The point of view is that of a clinician who is standing at the bedside. Each scenario is approximately two minutes in duration, with clinical situations that range from simple to complex. We produced scenarios that are nonspecific to a particular medical diagnosis. The lack of specificity allows the instructor to build cases around the learner's needs and objectives. This approach provides versatility in creating a scaffolding to increase scenario complexity as learning advances.

The library, copyright 2019, is housed on departmental Oculus Go wireless headsets or accessed through a private YouTube channel on a computer.

Classroom Implementation

The cine-VR library is a tool designed to enhance the delivery of acute care physical therapy education. It was not designed to be a stand-alone activity nor intended to replace simulation. Cine-VR alone does not translate to improvements in performance. When used as a pre-simulation activity, it does influence the student's reflective process. Reflection is defined as "serious thought or consideration" and traditionally occurs at the end of a learning experience. Cine-VR as a pre-simulation activity can facilitate an earlier reflective process since the student must consider the pre-planning component of care. Use pre-simulation reflection as part of the part-practice. When implemented as a component of more comprehensive learning activity as outlined below, nontechnical skill development can progress to technical skill development using a part-practice to whole-practice strategy. The following describes in more detail how we integrated cine-VR in my classroom.

1. Students use the scenarios as a pre-simulation exercise to facilitate nontechnical skills such as situational and safety awareness, clinical decision-making, and communication. Once immersed in a scenario, physical therapy students create a strategic plan for patient mobilization using visualization while considering how factors such as patient status, medical support equipment, lines, drains, and monitors will impact their plan. (See example A.)
2. Students use the scenarios as a blueprint to set up and implement a simulation in the simulation lab to facilitate technical skills development. Students have access to the simulation space and all of the same equipment used in the scenarios. Because faculty supervision is not required, students can work through simulations on their own.
3. Students use an extensive and detailed peer evaluative rubric to assess one another's performance. The rubric reflects an evaluator's specific thought process. Peer evaluators are required to provide comments on individual tasks and summative performance. Knowledge is gained from multiple viewpoints as students are required to portray the patient, physical therapist, and the peer evaluator. The rubric includes simplistic tasks such as the introduction of self, discipline, purpose, hand washing, and asking for consent and addresses items such as appropriate patient draping and ensuring all patient needs are within reach before departing the room. While these tasks are considered standard care and simple in isolation, they become challenging when the student's attention splits between the patient's demands and the environment. The checklist format helps the student take a comprehensive approach and sets the stage for acceptable practices because the learning activity incorporates peer reviews. Every member of the group benefits from the feedback received during the peer-review process.

The Academy of Acute Care Physical Therapy (AACPT) of the American Physical Therapy Association published a document in 2017 that outlined the minimum criteria for an entry-level practice called the *Core Competencies for Entry-Level Practice in Acute Care Physical Therapy*. The core competencies include clinical decision making, patient management, safety, communication, and discharge planning. Photo 3.1 illustrates how cine-VR can address the core competencies as a pre-simulation exercise.

Clinical Decision Making

- ■ Describe the patient's presentation.
- ■ What does each line/tube/support equipment/monitor do, and how might it affect a physical therapy session?
- ■ What information is needed to determine if the patient is appropriate for treatment today?

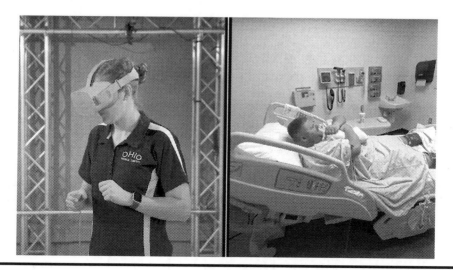

Photo 3.1 Split-screen image of a DPT student (left) engaged in a cine-VR room assessment (right)

Patient Management

- What types of assistive devices and equipment might be needed to complete an out of bed assessment?
- Based on the environment, describe a logistical plan for mobilization. Do you need to create space? What can be unlocked/moved/locked?
- Which lines are mobile already? What lines need to become mobile?

Safety

- What safety mechanisms can be put in place to reduce risk to the patient and therapist if working alone?

Communication

- How does the style or strategy of communication change in the following situations?
  - The patient is deaf or hard of hearing
  - The patient does not speak English
- If the patient is not appropriate today, how and what do you say to the nurse, the physician, and the anxious family member who is eager to hear about the patient's status? Practice aloud.

Discharge Planning

- What are the minimum mobility tasks that the patient needs to be able to accomplish in order to discharge home safely?

The cine-VR library works in both live and remote learning. Small group or whole-class discussion can be facilitated easily through screen sharing capabilities. Addressing responses to student questions can increase or decrease case complexity.

This teaching strategy addressed the needs of my students and myself. It allowed students to have more time for practice in different clinical situations, and then I was no longer limited by resources. With the cine-VR scenario library, the students had immediate and easy access to a high volume of scenarios and the physical space and resources available to reconstruct a simulation scenario.

Audience

This tool was designed with early learners in mind and geared toward physical therapy students specific to the acute care environment. Similar but distinctly different healthcare education programs such as Physical Therapy Assistant, Occupational Therapy, and Occupational Therapy Assistant PTA, OT, COTA may use the tool in a similar acute care education capacity.

Healthcare organizations may use the cine-VR library as part of an initial or ongoing assessment process. If implemented as part of an interview or onboarding, it may help an organization select the right candidate and avoid the costs associated with a poor-hire. Regularly assessing competency assessments of staff is possible.

Production Approach and Process

Actors portray hospitalized patients. They were donned with various degrees and combinations of medical equipment, including but not limited to intravenous lines, urinary catheters, oxygen delivery devices, drains, telemetry monitoring, bandages, and bracing.

Recording occurred in Ohio University's College of Health Sciences and Professions Interprofessional Simulation Suite. The simulated patient's room size is comparable to actual hospital rooms – the most considerable requirement for recording in these rooms related to visibility and resolution of monitors and signage. The production team experimented with camera placement to determine the best location for visibility. A camera was placed five feet high, with the monitor approximately four-to-five feet from the camera and the patient approximately five-to-six feet from the camera (see Figure 3.1). No additional lighting was used aside from the light provided from the room.

We chose a prosumer cine-VR camera recorded in 6K video quality required stitching the captured images in post-production. We recorded in four-channel surround sound audio to create 360° spatial audio of the room. The sound mix allowed the students to hear the beeping of the monitor "behind them" as they looked at the patient – reminding them to turn around to see the monitor. Further equipment explanations are available in Chapters 7, 12, and 20.

Tool Presentation

The cine-VR scenario library concept as a teaching tool was presented at the American Physical Therapy Association's Combined Sections Meeting and the Academy of Acute Care Physical Therapy's Bridge the Gap Conference to audiences primarily comprised of faculty. Many have expressed excitement at its promise and utility. Additionally, presentations at university and college-wide events at Ohio University have excited colleagues about their potential use.

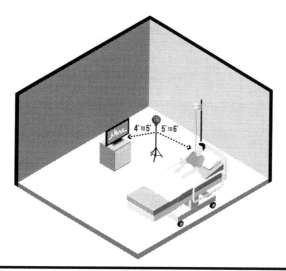

Figure 3.1   The production team experimented with camera placement to determine the best location for visibility

Quantitative data was collected as part of a pilot confidence study examining the tool's impact on self-reported student confidence. The sample size is too small to derive any significant or conclusive results. However, trends in scores suggest that exposure to cine-VR in their educational preparation for acute care clinical rotations had less change in self-efficacy ratings after their actual acute care clinical practicum. This trend suggests that classroom exposure to acute via cine-VR provided such a realistic environment that the students were unsurprised by the environment once actually there.

Student Comments

Here are some post-experience comments from second-year physical therapy students:

> *The skills check off, time in the suite to practice for our practical, and dry lab time were all tremendously helpful. Virtual reality proved most helpful in the beginning for me to assess a situation and make a game plan. After getting better at that, it was more beneficial for me to practice in the lab and get better hands-on work physically. All three helped build my confidence for patient care and better prepare me to succeed on clinical!*
>
> *These activities greatly prepared me for my acute care rotation. Being familiar with all lines, tubes, and so forth was extremely helpful. I did not feel super overwhelmed when walking into rooms with patients with several lines. I felt like I could handle it.*

Lessons Learned

Some users experienced motion sickness known as visuomotion sensitivity while using the cine-VR technology. Motion sickness is the result of a sensory mismatch between two or more sensory inputs. The orientation of self-concerning space is related to integrating one's vision, vestibular, and somatosensory senses. Utilizing the cine-VR technology in a headset creates a mismatch between visual and vestibular input, creating the by-product of motion sickness. The 6K video quality possibly contributed to the mismatch because it may not create the smoothest playback while being a high resolution. It may be advisable that users sit instead of stand and utilize a graded exposure approach to viewing content to allow for habituation development.

What Is Next?

Creating a library of cine-VR scenarios with the early learner in mind will create more complex and dynamic scenarios to target the intermediate and advanced learners. This library involves producing more extended and more complex scenarios. An intermediate and advanced level cine-VR library would require a higher level of thought processing by the student. An example of an intermediate level scenario would involve a patient who is actively moving or completing a task. Asking students to determine a course of action or make a clinical decision based on experiencing the scenario is required. An example of an advanced scenario would be an entire patient and therapist interaction, such as during an evaluation or treatment session.

Lastly, exploring marketability and partnerships with other academic programs or healthcare organizations may be pursued.

Financial Implications

A small internal grant procured the resources needed to build the cine-VR library. The collaboration with the GRID Lab at Ohio University allowed for some cost savings. No camera or sound equipment needed to be purchased, and university computers and software were used. The GRID Lab's million-dollar VR infrastructure was already in place, so there were no additional technical supplies to create this experience. The remaining costs were associated with the time required in post-production editing, purchasing props for the scenarios, and paying patient actors. After the initial investment to create the scenarios, potential cost savings can come in many forms.

Cine-VR used in conjunction with hands-on learning activities may replace costly high-fidelity mannequin simulation without expensive simulation laboratories. Also, reductions in costs associated with faculty time are possible. If used as an alternative learning experience in clinical education or remedial work, it may prevent graduation delays for students studying physical therapy. Lastly, there may be savings associated with onboarding costs in hiring if used as part of an evaluative process for new hires or ongoing competency.

Viewing

To view and download cine-VR examples mentioned in this chapter, please visit: https://vimeo.com/channels/cinevr4healthcare/ (**password:** *cineVR4health*).

Notes

1. Mori B, Carnahan H, Herold J. Use of Simulation Learning Experiences in Physical Therapy Entry-to-Practice Curricula: A Systematic Review. *Physiother Can.* 2015 Spring;67(2):194–202.

2. Ohtake PJ, Lazarus M, Schillo R, Rosen M. Simulation Experience Enhances Physical Therapist Student Confidence.
3. Silberman NJ, Litwin B, Panzarella K, Fernandez-Fernandez A. Student Clinical Performance in Acute Care Enhanced Through Simulation Training. *JACPT.* 2016;7(1): 25–36.
4. Silberman NJ, Panzarella KJ, Melzer BA. Using Human Simulation to Prepare Physical Therapy Students for Acute Care Clinical Practice. *J Allied Health.* 2013 Spring;42(1):25–32.
5. Undre S, Koutantji M, Sevdalis N, Gautama S, Selvapatt N, Williams S, Sains P, McCulloch P, Darzi A, Vincent C. Multidisciplinary Crisis Simulations: The Way Forward for Training Surgical Teams. *World J Surg.* 2007 Sep;31(9):1843–53.
6. Sabus C, Sabata D, Antonacci D. Use of a Virtual Environment to Facilitate Instruction of an Interprofessional Home Assessment. *J Allied Health.* 2011 Winter;40(4):199–205.
7. Stefanic D. Virtual Reality Check. *TD.* 2016;70(1):88.
8. Baus O, Bouchard S. Moving from Virtual Reality Exposure-Based Therapy to Augmented Reality Exposure-Based Therapy: A Review. *Front Hum Neurosci.* 2014 Mar; 8:1–15.
9. Huhn K, McGinnis P, Wainwright S, Deutsch J. A Comparison of 2 Case Delivery Methods: Virtual and Live. *J Phys Ther Educ.* 2013 Fall;23(3):41–48.
10. Pierce J, Gutiérrez F, Vergara VM, Alverson DC, Qualls C, Saland L, Goldsmith T, Caudell TP. Comparative Usability Studies of Full vs. Partial Immersive Virtual Reality Simulation for Medical Education and Training. *Stud Health Technol Inform.* 2008;132:372–377.
11. Wilson CJ, Soranzo A. The Use of Virtual Reality in Psychology: A Case Study in Visual Perception. *Comput Math Methods Med.* 2015: 1–5.
12. Campbell A, Amon K, Nguyen M, Cumming S, Selby H, Lincoln M, Neville V, Bhullar N, Magor-Blatch L, Oxman L, Green T, George A, Gonczi A. Virtual World Interview Skills Training for Students Studying Health Professions. *Journal of Technology in Human Services,* 2015;33(2): 156–171.
13. Huhn K, Deutsch J. Development and Assessment of a Web-Based Patient Simulation Program. *J Phys Ther Educ.* 2011 Winter;25(1): 5–10.

Chapter 4

Capturing Bedside Care in Clinical Settings

Petra S. Williams

Contents

Introduction

This chapter describes how our doctoral physical therapy (DPT) program on the Flagstaff campus of Northern Arizona University (NAU) used cine-VR to create PREality experiences of actual patient care, captured at the patient's bedside in a local hospital. It also discusses how we use PREality as part of our Integrated Clinical Education (ICE) curriculum.

DPT programs prepare students for success in full-time terminal clinical education (TCE) experiences with didactic content, laboratory-based simulation practice, and occasional early patient exposure experiences at community clinic sites. However, once in the actual clinical setting on their TCE, students often report feeling unprepared for and intimidated by an unfamiliar environment, complex patient interactions, and interprofessional collaboration fundamental to dynamically evolving acute care reality. While traditional simulation's strength lies in providing repetitive technical skill practice opportunities, these tools only mimic reality by using problems derived from real life. Additionally, the need to suspend reality during simulation limits the capacity to address non-technical soft skills essential to successful patient outcomes in challenging, high

DOI: 10.4324/9781003168683-6

acuity healthcare settings, including situational awareness, communication, emotional acclimation, and critical thinking. Unlike preplanned simulation cases, PREality captures the successes and failures where it happens: at the bedside.

Using cine-VR to record live patient care from the perspective of the practicing physical therapist (PT) gives the learner what we describe as "the super-power of invisibility" in the actual clinical environment where they will be practicing. Although traditional video instruction remains a valuable component of medical education, PREality takes advantage of the sense of presence delivered by complete immersion in a virtual environment. This immersion consumes the learner's awareness visually and aurally, commanding the same attention as if the learner is "right there" at the bedside shadowing the PT for the day. Yet, unlike a shadow experience, PREality created with cine-VR provides the educator with a digital experience that allows the learner to pause and revisit every aspect of a "live event" in 360°.

"Leaders in physical therapy assert that 'early patient exposure in genuine clinical environments provides students with the critical skills necessary for future professional practice.'"[1] In 2017, the American Physical Therapy Association (APTA) published their "Best Practice for Physical Therapist Clinical Education Task Force Report."[2] In this report, the APTA identified key challenges facing PT education today, including lack of early patient exposure in clinical environments due to fiscal demands, inconsistent quality of clinical education experiences, and diminished capacity for clinical education placements. Depending upon the PT Clinical Instructor's (CI) caseload that day, some students may have a full day of observation with various patients. In contrast, others may have a truncated experience dictated by the patients in the hospital at the time. These challenges are even greater for programs in rural counties like NAU's (in Flagstaff). We annually have two cohorts of forty-eight students to place in a minimum of two settings each year with a finite number of local healthcare venues.

PREality experiences created with clinical partners can offer academic programs access to genuine clinical environments that may be limited, inconsistent, or even restricted (as with the COVID-19 pandemic stay-at-home orders). With PREality experiences of actual patient care, acute care exposure is not dictated by today's caseload; instead, everyone can be virtually in the same room with the same patient. PREality experiences can also reduce the burden that students place on clinic sites. A single PT CI could simultaneously mentor hundreds of DPT students as they all "peek over the shoulder" while the PT CI delivers patient care. A "caseload" of PREality experiences allows the entire cohort of DPT students to learn from the same clinical encounters, thereby giving programs the capacity to prepare DPT students to learn from the successes and mistakes of practicing PTs. They all can learn to handle both the most common and rare clinical situations.

These factors make PREality ideally suited for ICE. ICE is "designed for students to become familiar with the clinical environment, integrate didactic knowledge, gain confidence with patient management skills, and enhance self-awareness of professional behaviors."[3] With this in mind, we believe that PREality experiences, when implemented as a fundamental element of ICE, can be a novel and innovative strategy to provide early patient exposure in a variety of healthcare environments and to tackle some of the challenges to clinical education identified by the APTA.

Creating a Clinical Environment Library

We set out to create a collection of eight-to-ten PREality experiences of actual patient care that would allow us to replicate a typical caseload observed by a first-year DPT student while shadowing a PT CI during an Early Patient Exposure day in the clinic.

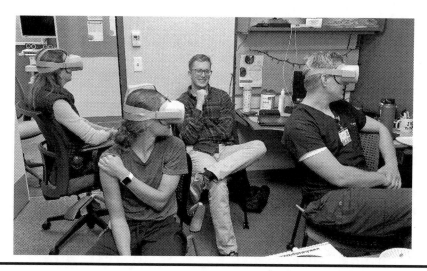

Photo 4.1   Students observing PREality cases as part of NAU's ICE program

Our intention with the library was to use PREality to provide our DPT students the opportunity to observe a consistent slate of real bedside patient care experiences in the clinical setting. Thereby eliminating the challenges inherent to "shadowing" for a day and reducing our clinical partners' burden to provide these early patient exposure experiences. By combining PREality experiences with instructor-guided debriefing, discussion, and follow-up simulation practice, we would create a consistent educational program for the students before entering their TCE's (see Photo 4.1).

We theorized that the PREality library would serve various purposes:

1. For those who will complete their TCE at VVMC, this library would serve as a "by definition" PREality experience. Ideally, when they arrive at VVMC for their TCE, they will be better prepared. A better-prepared student will make more effective use of their time while on their internship. They will acclimate faster to the facility and have a longer time functioning at their highest level of competence.
2. Regardless of whether a DPT student is assigned to VVMC, the cine-VR library would provide a consistent reference point for discussing clinical experiences. Assuming that we could capture a wide variety of actual patient care cases recorded at the bedside from the point of view of the healthcare provider, students with limited experiences on their actual early patient exposure days would (at the very least) have had a broad *observational* experience.
3. Ideally, this model could be replicated with other clinical partners who are unable to take our students for early patient exposure experiences or those non-local clinical settings that have our students for TCE. With site-specific PREality, our goal is to potentiate the DPT students' clinical experiences by accelerating their transition into a specific clinical environment and reducing the orientation burden on CIs.

Securing Clinic Site Participation with Patients, Clinicians, and Leadership

To obtain initial approval for this project, we collaborated with one of our dedicated regional clinical partners, Verde Valley Medical Center (VVMC), part of Northern Arizona Healthcare (NAH). Approximately 15% of our students complete at least one terminal clinical experience at VVMC. Up to 50% of each cohort complete an acute care early patient exposure day there during their first didactic year. Over five months, we met with interested PTs who also serve as CI's and the leadership of VVMC Rehabilitation Services to identify our PREality CI's and to establish our protocol for obtaining consent from patients and clinicians to record their interactions. Additionally, we mapped out our procedures for recording the scenarios and protecting the privacy of the digital images and files.

Members of the research offices at both NAH and NAU conducted a review of the proposed project. They determined that because the purpose of this project was to prepare NAU DPT students for clinical internships, the DPT students viewing the PREality scenarios were the "subjects" of any research (not the recorded patients or clinicians). Therefore, the creation of the PREality scenarios did not fall under IRB oversight for human research activities. With this non-research determination, VVMC asked us to use their preexisting Communications Department media consent forms for patients, families, and employees. We decided that I would obtain consent from participants because patients or families may feel obligated to give permission to be recorded if their treating clinician asked them to participate.

Before recording a session, the PT CI introduced me to the patient and any family members present. I described the project's purpose, showed them the recording equipment and where it would be placed in the room. I emphasized that the viewers of the recordings will be NAU DPT students as part of their training to prepare them to work with patients like them in the future. I explained the process for protecting video files and images in non-technical terms to clarify how the files would remain private and how they would never be viewable by the public on the internet. Specifically, the files are transferred from the memory cards in the cameras to password-protected external hard drives and then to the viewing headsets which do not have access to the internet. As most of the patients were over 60, I said the card in the camera is like a roll of film that gets developed. The files are then loaded onto a headset or hard drive, like placing pictures in a scrapbook. I further emphasized that files will not be shared outside of NAU DPT, nor will they be posted in any location where the public could view them (i.e., not on YouTube, Vimeo, etc.). Patients and families agreed to participate by signing the VVMC consent form. We used a similar procedure to obtain consent from all clinicians (i.e., PT CI, nurses, physicians, etc.) who may be involved in the patient's care during the session. We remain intentional about this limited use because of these agreements we made with the patients and the clinicians who gave us this tremendous opportunity to learn from them.

The Low-Cost Rapid Implementation Strategy Production Process

We refer to the production process we developed for capturing Bedside Patient Care as "Low-CRIS," which stands for *Low-Cost Rapid Implementation Strategy*. This process compares to the productions described in Chapters 3 and 5. Low-CRIS design captures actual patient care in a healthcare setting expeditiously to minimize patient care interference and facilitate rapid turnaround for implementation in weekly ICE activities. *What we record today can be ready for use in the classroom tomorrow.*

Low-CRIS meets three objectives:

1. To capture bedside patient care in a dynamic and unpredictable hospital setting where opportunities can present at a moment's notice, the production process needed to be quick

and easy for one person to set up. It also had to be readily mobile and dependable to follow the PT from room to room. Speed and simplicity were more important than a polished final product.

2. To reduce any distraction or the potential for interference that recording a clinical encounter could cause, the equipment used had to be minimal to be essentially kept "out of sight and mind" for the PT and the patient during the treatment session. Getting the gestalt of the clinical encounter was more important than a perfect, high-quality image.

3. To make the PREality experiences readily available, post-production was kept simple. The camera stitched the images automatically and created new files for every five minutes of footage recorded. As most sessions were 20–30 minutes in length, we had to edit these clips together after cutting the heads and tails off of the first and last videos (i.e., before the PT entered the room and after they left). We labeled each cine-VR experience with its date and case number, but we did not create any graphics, title cards, or credits. The experiences were edited together quickly, loaded to the head mounted display (HMD), and available within a day for student use.

Daily Logistical Considerations

One VVMC Physical Therapist (Kelly Hughes PT, DPT), an alumna of the NAU DPT program and CI for our acute care early patient exposure experiences, volunteered to be the primary PREality CI. Patient treatment sessions were recorded on four different dates over eight weeks. During that time, Kelly also had an NAU DPT student (Sara Patterson) completing her ten-week acute care TCE at VVMC. We decided to include Sara in the videos to give the DPT audience someone to relate to specifically and to demonstrate how a CI and DPT student work together in this setting.

At the beginning of each day, Kelly, Sara, and I discussed the patient roster for the day. We decided which patients might be best for the day's shoot, and then I approached each one individually to obtain permission. Once the patient authorizations were accepted, I simply shadowed Kelly and Sara with our equipment during the day. We confirmed the consent to participate again immediately before recording the session from patients, family members, and clinicians in the room.

Technical Considerations

Consistent with the low-CRIS objectives, the only equipment in the room was the fist-sized camera mounted on a lightweight tripod set so the camera lens height was approximately 5'5". We used the on-camera microphone to record audio. We did not use any additional lights other than the lights in the patient's room. To optimize the available room lighting, as the Arizona sun can be very bright during the day, after placing the camera, we turned on all of the lights in the room and closed all of the window blinds. This setup allowed for adequate light with the least amount of contrast and risk for silhouetting people and objects when they pass in front of the window. The size of the currently available prosumer 360° digital video-audio cameras (combined with the lack of a production crew in the room capturing the footage) makes it more likely that the clinicians and patients forget that they are being recorded.

To create PREality experiences that gave the learner the sense of a physical presence "right there" at the bedside, camera placement had three concurrent objectives to meet:

1. Put the student in the room where they would be standing if they were at VVMC with Kelly and Sara to observe that day;
2. Prevent unnecessary exposure of the patient's body; and
3. Be enough out of the way of the activity so that everyone could forget that they were being recorded.

To achieve these objectives while optimizing the "over the shoulder" visual and auditory experience, we strategically placed the camera on its tripod adjacent to the head of the bed in the patient's room (see Figure 4.1). There may also be a chair, IV pole, and oxygen next to where the student is "standing" in the room. One final element to consider with camera placement was to ensure that the stitch line would fall in locations where the clinician and patient were least likely to cross it during the session. With the camera in this location, the student can watch the treatment session in front of them, with the patient and clinician within a virtual arm's length. It is interesting to watch students while they view one of the challenging patient encounters. With the HMD on, we often observe that students reach out as if they are trying to assist the PT CI during the session.

Once the camera was in place, I turned it on, started recording, and then left the room to wait in the hallway until the treatment session ended. Kelly and Sara then joined to start the session. Using this protocol, the camera is already recording with the patient before the PTs enter the room, reducing their awareness that they are being recorded. To ensure privacy during the session, the PT CI and DPT student refer to the patient by their first name only and do not offer any other identifying information about the patient typically requested by a hospital (e.g., date of birth, hospital id number). After Kelly and Sara ended the session, I would stop the camera, wipe down the tripod and camera housing for infection control purposes before removing the camera from the room. After replacing the battery and data card, we moved to the next patient. This routine

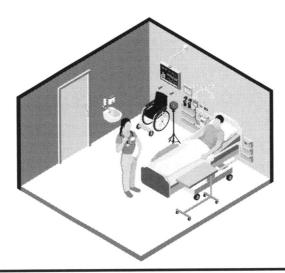

Figure 4.1   To optimize the experience, the camera is strategically placed adjacent to the head of the bed

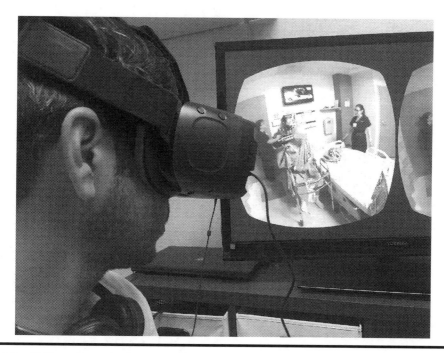

Photo 4.2   DPT student watches scenarios recorded at VVMC through a Samsung Gear HMD

was easy to repeat throughout the day and allowed us to record in real-time without interrupting Kelly's schedule.

After we completed the post-production edits described above, we transferred files to password-protected external hard drives. We then loaded them to wireless HMDs, which remain disconnected from the internet when viewing loaded cases. When we first started, we used the Samsung Gear, which was technically challenging for novice VR users (see Photo 4.2). Now we use the Oculus Go, which is more cost-effective and straightforward.

Implementation of PREality Experiences in ICE

While implementing our library has been multi-faceted (especially during the COVID-19 pandemic), this section describes one particular implementation that pairs PREality experiences with simulation practice as part of our ICE curriculum. Groups of four first-year DPT students in their second didactic semester attend one three-hour session on campus in one of our labs set up to mimic a hospital setting with hospital beds and other equipment. This experience was particularly welcomed by the DPT students in 2020 and 2021 as our clinical partners could not take students for early patient exposure experiences in acute care due to the pandemic.

After describing the session's purpose, students are introduced to the VR environment and the Oculus Go HMD. Students are invited to either stand or sit in a swivel chair to fully explore the 360° environment.

Students who report feeling disoriented or experience some motion sickness in the VR environment are advised to look down for footprints or the tripod's legs and then stamp their own feet in place to "feel" the floor they see in the image. Another strategy, depending upon the room

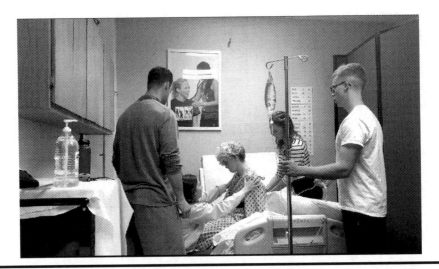

Photo 4.3 Based upon the PREality case, first-year DPT students implement their treatment plan with a second-year student acting as the patient and instructor acting as CI during simulation practice

setup in the PREality scenario, is to position a table or other stable object in the lab where a bed or chair is located in the students' PREality environment to touch with one of their hands while viewing the scenario. Finally, some students report that seeing a little bit of the "outside" world through the bottom of the headset near their nose or cheeks is helpful. Once students orient to the environment and understand how to use the HMD controller, they can access the three scenarios.

All of the PREality scenarios we have recorded are considered "treatment sessions" – the PT CI and the DPT student intern are already familiar with the patient, and they are carrying out their treatment plan. Thus, we instruct the students to view the session with the intention that they will treat the patient at the "next" session. Before viewing each PREality treatment session, students receive a brief paragraph about the patient's medical history and anticipated discharge destination (e.g., home, nursing facility). After viewing the PREality treatment session, we invite students to ask questions and share insights about what they observed, much like they would with the CI. We shift into a more focused discussion about the case with a series of questions designed to target the five elements identified in the "Core Competencies for Entry-Level Practice in Acute Care Physical Therapy." Created by the Academy for Acute Care Physical Therapy in 2015, the elements include clinical decision making, patient management, safety, communication, and discharge planning.[4] The students get some time to prepare their treatment plan to implement with the patient during simulation practice with an instructor acting as CI and a second-year DPT student acting as the patient (see Photo 4.3). Simulation practice is then followed by a debrief session about their performance and reflections on the whole experience.

To begin to evaluate the efficacy of PREality and simulation practice as a part of ICE, students completed a custom ten-item Confidence survey about acute care practice confidence before the session. Within twenty-four hours, students completed a second Confidence survey, a VR Presence survey, and they rated the Value of PREality and simulation practice.

- Mean Confidence survey scores increased by 17%±15% after the session (p<.000), and 91% want to use PREality with simulation again, while 31% would also use PREality alone.
- Compared to traditional video, 87% said PREality was more useful, and when compared to on-site visits, 93% said PREality was as valuable.
- DPT students found one session of PREality with simulation as valuable as an on-site visit and want to use it again to prepare for internships.

This evaluation suggests that immersive PREality libraries of actual patient care are a novel way to meet early clinical exposure goals and may be a solution to limited and inconsistent acute care exposure challenges.

Additionally, students were invited to share comments about the PREality experience:

"[PREality is] more engaging, and you forget that you are not there (until you take the headset off!). And I'm curious, so it allows me to look around the room to see what else is there."

"This makes me pay attention like I would if I were there that day. It is much more engaging, and I feel much more emotionally invested…it makes the experience my own memory, not just something I watched."

"It feels like you are a part of the case, which provides a different perspective/attention when viewing."

"I can get a feel for the room as if I am really standing there observing. On a screen, the cases might seem much more detached and impersonal, but with the VR, I felt like I was there and a part of the action."

"It was great to get a look into what this setting was like. I did not have any shadowing hours or experience in acute care, and viewing this while critically thinking about the case was a huge benefit and learning experience."

"I like any opportunity to be a fly on the wall; it's so great to get to just watch as if I am there. Even better than in-person in 'some' ways because I don't have to practice social niceties, and I can just focus on the learning experience. If I had a library of a bunch of these videos, I would watch them all."

"Getting the opportunity to see the interaction without any feelings of needing to move out of the way, being able to watch how people in the room act without being self-conscious of staring at them."

"PREality before simulation practice was essential for me to get the most benefit from this experience. I have never been in a hospital or had the chance to shadow a PT there."

"You feel that you are with the PT, but you can rewind it, and you're not in the way, and we all get to meet the same amazing patients. No more fear of missing out!"

Finally, one graduating student emailed me and said:

"I'm so grateful for all of those PREality experiences we did before the pandemic hit. I was so nervous for my TCE at the hospital because we had been at home for months, but then I walked in and realized, 'I've been here before…it's going to be OK,' and it was."

What's Next?

The DPT student and PT clinician feedback have been enthusiastic about these ICE experiences, and their insights into the utility of PREality for clinical education have provided the groundwork for some new projects, including:

■ **Sensitive conversation preparation:** Using PREality to detect nonverbal and verbal cues through evaluating actual conversations between patients and practitioners about sensitive topics such as bowel, bladder, and sexual function. This process would involve using cine-VR with simulated conversations and karaoke practice to provide repeatable immersive scenarios for students to experience and practice clinical discussions.

■ **Library expansion:** We plan to expand our library by adding more patients and different hospital areas (e.g., intensive care and critical care units). We would also like to include home care and nursing facilities in ICE experiences, as well as targeted scaffolding of experiences for our first-semester Foundations course and our fifth-semester Medical Therapeutics courses. We want to test if simulated cases presented with PREality are more effective than the traditional paper case.

In conclusion, please remember that the intention of PREality experiences is not to replace all early patient exposure clinical education experiences. On the contrary, by definition, PREality serves to prepare the students for the clinical environment's reality and bridge the gap between classroom preparation and the actual clinical environment through site-specific and role-specific immersive experiences. Fully immersive PREality of bedside patient care created with cine-VR provides a novel, innovative, reliable, and relatively low-cost rapid implementation strategy for training nontechnical skills vital for optimal patient outcomes. PREality has the potential to make a significant and transformative contribution to the future of medical education by optimizing DPT students' early exposure to clinical environments while simultaneously assisting DPT programs with limited access to clinical sites.

Viewing

Unfortunately, cine-VR examples mentioned in this chapter are unavailable due to HIPAA regulations and agreements made with patients, clinicians, and VVMC.

Notes

1. Haywood LM, et al. Student Perceptions and Understanding of Client-Therapist Interactions Within the Inpatient Acute Care Environment: Qualitative Study. *Physical Therapy* 2015;95:235–248.
2. American Physical Therapy Association Board of Directors. Best Practice for Physical Therapist Clinical Education Task Force Report. Alexandria, VA: American Physical Therapy Association; 2017.
3. Erickson M, Birkmeier M, et al. Recommendations from the Common Terminology Panel of the American Council of Academic Physical Therapy. *Physical Therapy* 2018;98(9):754–762.
4. Academy of Acute Care Physical Therapy Minimum Skills Task Force. The Core Competencies for Entry-Level Practice in Acute Care Physical Therapy, December 2015. https://www.aptaacutecare.org/page/corecompetencies

Chapter 5

Training Trauma Care Providers at a Level 1 Trauma Center

Amanda Sammann and Devika Patel

Contents

Postgraduate medical ("residency") training is often characterized by the "see one, do one, teach one" paradigm.[1] Residents (also known as trainees) watch a more senior person do a procedure, then do it themselves, then teach another resident. In this paradigm, trainees practice their skills on real patients which results in higher rates of medical errors, negatively impacting patient care and outcomes.[2]

Trauma care, or the care of acutely injured patients, is a unique and high-stress clinical situation where a multidisciplinary team of medical providers comes together to deliver urgent, life-saving medical care. At our hospital, for lower level trauma resuscitations or cases of less critically injured patients, the team consists of eleven people, including the emergency medicine attending, senior

DOI: 10.4324/9781003168683-7

trauma resident, junior trauma resident, trauma intern, trauma nurse practitioner, emergency medicine resident, emergency department registered nurses, a neurosurgery resident or attending (upon request), medical social service, a medical evaluation assistant, and a pediatric resident or attending for pediatric patients. For higher level traumas or cases of critically injured patients, the team consists of seventeen people, including all team members mentioned above, and additionally the trauma attending, anesthesia attending, trauma fellow, anesthesia resident, radiology technician, and respiratory therapist. While familiar with trauma care, these individuals may not know each other or have previously worked together due to the nature of rotating shifts and resident training schedules.

Studies suggest that 70–80% of healthcare errors are caused by poor communication.[3] Good teamwork can mitigate these errors, and implementing teamwork training has been shown to improve trauma patients' clinical care.[4] In trauma care, residents typically learn on the job while responding to high-stress, time-sensitive, life-or-death events. Formal training is often limited to a two-day Advanced Trauma Life Support (ATLS) training course that is renewed every two years and includes one day of simulation training with standard actors. The ATLS course focuses on the process and necessary procedural skills to evaluate and care for an injured trauma patient.[5] To our knowledge, few residency programs conduct additional formal trauma simulation training due to significant implementation barriers.

Exposure to quality trauma care training is highly inconsistent across residency training programs. This inconsistency results in trainees graduating from residency with variable exposure and comfort providing trauma care. Trainees with inadequate experience lack the effective leadership and teamwork skills necessary to coordinate multidisciplinary trauma care in acutely stressful situations.[6,7] The increased stress levels of inadequately prepared trainees also impedes performance on tasks requiring divided attention and decision-making in patient care.[7,8]

Current Solutions in Medical Education

One current modality is to provide team-based and clinical skills training in simulation-based education. Simulation-based medical education uses actors, mannequins, or trainers to create an artificial representation of a real-world process to facilitate experiential learning.[9] Simulation has been shown to improve teamwork and communication but is limited in scope for several reasons[9,10]:

- Significant human and financial resources: Simulation requires multiple stakeholders and considerable financial resources.[11]
- Expensive equipment: Equipment such as simulation mannequins or medical equipment are a required investment for many types of simulation-based education.[11]
- Complex coordination of multiple stakeholders: Simulations require the coordination of actors and mannequins, providers, and trainees.[9]
- Inauthentic environment and experience: Simulation remains a hypothetical scenario that fails to capture the graphic and unpredictable nature of certain situations.[12]

Cine-VR in medical education has the potential to address these limitations:

- Low resource: Only the trainee and educator need to be engaged in watching the cine-VR.
- Cost-effective: While there are initial start-up costs in buying equipment and editing videos, these are one-time and require only the trainee and facilitator for repeat use.

- Accessible and flexible: Individuals can practice and train on demand, in a location and time of their choosing.
- Authentic: Cine-VR captures real patient scenarios showcasing medical teams making decisions rapidly.

This chapter will describe how we developed a cine-VR trauma training curriculum at an urban, Level 1 trauma center and teaching hospital. We will describe our curriculum development and production process, the technical and production processes, and current best practices for future academic medical centers.

Developing Trauma Training Cine-VR

Understanding the Experience of Providing Trauma Care

Trauma care requires rapid decision-making, efficient communication, and precise teamwork to deliver care to critically injured patients. We used the human-centered design (HCD) methodology to understand how we might improve the trauma care experience. HCD is an innovative approach to problem-solving, centered on focusing on the end users' challenges and unmet needs.[13] The first step of the HCD process consists of the "Inspiration" phase, where we conducted thirty-five in-depth interviews with various trauma care stakeholders, including physicians, nurses, technicians, and trainees, and fifty hours of live observation of trauma care. Through our research, we found numerous challenges that providers face when delivering trauma care. Here, we will detail three of these challenges and supporting quotes from our qualitative research:

1. Due to varying trainee and staff rotations and shifts, every trauma team that assembles is an ad-hoc and unique collection of teammates, which hinders communication and collaboration.
   a. "The worst codes are when multiple people are going for the same role" – Emergency medicine resident, fourth year
   b. "It's hard to know who in the ED is doing what" – Surgery/Trauma resident
2. Due to the unpredictable and high volume nature of trauma care, providers and staff have no mechanism to debrief as a team, impeding formal, collaborative, interdisciplinary teamwork.
   a. "I'd like to see recognition that we rely on each other; [that we are] a necessary part of [the] team." – Emergency medicine resident, second year
   b. "[I want to see] more debriefings. How it flowed, how it went…always want to circle back…makes us stronger." – Senior nurse
3. Trainees are cognitively overloaded by the competing demands of providing trauma care to the patient and leading the team, compromising their ability to perform and learn.
   a. "It took me all of my training to learn how to do ABC's [resuscitation guidelines]…no one taught me how to run a room." – Emergency medicine attending
   b. [Referring to running a trauma] "We don't get practice and comfort here…" – Surgery resident, fourth year

Developing the Curriculum

In the next phase of the HCD process, "Ideation," we brainstormed solutions to address these challenges.[13] Through our ideation and subsequent research, virtual reality, particularly cine-VR, came forth as an appropriate and promising solution to these challenges. Cine-VR can address trauma care providers' unmet needs by providing a platform for immersive and authentic training used repetitively and flexibly to adapt to providers' schedules. Once we decided on cine-VR as the educational technology, the next step was to produce and develop the curriculum.

To develop our trauma training curriculum, we conducted qualitative research with twenty-eight junior-level residents, including first and second-year residents in General Surgery, Anesthesia, and Emergency Medicine. We used the cognitive load theory (CLT) approach as our evaluation framework. CLT states that an increased load on a trainee working memory can compromise the trainee's knowledge acquisition.[14] To understand the role of cognitive load for trainees during trauma resuscitations, we had each trainee watch a cine-VR video of trauma resuscitation. While watching the cine-VR video, the trainee participated in a "talk aloud," where they were asked to detail what they saw, their priorities during the case, and what they found to be essential and distracting while watching the video. Afterward, the trainee debriefed the experience with the research team. After conducting a thematic analysis of the data, these interviews revealed six sources of cognitive load for junior-level residents that interfered with their ability to learn during trauma resuscitation:

1. Orientation to VR technology: Cine-VR can be disorienting for trainees. Many do not realize that rotating in 360° is possible (i.e., look behind you).
2. The orientation of room layout: As a novice, it can be confusing to understand where people stand and work.
3. Knowledge of team members' roles and responsibilities: During a trauma resuscitation, it is integral to know who is doing what and why in taking care of the patient.
4. Medical knowledge of ATLS guidelines: ATLS guidelines are also known as the ABCDE's, and trainees need to be informed and practice the application of the ABCDE's.
5. The anticipation of next steps: Caring for a critically injured patient requires quick, accurate decision-making and evaluation.
6. Medical knowledge of specialized clinical content: There are certain clinical cases, such as pediatric trauma care and burns care, that require additional training on clinical management guidelines.

We used our findings from the qualitative research to develop the trauma training curriculum in cine-VR, which focus on four learning objectives and one orientation objective:

1. Acclimate to chaos and understand the roles and priorities of the team members.
2. Understand and apply the ATLS framework of ABCDE's for the care the patient.
3. Anticipate next steps in the management of the patient.
4. Understand how to tailor trauma care to particular cases, such as pediatrics and burns.
5. Orient to cine-VR technology and the 360° environment.

Recording the Curriculum

The first task was to identify a production partner with cine-VR production and editing capabilities that were compliant with the Health Insurance Portability and Accountability Act (HIPAA). We chose to collaborate with the Game Research and Immersive Design (GRID) Lab because they possessed the extensive experience in developing cine-VR in the academic healthcare space, with HIPAA-compliant technical infrastructure. We recorded twenty real and simulated patient trauma resuscitations described in detail later in this chapter. From those twenty videos, we chose eight to edit and four to augment with additional curriculum. We developed "augmented" or curriculum-based videos and "unaugmented" or naked videos for the four videos involved in the curriculum.

Production Process/Technical Overview

Video and Audio Capture

Given our work's real-world nature, the first important consideration was to ensure our patients' and providers' privacy. We collaborated with the Institution Review Board (IRB), the research ethics committee, and information technology staff to develop a robust data security protocol to ensure HIPAA compliance. We then worked closely with the GRID Lab to determine a data security protocol for capturing, uploading, downloading, and editing the video and audio recordings. The video data was stored on a secure hard drive and locked in a secure office. Data was shared between labs over encrypted WIFI to secure HIPAA-compliant cloud storage. Editing was completed in an air-gaped (connected to no networks) office with restricted access to assure strict adherence to HIPAA protocols.

Trauma care is multidisciplinary, and we felt it was essential to capture each of our providers' different perspectives. As a result, we recorded the cine-VR videos from six different perspectives in the trauma resuscitation room (see Photo 5.1):

1. The head of the bed: At the head of the bed is the airway team (anesthesia or emergency medicine), who manages the airway.
2. The left of bed: At the left of the bed is the resident (emergency medicine or surgery) leading the trauma resuscitation.
3. The right of bed: At the right of the bed is nursing, who obtains IV access to the patient and monitors the patient's vital signs.
4. The foot of the bed: At the foot of the bed is the attending physician (emergency medicine or surgery), who is overseeing the trauma resuscitation.
5. Charting Nurse: The back corner of the room is the charting nurse, who documents the case.
6. Patient: At the center of the trauma resuscitation is the patient.
    The trauma bay was configured to capture the six different perspectives by securely mounting camera booms from the ceiling panels. Several cameras were then hung from those booms at the locations of that perspective. The cameras were hung from 5′11″ height – 6′2″ height to accommodate our tallest providers' height so that the cameras would be above their heads during patient encounters. From the patient perspective, we attached the camera to rolling mic stands, and from the charting nurse's perspective, the camera was mounted to computer displays.

To capture a wide variety of clinical scenarios, our production and research team convened for two weeks over two different months. Our team recorded every high-level trauma resuscitation that came in during those two weeks, as well as simulations of unique trauma scenarios.

We stationed the production team and all equipment in a separate room near the resuscitation bay known as the "control room." When recording live subjects, the production and research team would be alerted to the incoming patient and enter the trauma bay to turn on the cameras and

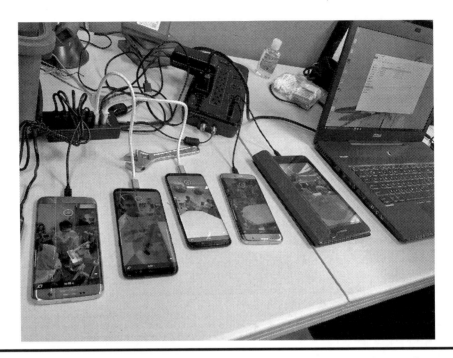

Photo 5.1   From the control room, our production team was able to monitor each camera via cell phone and quickly download footage onto a secured laptop at the end of each trauma

spatial microphones. The resuscitation would then occur, with all team members observing from the control room (see Photo 5.1). After the patient moved to another location, the production team would enter the resuscitation bay to turn off cameras and audio equipment. Our research team then worked with each patient's care team to understand if they could consent for themselves. If that patient could consent, a research team member held a consent discussion to inform the patient before discharging. If the patient was unable to consent, we sought surrogate consent for a maximum of three weeks post-resuscitation, as outlined by our IRB. If surrogate consent was unattainable or the patient did not consent, we securely deleted the video and audio files. We also obtained consent of all providers present in the room at time of filming, either at the beginning of the filming shift, immediately before the trauma patient arrived, or after the resuscitation. Additional details about our consent protocols are available in our paper *Developing Virtual Reality Trauma Training Experiences Using 360° Video: Tutorial* in the Journal of Medical Informatics Research.[15]

When recording simulations, we used volunteer actors and moulage artists to simulate patients' injuries. We recruited providers to participate in various pre-planned patient scenarios (examples include patients with a traumatic amputation, a stab wound, and involved in a motor vehicle collision). These simulations were unscripted, meaning that providers came into the simulation only knowing the essentials of the patient's injuries.

The nature of working within a 360° video meant that everyone and everything is captured, including those walking by open doors, as well as identifiable patient data. We worked with the production team to implement techniques such as blurring open doorways and exposed body parts during the editing phase.

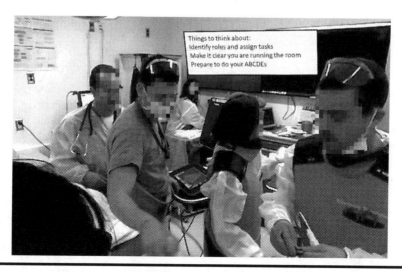

Photo 5.2   Screen grab demonstrating how graphics provided ideas for users to contemplate

To build the curriculum content, we assembled an expert provider team comprised of attending physicians in surgery, emergency medicine, and anesthesia to develop graphic and audio overlays to augment the videos. These graphics included specific questions for trainees to answer, educational content for trainees to read and contemplate (see Photo 5.2), and arrows to identify different providers. We worked with the expert provider team and GRID Lab staff to insert these graphics at the relevant video timestamps to correlate with clinical learning objectives.

We also worked with the GRID Lab to implement eye-tracking within a VR headset into the curriculum (see Chapter 21). The goal of eye-tracking was to understand the relationship between the trainee's gaze and their attention. To implement eye tracking, we created a grid overlay on the four augmented videos and marked each box in the grid as either a "relevant" or "irrelevant" stimulus, as defined by the expert provider team. For instance, a relevant stimulus might be the monitor or the patient's body part. An irrelevant stimulus might be someone walking by the open door to the resuscitation room. We also created points of interest, or hitboxes, tracked separately on top of the grid. Hitboxes are invisibly tracked regions we add on top of the videos. The points of interest that we tracked included the patient, monitors, and medical staff moving around the space. We created hitboxes for each individual. The headset recorded the time and duration of gaze for each relevant and irrelevant stimuli. The purpose of incorporating eye-tracking into the training is to understand the trainee's cognitive load by identifying how often and for how long each trainee looks at different types of stimuli.

Technical limitations to consider during the recording of trauma resuscitations include the cameras' height and visibility of crucial visuals during the resuscitation. The cameras had to be high enough that our tallest providers would be able to navigate through the trauma bay without hitting their heads. However, for shorter providers orienting to VR, the video feels as if they are watching it from above, which can be disorienting. The "orienting to VR" video attempts to acclimate the trainee to the height difference before moving to the trauma resuscitation videos. Additionally, some key visuals, such as the vitals monitor's details, can be challenging to view in the VR headsets due to video resolution. In the future, we would recommend using graphical overlays to augment the resolution of those critical visuals. It is also worth noting that the

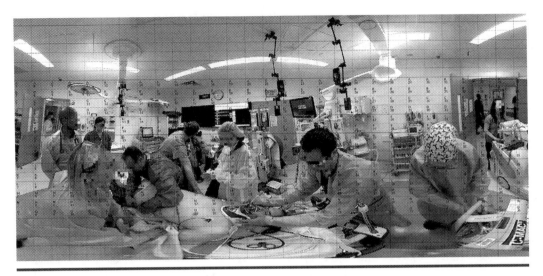

Photo 5.3 Eye-tracking grid overlay

resolution of cine-VR cameras is constantly improving, and the resolution of today's cameras may be sufficient. Further technical details of our production process details are available in the following publication: *Developing Virtual Reality Trauma Training Experiences Using 360° Video: Tutorial* in the Journal of Medical Informatics Research.[15]

Best Practices

Developing novel cine-VR experiences for trauma training requires meticulous planning and multidisciplinary collaboration. Ensure you have a detail-oriented and tech-savvy project manager who can communicate both to your production partner and the rest of your clinical team. Additionally, prioritize selecting a production partner with healthcare and HIPAA-compliance expertise. Develop a robust data security infrastructure with relevant stakeholders that meets your institution's requirements. Test and practice with different camera configurations and attachment configurations in the trauma bay to maximize capturing the best overall video perspective of the trauma care, while not hindering or obstructing necessary patient care. Lastly, work closely and collaboratively with trainees, medical educators, physicians, and other stakeholders to iteratively design the curriculum to best meet trainee's educational needs.

What We Learned

Developing cine-VR experiences for trauma care training is feasible, and lessons learned from our process can hopefully guide future endeavors. First, it is critical to ensure broad stakeholder buy-in, from the care providers to facilities staff to the data security specialists. Second, given the unpredictable nature of trauma care, budget for time delays, which include overestimating the time required to capture the correct footage and for setting up the technical infrastructure to carrying out the project. Finally, make sure to run realistic simulations with the team to ensure that the production equipment does not interfere with life-saving patient care and acclimate the care team to the room's additional equipment.

Project Reception and Impact

Early project reception has been positive. Given the novelty of the technology and the lack of studies on cine-VR's effectiveness, multiple stakeholder groups are very excited about the use case and its implications in trauma care training. In pilot studies, trainees express enthusiasm with the cine-VR training, and the project has garnered early military interest.

What's Next?

To understand the effectiveness of the curriculum as an educational tool, we are in the process of testing the curriculum with first and second-year residents in surgery, emergency medicine, and anesthesia and have several additional research questions:

- In what order should videos be viewed? Should we view the augmented video first or the un-augmented video first for each trauma resuscitation? Is there an optimal order of the trauma resuscitation scenarios themselves?
- What are the short and long-term impacts on knowledge retention?
- Do performance improvements in cine-VR result in improved performance in real-world trauma care?
- In cine-VR training, what is the relationship between the training and stress reduction using physiologic markers?

Innovation in medical education is beginning to utilize and embrace virtual reality. In trauma care training, cine-VR provides an on-demand and repetitive opportunity for trainees to practice their clinical and nonclinical skills without harming the patient in an authentic, high-stress chaotic environment. In the long-term, cine-VR video libraries can be shared or exported to other trauma centers and teaching hospitals nationally to democratize access to trauma care training. The potential of cine-VR to positively impact trainees across the world is excellent.

Viewing

To view and download cine-VR examples mentioned in this chapter, please visit: https://vimeo.com/channels/cinevr4healthcare/ (**password:** *cineVR4health*).

References

1. Kotsis SV, Chung KC. Application of the "see one, do one, teach one" concept in surgical training. *Plast Reconstr Surg.* 2013;131(5):1194–1201. doi:10.1097/PRS.0b013e318287a0b3
2. Al-Elq A. Simulation-based medical teaching and learning. *J Fam Community Med.* 2010;17(1):35. doi:10.4103/1319-1683.68787

3. Schaefer HG, Helmreich RL, Scheidegger D. Human factors and safety in emergency medicine. *Resuscitation*. 1994;28(3):221–225. doi:10.1016/0300-9572(94)90067-1

4. Capella J, Smith S, Philp A, et al. Teamwork training improves the clinical care of trauma patients. *J Surg Educ*. 2010;67(6):439–443. doi:10.1016/j.jsurg.2010.06.006

5. Simulation in trauma education: Beyond ATLS. *Injury*. 2014;45(5):817–818. doi:10.1016/j.injury.2014.01.010

6. Ford K, Menchine MDM, Burner ME, et al. Leadership and teamwork in trauma and resuscitation. *West J Emerg Med*. 2016;17(5):549–556. doi:10.5811/westjem.2016.7.29812

7. Groombridge CJ, Kim Y, Maini A, Smit DV, Fitzgerald MC. Stress and decision-making in resuscitation: A systematic review. *Resuscitation*. 2019;144(July):115–122. doi:10.1016/j.resuscitation.2019.09.023

8. Leblanc VR. The effects of acute stress on performance: Implications for health professions education. *Acad Med*. 2009;84(SUPPL. 10):25–33. doi:10.1097/ACM.0b013e3181b37b8f

9. Okuda Y, Bryson EO, De Maria Jr S, et al. The Utility of Simulation in Medical Education: What Is the Evidence? *Mt Sinai J Med*. 2009;76:330–343. doi:10.1002/msj.20127

10. Flanagan B, Nestel D, Joseph M. Making patient safety the focus: Crisis Resource Management in the undergraduate curriculum. *Med Educ*. 2004;38(1):56–66. doi:10.1111/j.1365-2923.2004.01701.x

11. Zendejas B, Wang AT, Brydges R, Hamstra SJ, Cook DA. Cost: The missing outcome in simulation-based medical education research: A systematic review. *Surg (United States)*. 2013;153(2):160–176. doi:10.1016/j.surg.2012.06.025

12. Quick JA. Simulation Training in Trauma. 2018;(October):447–450.

13. IDEO.org. *The Field Guide to Human-Centered Design*; 2015.

14. Chandler P, Sweller J. Cognitive load theory and the format of instruction. *Cogn Instr*. 1991;8(4):293–332. doi:10.1207/s1532690xci0804_2

15. Patel D, Hawkins J, Chehab LZ, et al. Developing virtual reality trauma training experiences using 360-Degree video: Tutorial. *J Med Internet Res*. 2020;22(12). doi:10.2196/22420

Chapter 6

Preparing for Cine-VR Production in Medical Environments

Eric R. Williams

Contents

It takes coordinated preparation to safely and effectively execute cine-VR projects in a medical environment. These projects require special consideration, far beyond the preparation and planning for a typical media production. This chapter is for media professionals new to shooting in real medical environments and might be a useful reading for medical professionals to share with incoming production crews before the actual work begins.

From experience, I can tell you that even though I had worked for three years as "the video guy" in a hospital and owned my own production company for more than twenty years, I was in for a surprise revisiting media production in an active hospital in 2016. The amount of legal and logistical wrangling required has increased exponentially since the 1990s. Add to the equation that 360° images literally "capture everything," and you've created a scenario where production, legal, and logistical details are significant factors.

DOI: 10.4324/9781003168683-8

To those production crews new to the hospital setting, I offer critical points of consideration. Please spend time assessing the following elements of your next cine-VR production:

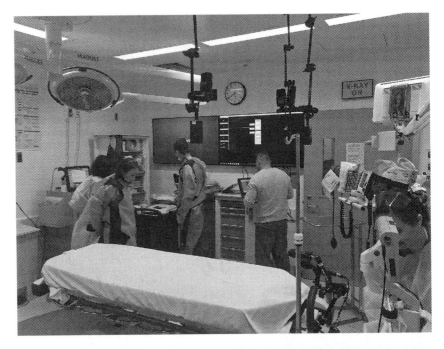

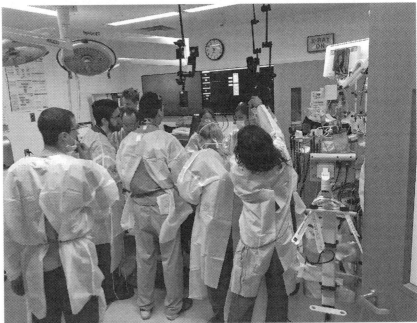

Photo 6.1   A quiet hospital setting (above) can erupt with activity (below) in a matter of moments

Authenticity and Permissions

Authenticity is essential in PREality. Therefore, you will have to shoot in live medical environments. Start the permission process early. It may take many months to work out legal permission to record in a hospital.

In addition to receiving permission from the hospital (and its various units), you will also need to secure patients' consent. This process is complicated and time-consuming. If the patient can provide permission before recording, that is preferable. However, in the case of recording traumas, that wasn't possible, and we received approval retroactively. If this is the case, a process must be put in place to track the patient, as they may not be conscious for hours or even days after the event.

HIPAA Regulations

You will be required to follow all HIPAA regulations to protect patients' rights. Created by the Health Insurance Portability and Accountability Act, these regulations are legally binding requirements. All members of your team will need to demonstrate appropriate HIPAA training. As part of the hospital approval process, you will undoubtedly need to design and implement a HIPAA compliance plan.

The HIPAA Privacy Rule establishes national standards to protect individuals' medical records and other personal health information and applies to health plans, health care clearinghouses, and those health care providers that conduct certain health care transactions electronically. The Rule requires appropriate safeguards to protect the privacy of personal health information, and sets limits and conditions on the uses and disclosures that may be made of such information without patient authorization.

– U.S. Department of Health & Human Services

Communication with Hospital Personnel

Once the production team has secured legal agreements and various permissions to enter an active area of the hospital, the work has only just begun. The GRID Lab cannot overemphasize the importance of communicating with the hospital personnel that you will be working with on the project. Their jobs are highly stressful, and you will be adding to their stress. We recommend the following:

1. Get to know <u>all</u> of the players involved. Have people who are already trusted introduce you to everyone.
2. Meet with people face-to-face to explain the project. If you plan to work around the clock, then meet with each shift employee during <u>their</u> shift. Don't make them work around <u>your</u> schedule.
3. Show off what you are doing. People are intrigued by this technology. Let them put on the headsets. Show them the cameras and microphones. The more that people understand what you are doing, the more helpful they will be.

4. Talk with the doctors, nurses, and technicians. Listen to their concerns. Do not try to solve their problems on the spot; their concerns are typically very nuanced. Take time to problem-solve any issues with the hospital experts.

5. Make sure to consult the maintenance department early and often. You will need to run wires and hang cameras – and you will need them to help you do all of this. There may also be specific legal requirements that you may not know about *(e.g., California earthquake regulations forbade us to hang more than five pounds from a single point on the ceiling).*

6. Make sure to consult the custodial department to understand sanitation. Your crew will most likely need to wear gowns, gloves, booties, and so forth. You may need to replace them often. You will need to know what to do if you get (someone else's) bodily fluids on your clothes or equipment.

Once you have gained the trust and respect from the hospital employees and have established buy-in from all of the key players, you will need to determine a reliable (yet flexible) workflow for your team.

Our checklist for establishing our workflow:

A. You need a defined space to:

Create a command center: Your team will need to quickly set up the cameras and microphones and then promptly leave. Try to avoid capturing any crew members in the footage. The relocation area needs to be close enough to the recording where they can (hopefully) monitor the cameras wirelessly. We call this the "command center." Your command center will need access to electricity for charging and reliable Wi-Fi connections for device communications.

Store and access equipment: You will need quick access to back-up equipment. On one project, we hung six camera/microphone combinations at a time, and we rotated these units with six others for every other patient. Additionally, we had three back-up units "just in case." That was fifteen cameras and microphones, thirty-six batteries, and twenty-four memory cards – not to mention the card readers, battery chargers, etc.

Rest and recuperate: Your team will work long hours – everyone in a hospital does. If you are recording traumas, you will work around the clock for possibly days on end. When this is the case, you will need a place away from the control center where your team can relax and rejuvenate – but close enough to the action that they can get back at a moment's notice!

B. You need a defined space within the command center to:

Stage the outgoing equipment: Most likely, you will not have a lot of space to work. Your crew will feel like they are stepping over each other – and they literally might be. It is vital to create a natural flow for swapping equipment and backing up data.

Download incoming data: In a high-activity location, we swap out equipment after every use. Once a camera records a patient, we immediately swap it out with a charged and sanitized camera. That way, there is a new camera ready to go if a new patient suddenly arrives. It also gives us time to pull the battery and memory card from the first camera. That data is then immediately labeled and stored on a keypad-protected drive according to HIPAA requirements. We dedicate a specific naming protocol for each project and typically assign one person per shift to transfer data. The media files can be quite large, so plan accordingly.

Photo 6.2   Once a camera records a patient we replace it with a freshly charged and sanitized unit

   Clean and repair: After pulling the batteries and memory cards from the camera and mic, the equipment is inspected and sanitized if required. We look specifically for bodily fluids anywhere on the camera and fingerprints on the lenses. The cameras are cleaned and loaded with fresh batteries and cards. This process completes a "new" camera/mic unit and is ready for rotation.
C. You need to define specific roles and duties:
   For each member of the team: You will have limited time to perform tasks, and you will often be choreographing with medical professionals. Each team member needs to know precisely what they are doing and the order in which they are doing it. We recommend practicing your routine outside of the hospital days in advance. A well-practiced team is essential to being able to problem solve and adjust to complications in the field.
   For data identification: HIPAA protocols and academic protocols may force you to "blind" your patient data. Meaning: you may need to prescribe a random identification code associated with a patient while simultaneously tracking that patient for days to obtain permission to use the footage. If a patient is unwilling to consent, then destroy that footage immediately. Track and document all of these details for later reference. It is essential to assign at least one person per shift who intimately understands the data identification protocol.
   For shift handoffs: Whether your team is working around the clock or periodically returning to the same location, information and processes must stay consistent from one shift to the next. For instance, a crew arriving to start a new shift should talk with the previous shift to ensure that all of the cameras are still on rotation. We recommend at least a fifteen-minute overlap between shifts. If shifts are day-to-day, then we recommend

documenting written summaries at the end of each day – even if the crew is writing notes to themselves for the next day.

For post-production communication: It is also crucial to create written production notes for post-production purposes. Even if your production crew is also your post-production crew, make a habit of taking notes in real-time. This documentation will save a tremendous amount of effort and confusion in the long run. We have found that memories fade over time (even over a short amount of time). Details get misremembered when crew members leave or get reassigned to other projects, which makes orienting new crew members troublesome. We ask our crew to write notes – not for themselves, but for "the new person" who may join the project a week from now. That new person should be able to read the notes and understand the information.

Following this short checklist will help focus your production efforts in a live medical environment and hopefully increase your project's effectiveness. It takes coordinated preparation to safely and effectively execute these types of projects in a healthcare setting. Working in these sorts of intense locations requires preparation, practice, and professionalism.

Photo 6.3 illustrates the equipment used on one of our key projects. Did you also notice the drain on the floor and the shower handle on the wall above the computer? For this project, our staging area was in the shower room – the closest location to the emergency room was also out of the way and was close enough for the smartphone to access the 360° cameras wirelessly – allowing us to monitor the footage live.

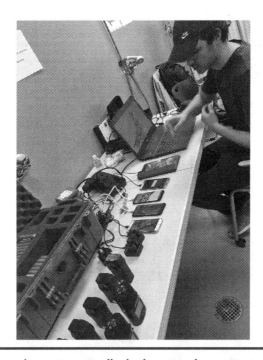

Photo 6.3 Production equipment on standby in the control room (note the shower drain on the floor and the nozzle on the wall above the computer)

Each production is unique. Each varies in terms of length, complexity, and subject matter. But we have found that medical cine-VR projects tend to fall into two categories with unique considerations: live capture and staged capture.

Staged Capture

A staged event in a hospital does not use real patients. Instead, they use actors to play the role of patients. Often, the medical professionals respond to the patient and their situation as if it were real. Sometimes, as is the case with child patients, mannequins can substitute for actors. Technology today can allow mannequins to cry, scream, bleed, and even blink – making them seem almost real in specific situations.

Staged cine-VR capture creates a lower sense of pressure. The experience is often rehearsed – if not by the medical professionals (who need to perform as if this were a new experience to them) then at least by the crew. Ideal locations for cameras and microphones need consideration and possible adjustments. If mistakes happen, there may be an opportunity to reset the room and "do another take."

However, staged capture typically occurs only at odd hours because during "normal business hours," most hospitals and their personnel are busy saving lives and treating patients. Identifying and coordinating short time windows to shoot a staged production in a live emergency room may be difficult but necessary. During our San Francisco project, we found that 4:00 am to 5:00 am was typically a good time to shoot and, if we stitched together three or four days in a row, we could accomplish four hours of production recording.

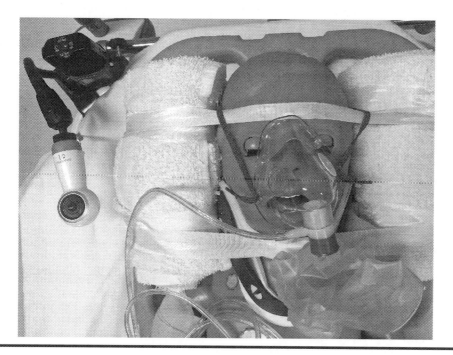

Photo 6.4 Mannequins can play a useful role during staged capture events. The cine-VR camera can be placed close for a patient POV perspective while the staff performs procedures

Live Capture

Live captures, on the other hand, can (and will) occur at any time. The crew must be ready to shoot day or night. There are no "do-overs" in live cine-VR capture. You either capture the event as it happens, or you don't. And the more variables that you introduce into the equation (adding more cameras, microphones, people, and consents), the more likely it is that something will go wrong. The experience may fail to capture in full or result in partial yet unusable content. The people are real. There are no rehearsals. Your crew and your equipment need to be on constant standby and be willing and able to roll with the punches – sometimes quite literally.

Both live capture and staged capture events still require the same meticulous planning and relationship building described in this chapter. The only difference is the use of the hospital spaces. Regardless though, authenticity is vital. Permissions must be acquired (if not from the patients, from the actors), and all HIPAA protocols followed.

Remember, communication and organization are key. Without them, the complexity of a multi-camera cine-VR shoot in a high-pressure situation will often overwhelm a crew and cause production to collapse in on itself.

Final Thoughts

In conclusion, cine-VR production in a healthcare environment is unlike any other shooting scenario. Often on shoots, the production needs are the top priority. In a medical setting, the cine-VR production is secondary – often tertiary to the patients' and medical staffs' needs. Success depends on the production team's understanding of this dynamic.

Medical professionals pride themselves on proper processes and procedures, and so too should the cine-VR team. Documentation is necessary and often a legal requirement. There are rarely "second chances" in these sorts of environments which may add more pressure. Capturing live patient care is a "use it or lose it" opportunity, but the ability to return to a location may be difficult even for a narrative piece with actors. Securing areas inside an active nursing home or hospital waiting room may be a special privilege requiring someone to call in favors to obtain. You may not be able to "reschedule" in the same location. Some locations are so challenging to obtain that you may only get one shot.

Professionalism and accountability are requirements to working in the medical arena – and I'm not talking about "production professionalism" (although that is a given) – we need to meet the professionalism and accountability levels that the healthcare profession expects. We are entering their world; they are not entering ours.

Viewing

There are no cine-VR examples to view for this chapter. Images are from a project detailed in Chapter 5.

Chapter 7

Choosing Cameras and Head-Mounted Displays

John Bowditch and Matt Love

Contents

Production Overview

Choosing a Camera

As we mentioned in Chapter 2, many different camera configurations are available to capture cine-VR content. In this section, we'll explore some of the reasons you might choose one over another. We will start with inexpensive and simple to use, then pivot to expensive and more complex.

The most straightforward 360° cameras are small, fit in the palm of your hand, and cost less than $500. They typically have two fisheye lenses and frequently offer software onboard for image stabilization. Image stabilization reduces the likelihood of motion sickness-inducing content. These cameras provide the benefits of small size and simplicity but output lower image quality. While reduced, their image quality improves with proper lighting. We've gotten great results with these tiny cameras in situations where larger cameras wouldn't have worked. Smaller cameras can be attached to a helmet, the front of a scooter, and drones with ease. They were crucial to capturing traumas at Zuckerberg San Francisco General Hospital (Chapter 5). We needed a solution that would not interfere with the medical staff. In addition to the smaller sizes, the two-lens setup means fewer stitch lines, which is advantageous.

DOI: 10.4324/9781003168683-9

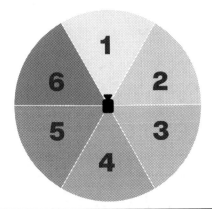

Figure 7.1 Parallax issues can be eliminated by leveraging a panoramic head and shooting in slices

Increasing the level of complexity, we have dedicated 360° cameras with four or more fisheye lenses. Some of these cameras can have more than a dozen sensor lens combinations, and prices for this camera category can run from a couple thousand to almost one hundred thousand dollars. These cameras typically have higher resolution and image quality compared to the more straightforward two-lens cameras. In this tier, we see stereoscopic capture as an option. Stereoscopic video captures two slightly offset images to provide a type of 3D effect for the final image. On the flip side, post-production requires more effort due to the additional stitch lines, and more care is necessary to avoid the stitch lines while shooting.

Furthermore, getting too close to the camera while on a stitch line can lead to strange distortions in the final image. This approach can be a tricky affair in a tighter setting, such as a hospital room, but thorough testing prevents post-production surprises. The more significant the parallax difference between each slice of the image, the more problematic this becomes. For this reason, a camera with many lenses but little parallax difference between them may have less noticeable stitch lines than a camera with fewer lenses.

The complex category we'll discuss is shooting with traditional cameras. Traditional cinema cameras can capture cine-VR content with impressive results. This process uses standard photo lenses, wide-angle lenses, or most commonly fisheye lenses. Recording more of the scene with each shot means fewer slices and allows characters to move about more within the scene. There are two primary approaches when using cinema cameras. One is to leverage a panoramic head, rotating the camera after each shot to capture an entire 360° scene – an example would be six angles 60° apart, which capture 180° vertically (see Figure 7.1). The scene's action would need to be contained within that specific space and not pass into any other since you are only capturing one at a time. The advantage is that parallax issues can become almost nonexistent, making for an exceptional final product.

The other approach is to rig two or more cinema cameras together to capture an entire 360° scene at once (see Figure 7.2). This configuration allows for the action to move from one slice into another but re-introduces parallax issues which can be more challenging to work with than those found in the all-in-one systems.

Using cinema cameras requires the most significant amount of work in post-production. The individual slices will need to be timed together and then taken into third-party software

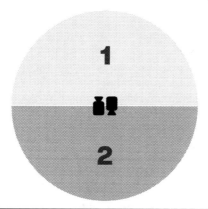

Figure 7.2   Two cinema cameras can be rigged together to capture an entire 360° scene at one time

for stitching. As of this writing, the software required for stitching these images has a reasonably steep learning curve. Even once an individual is familiar with the process, it can still be a time-consuming operation. There will also be increased storage requirements as these cameras tend to create larger, less compressed file sizes. With all these things taken into account, there are undoubtedly situations where the increased quality justifies the effort. No existing all-in-one 360° camera on the market today can match the image quality and dynamic range (ability to retain shadow and highlight detail) of even a modest cinema camera.

When starting, we recommend a smaller two-lens camera. These offer good results in the right lighting conditions and provide a much simpler workflow for becoming accustomed to working with 360° footage. Over time and as needs dictate, one could transition into higher-end options to meet specific needs.

Field of View

As you become familiar with utilizing your camera to create cine-VR content, it will help develop an understanding of how a particular headset's field of view can affect how viewers see your content. Knowing your playback capabilities will inform the way you capture things on set. Consider the following situation: You want to replicate a scenario where a medical professional is speaking with a patient while also monitoring a piece of equipment attached to the patient. You may want the viewer to see both the patient and the equipment simultaneously, or you may want to force the viewer to choose between looking at one or the other. To create either experience, you'll need to understand how your particular headset will display the final product.

Try this: while seated and looking straight ahead, look as far as you can to your right and left without moving your head, just by looking with your eyes. You can likely see a full 180° or more in your periphery. Try the same exercise with a headset, and the reality is that you will see far less. This range is known as your field of view (FOV).

We have found that producing content for broad distribution on various platforms and headsets requires framing shots within a safe production area of about a 70° FOV. Headsets display from 90–200° FOV depending on the make and model, but we have found producing with a narrower field of view in mind has avoided possible framing problems. You can learn how to test your field of view by reviewing *Virtual Reality Cinema* (Routledge 2021), but even if you don't want to go into great detail, it's still a good idea to have a grasp on what your viewer will have in front of them at any given moment. In our experience for many consumer-grade headsets, the following is pragmatic: if your camera is about six feet away from a wall, you'll be able to see about an eight-foot chunk of it.

Camera Tips and Tricks

Here are some tips and tricks we at the GRID Lab have picked up along the way.

- When placing your camera, consider the likelihood of someone bumping into it or the camera stand. This problem is particularly tricky in tight spaces, but camera bumps can quickly make footage nauseating and unusable once in a headset. One way we've gotten around this is by sometimes suspending the camera from the ceiling. It can go a long way to keeping things steady and free from the possibility of getting bumped.
- Stitch lines are also a critical aspect to keep in mind. Sometimes differing the camera positioning can place the stitch line in an area without activity and make all the difference. Viewers are much less likely to notice a stitching issue with a static object than they are when it's a person's body or an item in motion (see Photo 7.1). Generally speaking, 360° cameras are placed upright but remember that since we're capturing a 360° sphere, both horizontally and vertically, it really doesn't matter if the camera is right side up, upside down, or sideways. Some cameras will help auto-orient in real-time, but it is a simple matter to reorient the image in post-production.
- In mounting the camera, you should consider mounting the audio equipment as well. Placing it as close to the camera as possible can help keep it hidden in the final product, but you also run the risk of picking up any noise made by the camera. Some cameras have built-in fans to prevent overheating and to protect the electronics. Some fans can be temporarily disabled to stop running while the camera is recording but will have safety measures in place, turning them back on if the camera becomes too warm. Be sure to familiarize yourself with your camera's settings and behaviors to avoid being caught off guard on set.

Photo 7.1 Stitch lines can be an issue, especially when a person's body crosses one too close to the camera

■ Some cameras, especially of the smaller variety, offer optional underwater and weatherproof housings. These can prove quite helpful if you find yourself in an environment where liquids, including blood and other biologicals, may splatter onto the equipment. It is much easier to decontaminate a housing than a camera.

Headset Overview

Before selecting a VR headset, also referred to as a Head Mounted Display (HMD), you must consider the requirements for developing and disseminating your content. Will the cost be a barrier for your project? Is pixel resolution or other technical factors essential for publishing your project? Does your experience require a user to walk around in a room physically, or will they remain stationary (either standing or seated)? How will the audio be played back to preserve the immersive experience and dampen environmental noise? Will controllers or hand tracking be required? What accessibility challenges need addressing? These are just some of the factors to weigh when selecting headsets. Headsets range in price from $200 to $5,000+ depending on features. The headsets we use for large events with up to a hundred simultaneous viewers are usually in the $300–500 range (see Photo 7.2). We primarily use Oculus and Pico brand headsets for large events.

An excellent place to start, and a common way to sort headsets, is to determine whether the experience's playback will require you to be wired or directly connected to a PC for performance reasons, or can you be wireless requiring no computer. There are advantages and disadvantages to both wired and wireless headsets.

The VR industry is trending toward wireless as the default option due to consumer demand and ease of use; however, the overall quality will never match the performance of headsets wired to a PC. Some wireless headsets support wired connections to computers (usually with a USB cable) for more process extensive applications. Wireless headsets are generally less expensive because they do not require a PC to operate. Most wireless headsets can be initially configured with a smartphone and then run independently by downloading or streaming content through a Wi-Fi connection.

Photo 7.2 Conference attendee in a wireless HMD

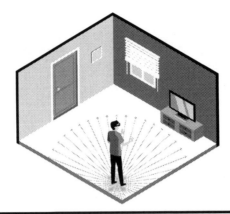

Figure 7.3 Wireless headsets work well in a space that allows for free exploration within a defined area

Wireless headsets tend to be more comfortable, easier to transport, and work well for both seated and room-scale experiences. Room-scale refers to a space that allows for free exploration within a defined area. You can empty your living room or workspace and turn it into a safe, navigable space (see Figure 7.3).

While this concept is exciting, it is unlikely that stationary cine-VR experiences will need room-scale capability. Most cine-VR playback is either seated or standing and will not require walking around. Swivel office chairs that rotate 360° with ease are our preferred furniture (see Figure 7.4). However, any furniture that doesn't restrict your user's movements is usable.

Individuals unfamiliar with VR experiences should start in a seated position for safety. First-time users may become disoriented and fall if they are standing. Allow them to acclimate to being in a virtual environment seated at first, and then you can determine if it is safe enough for them to stand.

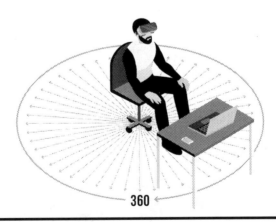

Figure 7.4 Most cine-VR experiences can be viewed seated or standing – swivel office chairs that rotate 360° are ideal

Wired Headsets

Wired headsets like the HP Reverb 2 or HTC Vive Pro rely on the PC to manage rendering and other computations. This configuration is advantageous because PC-based processing is significantly better than wireless headsets.

The advancements in computer graphic processing units (GPUs) have had a notable impact on VR development/playback. The GPU is a common computer component that carries out complex calculations and renders computer graphics. A decent GPU is likely to be the single most expensive component in a VR-ready computer and is commonly the most frequently upgraded component for VR enthusiasts. In a production setting, wired headsets are beneficial because they allow quicker playback and are powered either by the computer or an included power plug. Wireless headsets that can link to a computer, usually by USB cable, also get the benefits of wired systems.

All digital images displayed are composed of millions of pixels – so small that they are typically invisible to the naked eye. An individual pixel displays only one color, but it creates impressive graphical compositions when densely packed into a screen. The more pixels you have in an area, the higher the image quality. Higher pixel density is a common perk of wired headsets due to a desktop computer GPU's rendering capabilities. Pixel density is the number of pixels you can squeeze into a display's space and measures as pixels per inch (PPI). With higher pixel density comes enhanced clarity, definition, and sharpness for still images and video. Lower resolution/PPI headsets can give the illusion that you're looking through a screened door. This undesirable effect is shared by all digital screens and is known as the screen-door effect. If you focus your eyes near the surface, you may see a light grid pattern on some of your screens; others are so pixel-dense that the effect is only visible with a magnifying glass. As digital display technology evolves, this effect will reduce with every new headset iteration.

Advertising overall resolution as a "number + K" amount is customary for displays. Pixel resolution is commonly marketed as 2K, 4K, 6K, 8K, etc., especially for high-definition televisions. The 'K' amount refers to the number of horizontal pixels in "thousands" on a screen. A 4K screen advertises as having approximately four thousand (4K) horizontal pixels per display. Technically, 4K screens typically have 3,840 pixels (marketed as Ultra High Definition or UHD) or 4,096 pixels (True or Cinema 4K) lines but round to the nearest thousand for marketing simplicity. A 2K screen has approximately 2,000 pixels.

It might be easy to assume that a 4K screen has twice the resolution amount as 2K, but it actually has four times the resolution because both the horizontal and vertical line count doubles (see Figure 7.5).

Regardless of your headset's pixel density, the cine-VR playback quality is only going to be as high as the resolution in which you shoot and process your 360° video. If you shoot with a 2K camera and display the video on a 4K display, you will get a blocky, pixelated project – think of what happens when you zoom-in on digital photos. The more you zoom in, the more jagged the edges of an image appear. This undesirable outcome is called aliasing and is responsible for distorting and pixelating images. Our advice is to shoot with a higher quality camera and, if needed, downscale the quality to a lower resolution for headset playback. You will see minimal differences in quality if you shoot in 4K and need to shrink it down to a 2K video.

Shooting at a higher resolution can also extend the shelf life of your project. If your current headset is incapable of playing your content at the resolution used for recording, it will be a safe bet that headsets may support that quality in one to two years. For example, if you shoot at 6K,

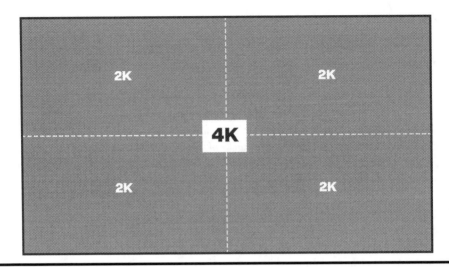

Figure 7.5 **A 4K screen has four times the resolution as a 2K screen because both the horizontal and vertical line count doubles**

you may have to reduce the quality down to 2K for playback purposes currently, but that may change soon.

If you chose a headset for pixel resolution, check the "per-eye" resolution. Some headsets are marketed as a 4K headset but have closer to a 2K resolution per eye.

There are disadvantages to wired headsets as well. It can be frustrating to get tangled up in wires, so wire management is essential. You can use Velcro straps to bundle the cables together or attach them to the back of a chair – make sure you leave enough slack so that the user is not whiplashed while moving.

Another solution is to mount the headset from the ceiling. Mounting the headset keeps all of the wires above and out of the user's way. We use extendable dog leashes to manage cable slack if someone moves around. Our solution is quick and dirty, but you can buy ceiling mounts designed for VR cable and headset management that work similarly. If ideal cable management is not possible, someone should be on hand to prevent wire tangling so that the user is safe and comfortable. If you travel with your headsets to conferences, classrooms, or exhibitions, make sure you have a plan for managing loose cables.

Wireless Headsets

Wireless headsets like the Oculus Quest 2 and HTC Focus are growing in popularity. Size, the convenience of use, and not being tethered to a PC are attractive features. Wireless headsets process everything onboard the device, similar to a smartphone because hardware size is limited. Due to this space restriction, wireless technology will naturally lag behind what desktop computers can process. Most wireless headsets require you to send content data files over a USB cable connection manually or may be downloaded or streamed directly to the device.

The GRID Lab exclusively uses wireless headsets for playback at conferences and workshops because they are easy to set up and scale up. There are no significant concerns about cable management as well. Not requiring a PC for playback also makes it considerably more affordable for large crowd demonstrations. Wireless headsets can be synchronized to deliver the same experience to all connected devices at the same time. For example, if you have twenty headsets, you can broadcast identical play and stop commands to each device. You will need a PC and dependable Wi-Fi access to make this work. We bring our own Wi-Fi router to avoid potential issues connecting to restrictive networks at hospitals or conference centers.

We have found synchronization valuable at conferences and workshops because it enhances the presentation flow and reduces tech support. You do not need to explain how to navigate to an individual file, thus eliminating the need for controllers. Controllers have been problematic for us because of the confusion created by something as simple as pressing the wrong button. The most extensive synchronized playback we've had was sixty Oculus Go headsets (Facebook has discontinued this headset). We use an off-the-shelf product called VR-Sync to achieve synchronous playback, but other comparable solutions are available.

There are many production and playback solutions from which to choose. If your budget allows it, try different technologies to weigh the pros and cons yourself. Keep in mind that headsets, cameras, and microphones may need to be repaired or replaced often. The GRID Lab expects all headset and camera technology to survive less than two years with continuous use. We plan our project budgets to reflect this expectation.

Chapter 8

Eye Tracking

John Bowditch

Contents

Tracking where eyes look on screens is not a new innovation. In fact, eye-tracking techniques have been used in the hopes of demystifying human cognition for over a century.[1] Marketers use eye-tracking data to identify the most appealing placements, designs, and colors for advertisements. A well-placed, visually appealing web advertisement may entice a consumer to purchase a product. Making decisions based on consumer cognition is attractive beyond marketing as well. This chapter will provide a basic overview of eye-tracking technology and how the GRID Lab has integrated it with cine-VR.

Eye Tracking in VR

Eye-tracking in virtual reality was first used in 2000 by a team of researchers wanting performance measurement information for an aircraft inspection simulator.[2] Over the last twenty years, affordability has generally limited use to research and development-intensive applications. Thankfully, prices are beginning to drop, making the technology more accessible. Researchers and developers, including the GRID Lab team, are finding powerful ways to integrate this technology. The GRID Lab has used VR eye tracking to record how effectively hospital residents scan a trauma bay captured with cine-VR. The technical details of that project will be discussed later in the chapter.

The basics of eye tracking are easily comprehended. Cameras are aimed at mirrors located behind, below, or above each headset lens. Specifically, these cameras record gaze-based motion by

DOI: 10.4324/9781003168683-10

targeting each eye's pupil. Pupils are the dark circles located in the center of the iris that contract and expand based on changes in stimuli, such as light intensity.

The technical overview is also relatively straightforward. Eye-tracking cameras track what part of an image, video, or website your pupils are focusing on and for how long. Sometimes infrared lighting is used to improve the precision of the capture. Infrared (IR) light is not visible to the naked eye. IR lighting reveals enhanced details when captured by specialized IR digital cameras. IR lights enhance the tracking precision of minute pupil movements. Algorithms can assess where the user gazed, for how long, and in which sequence to improve the delivery and quality of content. The techniques are sophisticated enough to accurately track dozens of subtle movements per second.

Tracked eye movements will naturally inform marketers and researchers, but they can also lead to better virtual experiences. They can enhance rendering, reduce cases of motion sickness, and function as a controller.

There are many practical applications for using eye movements as an input device. For example, focusing your gaze could launch an application, navigate to a specific space, or function as a simple "click." Eye movements and other inputs like voice commands, hand gestures, and haptic feedback can enhance virtual experiences.

Eye movements can also influence rendering priorities resulting in higher definition graphics and videos. This approach is known as foveated rendering, a technique derived from computer graphics. As part of the eye's retina, the fovea helps us focus our eyes on a specific spot or movement. We use our foveal vision when concentrating on reading important text, spotting enemies in video games, or avoiding dangerous situations while driving. Based on how our foveal vision works, foveated rendering instructs the computer to assign greater importance and computational resources to what your eyes are focusing on. Less significant areas receive reduced computation.

Your foveal vision makes the focus spot of a digital image look crystal clear, and the surrounding visuals appear slightly blurred. The image detail you're focused on may be as small as 5° of your overall visual range.[3] While simultaneously focusing on a specific spot, the pixel resolution surrounding the spot begins declining. An image's overall pixel resolution decreases the farther from the center you get. This transformation is known as blending. The outermost edges, known as the peripheral, may be reduced to vague shapes and muted colors.

While not all VR hardware or software support foveated rendering yet, this will likely be a standard feature on all future headsets.

Cine-VR Example Project

Ohio University's GRID Lab and the Better Lab from the University of California San Francisco designed a project using eye-tracking to collect medical training data from a series of cine-VR experiences.

Traumas were captured with 360° cameras at the Zuckerberg San Francisco General Hospital (SFGH) over one week. Six 360° cameras and spatial microphones were positioned to maximally capture all perspectives of emergency room operations (specifics highlighted in Chapter 5).

We hypothesized that recording these events would allow new SFGH traumatic care residents to familiarize themselves with the hospital layout and functionality before stepping foot in it. This familiarization includes getting a sense of the core medical team's positioning, supply cabinets, and vitals monitors. This is a perfect example of PRE-ality.

Our primary research objective was to capture data of when residents' eyes focused on a specific person or point of interest in our recordings. We also wanted to know how long the residents looked at a particular area and in which order they scanned the room.

Eye-tracking this cine-VR experience helped answer several questions from the large pool of data collected. These questions included:

- How often do residents check vitals monitors, and for what duration?
- In what order do residents observe the patient, monitors, colleagues, and then "fill-in-the-blank"?
- Are residents squeamish, spending portions of the experience staring at the floor?
- Are residents looking at irrelevant items in the room or relevant items at the wrong time?
- Can residents find each healthcare provider in the room when their names or qualifications are called for?

The budget for the eye-tracking phase of the project was limited compared to other project phases. A small budget created challenges. We knew of several companies developing eye-tracking VR technology, notably the Swedish company Tobii, but their tools exceeded our budget.

It took us several months to find an affordable solution that we could actually modify code on. There were many starts and stops throughout this phase. Thankfully, HTC released the Vive Pro Eye, a $1,500 modified version of their Vive Pro headset, which could capture various data. Example data includes gaze origin and direction, pupil size and position, and whether eyes are opened. It also came with an excellent set of analytical tools. This affordable platform arrived just in time for our project.

The Vive Pro Eye headset needs to be connected to a computer via video and data cables. Two tracking sensors called Base Stations are also required to track headset and controller motion. The Base Stations can be mounted to a wall or two tripods – tripods being a better mobile solution. We used a VR-ready Lenovo Legion laptop for controlling the headset and capturing data, which was reasonably priced and performed well. The GRID Lab configured three sets of laptops, each with Vive Pro Eye headsets, and shipped them to San Francisco to begin data collection. This was achieved with a budget of less than $7,500.

Our team had to custom design a Unity game engine application to make data collection possible. Developing software in-house can be expensive. Our team consisted of several faculty and students, and it was a great experiential learning opportunity for them. If you do not have developers on staff that can create an eye-tracking application, consider budgeting for an off-the-shelf solution like those offered by Tobii.[4] Developing internally or purchasing a vendor's solution can both be expensive, depending on the project requirements. Try to plan ahead and budget accordingly.

Data Collection

As mentioned earlier, the Vive Pro Eye is designed to capture various types of data. Initially, we only wanted to focus on gaze direction and time spent focusing on a particular area. The cine-VR experience would run through a custom application built with the Unity game engine. Unity exported the collected data as a standard file-type (.csv or comma-separated values). All of this data was stored on an air-gapped computer that also controlled the headset.

The Better Lab selected the cine-VR content they wanted to track. We used grid-based tracking to determine gaze direction. We also placed hitboxes which are invisible three-dimensional shapes placed over areas or persons of importance. Using hitboxes is a technique we often use when making video games. The process involves creating non-visual "boxes" that track specifically identified regions or persons. Computer code was written to detect if someone's gaze passed through

Patient Lower Left Quadrant	00:01	00:01
D30	00:01	00:01
Patient Lower Right Quadrant	00:01	00:01
Patient Lower Left Quadrant	00:01	00:01
Patient Lower Right Quadrant	00:01	00:01
Patient Lower Left Quadrant	00:01	00:01
Patient Upper Left Quadrant	00:01	00:01
Patient Lower Left Quadrant	00:01	00:01
H31	00:01	00:01
Patient Upper Right Quadrant	00:01	00:01
Patient Lower Left Quadrant	00:01	00:01
H30	00:01	00:01
Patient Lower Left Quadrant	00:01	00:01
Patient Upper Right Quadrant	00:01	00:01
Patient Lower Left Quadrant	00:01	00:01
D31	00:01	00:01
Patient Upper Right Quadrant	00:01	00:01
D31	00:01	00:01
Patient Lower Left Quadrant	00:01	00:01
Patient Upper Right Quadrant	00:01	00:01
Patient Lower Left Quadrant	00:01	00:01
Patient Lower Right Quadrant	00:01	00:01
Patient Upper Right Quadrant	00:01	00:01
Patient Lower Left Quadrant	00:01	00:01
Patient Lower Right Quadrant	00:01	00:01
Patient Upper Right Quadrant	00:01	00:01
Patient Lower Right Quadrant	00:01	00:01
Patient Upper Right Quadrant	00:01	00:01
Patient Lower Left Quadrant	00:01	00:01

Figure 8.1 Sample output of the eye-tracking data captured in early tests

a hitbox. We positioned these boxes over specific individuals and objects. We knew exactly when someone looked at a specific medical team member, the patient, and other points of interest.

The captured data eventually told us where the eyes focused and for how long. The data was exported to a .csv file and evaluated by statisticians. Figure 8.1 demonstrates a sample output of the eye-tracking data captured in early tests. The left column identifies the hitbox or grid position looked at. The middle column is the start time, and the right column is the time they looked away. You'll notice all of the gaze positions are recorded over one second's worth of movements. Though the image shows a select portion of what was captured, there were actually eighty-one recorded motions in the first second alone. We had to decrease the eye movement sensitivity going forward to produce digestible research information.

Unity

Unity is a game and simulation engine that we use to teach our VR and game development courses at Ohio University. Notable computer games, mobile games, architectural visualizations, and other simulated environments have been created on the Unity platform. The engine is free to

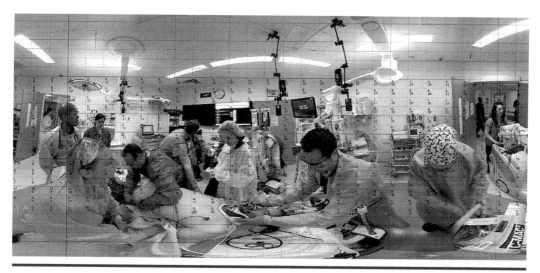

Photo 8.1   Example of a grid overlay applied to the SFGH footage (with an actor as a patient)

try, but it does have a steep learning curve for beginners. Unity develops freely accessible educational materials for learning how to use the engine (https://learn.unity.com).

In Unity, our team wrapped the cine-VR video around the interior of a sphere model. To help visualize this, imagine standing inside a giant sphere and watching cine-VR content playing in all directions around you. Next, we applied a grid overlay and assigned names to each grid space base. Each grid size will differ depending on the desired precision. If you expand the number of grid spaces, you'll increase the gaze tracker's accuracy. Each grid space was assigned a unique hitbox.

We were unsure how many grid spaces were optimal, so we estimated a grid size and started with that value. The first grid we created had over 500 grid spaces. This size created too much information because eye movements were tracked with way too much detail. Reducing the grid to less than 200 grid spaces worked best for our project. We also chose not to track several regions like the ceiling and directly below the camera, further reducing the number of grid spaces.

Grid space rows were assigned letters, and columns received numbers. Every grid space had a corresponding letter and number (e.g., A25, A40, B27, D12). We could also track an individual based on what coordinates they populated at any given moment. For example, if we wanted to track the attending anesthesiologist, we knew they were in specific grid spaces during particular moments in time and therefore trackable. Following someone in motion through multiple grid spaces is cumbersome to configure but potentially quite useful.

Final Thoughts

There are many ways to integrate eye-tracking into your cine-VR project. Make sure to budget accordingly and design your projects around recording specific information. Identify the best tools available for your project.

It is not necessary for you to utilize all of a headset's eye-tracking capabilities. Often, the amount of information that can be recorded is overwhelming. Know what research questions you're trying to solve and record data accordingly.

Viewing

There are no cine-VR examples to view for this chapter. Images are from a project detailed in Chapter 5.

Notes

1. Viviane Clay, Peter König, and Sabine Koenig, (2019), Eye Tracking in Virtual Reality. *Journal of Eye Movement Research*. 12. 10.16910/jemr.12.1.3.
2. Andrew T. Duchowski, Eric Medlin, Anand Gramopadhye, Brian Melloy, and Santosh Nair, *Binocular Eye Tracking in VR for Visual Inspection Training*. In Proceedings of the ACM symposium on Virtual reality software and technology (VRST '01). Association for Computing Machinery, New York, NY, USA, pages 1–8. 2001 DOI: https://doi.org/10.1145/505008.505010
3. Guenter, Brian, Mark Finch, Steven Drucker, Desney Tan, and John Snyder, *Supplement to Foveated 3D Graphics: User Study Details*. Microsoft Research, November 2012.
4. Tobii Eye-Tracking. https://www.tobii.com

SECTION III

Many media function as independent, stand-alone experiences. If you pick up a magazine, turn on a news program, or listen to the radio, you can get the complete story in one easy-to-understand experience. If you want to teach, a lecture might do the trick; or maybe an instructional video, a field trip, or a video game. These forms of non-fiction media can exist on their own.

Cine-VR, in its current state, does not seem to fit that mold. Yes, a cine-VR experience may have a beginning, middle, and end – allowing it to feel like a complete piece. However, in our experience, we have found cine-VR to be much more effective as just one element of a mixed or multimodal approach.

Mixed Media vs Multimodal Approach

A *mixed media* approach combines two or more forms of media into one final project. The final project cannot exist without each piece. For instance, consider teaching first-time drivers how to prepare to drive a car. Cine-VR might be used to have the student feel what it's like to sit at the wheel, while a 2D animation might be used as an overlay to illustrate how the driver will use the clutch, brake, and gas pedals. In this example, both 2D animation and cine-VR are used in concert to deliver the information. The final piece requires both forms of media. If either was removed, the piece would fall apart.

A *multimodal* approach utilizes more than one medium to create a final project, but each medium stands independently. As an example, consider a journalistic piece written about prison overcrowding. As an addendum to that piece, the reader had the option to access a cine-VR experience to feel what it's like to be inside an overcrowded prison. The written piece and the cine-VR piece each provide information that can be consumed as a complete experience. Ideally, they would be viewed in concert for each to be most successful – but they don't have to be viewed that way.

The GRID Lab began working with mixed media and multimodal approaches out of necessity to capitalize upon what we perceived to be cine-VR's fundamental strengths and to fortify its fundamental weaknesses.

Cine-VR Strengths

1. Cine-VR can immerse the audience in a location in a way that other media cannot. If done correctly, this immersion can make people feel like they are actually in the place (also known as a sense of presence).

DOI: 10.4324/9781003168683-11

2. When viewed in a headset, Cine-VR inherently forces the audience to focus on the task at hand. Cine-VR isolates the audience from all of the everyday world's distractions (e.g., class-mates, smartphones, laptops, butterflies).

3. Cine-VR captures people's attention. People are curious about the technology, and people will explore cine-VR content that they may ignore in traditional media. For instance, "Would you like to experience a VR canoe ride?" vs. "Would you like to watch a video about riding in a canoe?".

Cine-VR Weaknesses

1. It takes time to become familiar with the technology. Most people need to be guided through key aspects of a cine-VR experience:
   a. Menu navigation
   b. Cueing and/or controlling the video
   c. Adjusting for glasses, audio, headphones, hairdos, etc.
   Often it helps to introduce people to cine-VR through "desktop VR" (i.e., on a computer with no headset) as a "gateway" to understanding how true cine-VR works.

2. Today's audiences have been conditioned by film and television to such an extent that they expect specific visual storytelling techniques to tell them how to feel and what to expect in a story. These techniques include:
   a. Close-up camera shots,
   b. Camera moves,
   c. Frenetic editing.
   These techniques are less available in cine-VR.

3. New storytelling techniques are still being developed. While some cine-VR directors are developing these new tools, most audiences are not as familiar with them.

With strengths and weaknesses in mind, we started combining media into the same project – relying on the shortcomings in one medium to be covered by the other's strengths. The three projects in this section will illustrate the differences between a mixed media and multimodal approach. These chapters will lay the groundwork to better understand some of the other multi-layered approaches you will find with still other projects in this book.

Examples and Effects

Narcan Training Project (Chapter 9): Mixed Media

As you'll read in Chapter 9, *Training a Community How to Save a Life with NARCAN*, higher education frequently uses digital media and live simulation as successful teaching tools. Until last year, Ohio University's School of Nursing used a didactic approach (combining lecture and traditional video) to teach nursing students how to deploy a Narcan kit. Narcan is a drug that can potentially counteract an opioid overdose. The didactic approach was successful, but the faculty wanted to take the education a step further. They wanted to explore ways that students could experience the Narcan deployment process in real-world settings.

In 2017, the GRID Lab produced a cine-VR pilot project where the audience experiences a reenactment of two students finding a third student overdosed on heroin in a college dorm room. Back then, we thought that the cine-VR experience could operate as a stand-alone training experience – replacing the 2D video and much of the lecture. The pilot was well-received, garnering attention from National Public Radio's *All Things Considered*. However, focus groups revealed that while audiences were captivated by the intensity of the situation, the specific steps of using the Narcan kit were getting lost.

The details were getting lost for three specific reasons:

1. The environment is chaotic. Students frequently missed the deployment of the Narcan kit because they were paying attention to something else.
2. Even if the students were watching the person administering the Narcan kit, there were no close-up shots of the kit being used. Students had to rely on their previous knowledge of how a Narcan kit was deployed.
3. Students often didn't remember all the details from the previous day's lecture in this intense environment.

Upon reflection, we realized that we had eliminated vital information (the traditional video illustrating detailed steps to administer Narcan) in exchange for an intense emotional experience via cine-VR. We went back to the drawing board and determined that our project's primary objective was not only to create a moving scene, but also to deliver critical information. With that in mind, we quickly determined that one medium had to build upon the other – not replace it. The lack of close-up visuals (a cine-VR weakness) was standing in our way.

The following year, funding was secured for a follow-up project. Our approach this time was a mixed media approach – combining traditional video and lecture with three cine-VR experiences to create a complete educational package. Chapter 13 will discuss the project in more detail, but, in essence, we made a mixed media product by simultaneously simplifying and complicating the educational process.

We simplified the process through repetition and unification. Then, we complicated the project by creating three cine-VR experiences instead of one:

- One cine-VR experience in a private space (in a dorm room),
- One in a public area (in a parking lot), and
- One in a professional setting (in a home health facility).

Each experience was then coupled with a 2D video to create a three-part lesson:

Part 1: A didactic explanation of how a Narcan kit is used, complete with a 2D video to demonstrate the details to the audience.
Part 2: A complete cine-VR experience.
Part 3: A summary of the information from Part 1, reinforced with 2D video.

In creating this approach, we agreed on three fundamental tenets to the project as a whole. First, all three parts of the lesson were crafted as a complete educational unit and viewed as a whole. Therefore, there was no temporal disconnect between the didactic information and the cine-VR experience. Each piece just flowed into the next. Second, students would view all three parts of the lesson while in a headset, isolating them from distractions (one of the cine-VR's strengths). And finally, the didactic segments were similar in each of the three lessons. Since each student was required to watch all three lessons, the critical didactic information was repeated nine times.

Parkinson's Disease Project (Chapter 10): Multimodal Approach

At Ohio University's School of Nursing, professor Miller routinely teaches students how to work with patients suffering from Parkinson's Disease. Her typical mode of delivery is lecture and discussion. This approach has served her well over the years and has proven to be effective.

Cine-VR adds a second modality. The students can now experience the ideas they had previously heard about in lectures and discussed in small group meetings. Yet, each can potentially stand alone. The lectures mention the cine-VR experiences, but they are not directly tied to one another. Meaning: professor Miller does not have students don HMDs as part of the lecture. Nor do the students engage in the cine-VR experiences as part of their weekly discussion groups. A student needs to choose to engage with the experiences outside of lecture and discussion – similar, in many ways, to "recommended readings."

A multi-modal approach relies on confidence that students will seek what a student needs. Some students may be fully informed through lectures and discussion. If so, the cine-VR experience would be superfluous. For others, the cine-VR is a welcome augmentation of the lesson. In this case, the content's amount (and form) is for the student to decide.

Similarly, an educational program may select a multimodal approach for an entire unit. Imagine, if you will, a small library of medical cine-VR experiences. If a faculty were well-informed about the library's content, then each instructor could utilize the content differently – as needed for each content area. For instance, professor Miller might reference the PDP experiences to demonstrate the patient perspective of Parkinsonian hallucinations. But professor Smith might choose to use the same experience to demonstrate hygiene practices. Because the experiences are designed for multimodal use, each experience becomes "nodal" and can be used interchangeably within various programs of study.

Best Practices

Every project is unique, so the entire team needs to have planning meetings in advance of starting any project. We suggest that these meetings occur during the pre-funding stage, as the answers to crucial questions are necessary to determine an accurate budget and timeline. During these planning meetings, two key conversations need to happen.

1. ***What are the primary objectives of the project as they relate to using cine-VR?***
   Whether mixed or multimodal, most projects have one of four primary objectives when it comes to using cine-VR:

Knowledge	Delivering information or instruction to the audience.
Innovation	Capturing the audience's attention via new technology.
Transportation	Mentally transporting the audience to a new location.
Emotion	Psychologically engaging the audience

   If the project's primary objectives don't fall into one of these areas, you may want to question whether cine-VR is the right tool to use.

2. ***Discuss the pros and cons of various media***

Once the project's primary objectives have been determined, the following conversation is to recognize the context of how the experience is going to be used. Questions that you might consider:

Will cine-VR be used to augment a lecture or presentation?
Will cine-VR allow participants to practice a skill or technique?
Is cine-VR delivering a specific experience that will later be revisited?
Is the cine-VR piece augmenting another medium from the outset?

To date, we have found very few uses of non-fiction cine-VR as a stand-alone medium. In the following three chapters, we will explain how specific cine-VR projects were implemented with multi-media and multi-modal approaches. We hope that these projects inspire you to design more comprehensive projects and encourage you to practice different techniques to augment the cine-VR medium.

Chapter 9

Training a Community How to Save a Life with NARCAN©

Sherleena Buchman, Char L. Miller, and Deborah Henderson

Contents

Opioids were involved in 47,600 overdose deaths in 2017 (67.8% of all drug overdose deaths) and 46,802 overdose deaths in 2018 (69.5% of all drug overdose deaths).[1] Ohio ranked second in the nation for drug overdose deaths (46.3 per 100,000) in 2017[2] and remained in the top five (35.9 per 100,000) in 2018.[3] In response to the national opioid epidemic, Ohio University's School of Nursing developed a cine-VR series as a focused educational intervention. The cine-VR design provides layperson education regarding awareness and knowledge of opioid overdose recognition and management in the college campus environment.

DOI: 10.4324/9781003168683-12

87

To expedite treatment and improve outcomes in cases of opioid overdose, naloxone, an opioid overdose antidote, is being promoted and utilized for community-based use by laypersons and first responders, including emergency services personnel.[4] NARCAN (naloxone) is effective in minutes and can restore normal breathing and save the life of a person who has overdosed with opioids. The reversal of opioid overdose by layperson administration of naloxone has a 75–100% success rate.[5] The growing availability and promotion of community-based naloxone administration have led to a need to educate the public on recognizing an overdose and properly administering naloxone.

Existing solutions to this educational need prior to our implementation of the cine-VR experiences included traditional videos and written materials from various government and privately funded organizations. These materials failed to engage learners. Without engaging educational materials, students were unable to apply necessary skills to a realistic real-life situation.[6] Virtual reality (VR) is a tool for educators to enhance teaching and learning in a desirable format.[7] Cine-VR content is delineated from other media mainly through the immersive aspect of the experience. Cine-VR promotes experiential learning by allowing students to have immersive, concrete experiences with opioid overdose and then encouraging assimilation of that learning through reflection.[8]

Audience and Outcomes

The cine-VR naloxone experience is a seven-minute, fifteen-second immersive video experience used as a teaching strategy for laypersons to increase opioid overdose awareness and knowledge about suspected overdose response. The intended audience for this cine-VR project includes college students, faculty, staff, and administration. Each of these groups must be aware of overdose and naloxone uses to prevent opioid overdose death. The project had four primary objectives:

1. To increase recognition of possible opioid overdose symptoms.
2. To increase awareness of naloxone as an antidote to opioid overdose.
3. To educate laypersons on appropriate naloxone nasal spray administration.
4. To evaluate cine-VR as a teaching strategy for naloxone administration.

Project Evolution

Dr. Buchman, the project team lead and a registered nurse (RN), was working a night shift in the emergency department (ED) when a young adult patient arrived by ambulance from a local college with a suspected opioid overdose. This scenario was not unfamiliar. It had happened many times before. But for Dr. Buchman, this night became a turning point.

The overdose patient's family came into the waiting room, arriving just a few minutes after the patient, with heart-wrenching cries of why and how this was happening. While other healthcare team members worked to save the patient's life, Dr. Buchman, acting as House Supervisor, stayed with the family. The family learned that the patient's college roommate and some other friends discovered him; they did not know what to do other than call for help, which they did promptly.

At this point, the patient had received naloxone and was waking up. Dr. Buchman was holding the mother's hand and silently offering support. However, in Dr. Buchman's mind, questions were surfacing. The family was concerned about the patient and wondering where he got the drugs and why he took too much. Dr. Buchman contemplated what she could do to make a difference to the next patient, the next mother, the next family?

The patient responded to the naloxone and recovered. The family was thankful to the ED team for saving the life of their loved one. The patient's mother thanked Dr. Buchman, who had remained by her side as she wondered if her son would live or die. Dr. Buchman accepted the gratitude, knowing that just a few more minutes without the opioid antidote could have meant a very different outcome.

Project Beginnings

Dr. Buchman first developed a traditional role-playing simulation based on her ED experience. She did this as part of an interprofessional course she was teaching. Students from the class helped to draft the original script and scenario. The interprofessional students performed the simulation at the end of the semester at an event attended by several local community members, campus students, and faculty. Interest garnered from the event led Dr. Buchman to explore better ways to share this information with a broader and more diverse audience.

Team Development

Dr. Buchman approached the GRID Lab to propose her idea for a cine-VR naloxone experience. The nursing and GRID Lab faculty and students' partnership provided an open area for communication and innovation. Previous VR research indicated that immersive VR provides students with positive learning and feelings of presence and empathy.[9] The team discussed different VR delivery models, but cine-VR was selected to provide a meaningful and immersive learning experience due to its realistic, 360° viewing experience.

Learning Theory

Kolb's Experiential Learning Theory (KELT) was selected as the theoretical foundation for this project. According to Kolb, learning is a continuous process, and knowledge is created by transforming experiences into cognitive frameworks, thereby creating new ways of thinking or behaving. KELT follows the circular process of a learning cycle comprised of four adaptive phases: active experimentation, concrete experience, reflective observation, and abstract conceptualization.

The team explicitly chose this theory because students desire an active learning environment rather than a passive learning environment. The theory asserts that in the first phase (concrete experimentation), concrete experiences such as cine-VR simulation would provide the context for the second phase (debriefing), in which learners reflect on their experiences, draw conclusions, and consider options for future behavior.[10] In the third phase (abstract conceptualization), learners draw conclusions and experience learning. Or they modify existing abstract concepts resulting in a change in thoughts and behaviors, applying their new knowledge to future situations. In the fourth and final phase (active experimentation), learners apply their new knowledge to future real-life situations (see Figure 9.1).

Project Development

The project evolved from a live simulation (one that included a pre-brief, simulation, and debrief) into a cine-VR experience that utilized a live pre-brief, followed by a cine-VR experience, and finally a live faculty-led debrief. The audience optimally viewed the cine-VR with a head-mounted

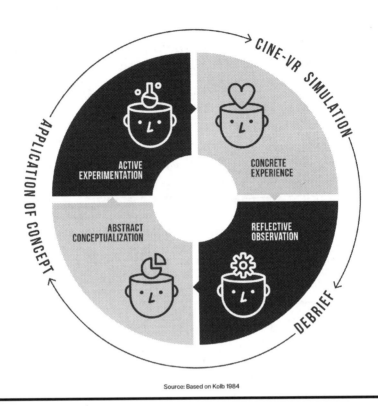

Source: Based on Kolb 1984

Figure 9.1 Depiction of the KOLB stages concerning the Narcan cine-VR experience. Based on Kolb 1984

display and earbuds. Upon completion, participants had the option to participate in a focus group experience to provide feedback.

There was only a shoestring budget for the initial cine-VR experience. It was shot and edited by undergraduate student employees at the GRID Lab, overseen by faculty member Eric R. Williams. Dr. Buchman and her team found volunteer students and staff to play the actors' roles of a college student who has overdosed on opioids and two peers who find him breathing yet unresponsive. The peers try to figure out how to respond and eventually call 911 emergency services for help as they administer naloxone. When the naloxone reverses the effects of the opioid overdose, the college student wakes up and is angry with his peers for "messing up his high."

Production Approach

The GRID Lab often provides low-cost production at the Proof-of-Concept stage to develop relationships with departments. These projects also serve as educational opportunities for undergraduate students who work at the GRID Lab.

The pilot naloxone project was recorded on-location within the College of Health Sciences and Professionals' interprofessional lab space with only a $100 budget. Bringing in additional furniture and wall/room décor, the crew transformed a room that typically serves as a mock hospital room into a college dorm. All actors volunteered for the project, using a script outline that ad-libbed their responses to the situation. Crew members donated costumes and props to create a sense of a college dorm life.

Figure 9.2 **The pilot project was recorded in a lab space with additional furniture and room décor transforming the space into a college dorm**

The GRID Lab team donated the production and post-production equipment and the time of faculty and student staff. The project was shot on one day and edited the following week.

This project used an Insta360° Pro camera and a Zoom H3-VR 360° microphone placed in the room's center (see Figure 9.2). The experience used only natural lighting and recorded the experience in its entirety without plates (see Chapter 20 for details on creating plates).

Pilot Stage

Students from thirteen disciplines piloted the cine-VR naloxone proof-of-concept. The volunteer participants completed the pre-brief, viewed the cine-VR naloxone, participated in a debrief, and then participated in focus groups of four-to-eight participants. The focus groups' compositions elicited feedback on reactions, preferences, perceptions, and suggestions regarding the cine-VR naloxone. The sessions were audio-recorded, transcribed, and subsequently underwent thematic analysis. All pilot data collected helped refine the cine-VR naloxone product.

Considerations

With cine-VR, there are no edits (or cuts) while recording, and rarely can you correct a blunder made on set by editing portions of a scene together, as is done in a traditional film. Additional challenges include equipment acquisition and proficiency with using technology in general. The GRID Lab equipment cost (for production and post-production) would have been approximately $9,000.00 if it had to be purchased solely for this project. The student crew learned to work on a project such as this one through games and virtual reality curriculum offered in the J. Warren McClure School of Emerging Communication Technologies.

Redesign Stage

The team reviewed the objectives, outcome measures, and all the data and feedback received from the variety of students who participated in the pilot study. While this review confirmed that the content was adequate, the pilot study highlighted critical areas of concern:

A. The location and characters (actors) were not believable. The scenario did not feel as "real" as desired. The main actor was not the traditional college age.
B. The production value was low. Some audio was difficult to hear, and particular locations needed improved lighting. Actors often blocked important information with their bodies.
C. Cine-VR was highly effective at placing the audience "in the scene" but was less effective when demonstrating "step-by-step" instructions (e.g., the specific process of preparing Narcan for use).

Simultaneously, Dr. Buchman's team determined that this cine-VR product could be an excellent educational tool for their large nursing student population. However, the live aspects of the pre-brief and debrief required for the project would be restrictive.

The team decided to seek funding to redesign the project. There were four critical decisions made for the redesign:

A. For the sake of authenticity, using a real dorm room located on Ohio University's campus was necessary. Casting actors from Ohio University's theater department and using a detailed script improved performance quality.
B. The production approach using plates, while more complicated, allowed the crew to use production lighting on set. The production crew did not need to hide because we captured only a portion of each scene at a time. We shot 90–180° and then repositioned the lighting equipment and crew to complete the full 360°. This approach required combining two to four separate shots in post-production but improved the scenes' overall cinematic quality (see Chapters 2 and 20 for production details regarding plating). Additionally, the audio specialists placed a multiuse Ambisonic microphone that captures sound from all directions in the room's center. Lavalier microphones recorded each actor's dialogue (see Chapter 12 for audio considerations). Synthesizing GRID Lab narrative strategies (see Chapter 13), the camera was moved away from the center of the room – allowing certain items to appear closer to the audience (e.g., the heroin that the students discover) while simultaneously using a 90° field of view to enhance the collection of information.
C. Combine traditional footage with the 360° footage to provide "close-up" illustrations of how to administer Narcan.
D. Create prerecorded, rather than live, prebriefing and debriefing materials for the project.

Photo 9.1   Important props are placed closer to the camera for careful observation by the audience

The team chose to create the entire experience so that it would occur inside of a head-mounted display (also known as an HMD). The experience would have three parts:

Part 1: The pre-brief would appear as if the viewer was sitting in a dark room watching a traditionally shot instructional video. The video would include instructional information from a student (accompanied by information graphics) and demonstrate Narcan's process.
Part 2: The traditionally shot portion would then "open up" to reveal a 360° cine-VR experience.
Part 3: The 360° element would return to a 2D approach for a verbal debrief session, including questions and self-guided reflections.

The additional funding allowed the GRID Lab to add a student from the School of Visual Communication to the team, who provided information graphics for the project. The budget further permitted the production of three plots rather than just one. The plots included:

■ Narcan use in a college dorm room;
■ Narcan use in a public setting (parking lot);
■ Narcan use in a healthcare setting (Skilled Nursing Facility).

These adjustments created a more realistic scenario (see Photo 9.1) and a consistent, quality delivery of information (see Photo 9.2). Cine-VR provides a real-life view of actual people in a situation that places the participants virtually in the location where the event occurs. Previous research has determined that this level of realism provides users with a feeling of presence.[11] The final Dorm-scene Cine-VR experience, including a pre-brief, the seven-minute, fifteen-second-long immersive cine-VR capture, and a debrief, concluded with an eighteen-minute encapsulated learning experience. The collection of materials is copyrighted and shared widely with others.

Best Practices

The cine-VR naloxone project had many successes. Promising data from the pilot informed iterations and allowed refinement of the process for participant orientation. Consolidating the content

Photo 9.2   Screen grab of 2D graphic viewed inside of an HMD. Illustration created by Kenzie Kress

and the educational approach into one unified educational experience viewable by students minimized the need for live interactions. Subsequently, the project permitted evaluation of cine-VR as a teaching strategy for focused, healthcare-related content.

The cine-VR naloxone project has been overwhelmingly well-received by the community, the campus, and professional colleagues in nursing and related fields. Several invitations to consult and collaborate with other universities have developed from presentations at conferences and community events. Our studies have demonstrated that cine-VR technology as a teaching modality can dramatically impact healthcare education, particularly healthcare simulation, as it represents a cost-effective supplement to traditional role-playing or human patient simulator-based education.[12]

This project provides six essential takeaway tips for those interested in creating their own cine-VR experiences, expanded upon in the next part of this chapter:

- Clinical experiences by faculty or students can translate into meaningful learning experiences through a team approach utilizing cine-VR;
- Clearly defining team member roles and timelines are essential to project success;
- Design cine-VR with evidence-based content and pedagogical considerations;
- Debriefing is an essential component of cine-VR;
- Cine-VR immersion experience combined with traditionally shot educational content appears to be the approach preferred by participants;
- Participants need to have a comprehensive orientation to the cine-VR 360° view to avoid stationary viewing of the product.

How to Create and Deliver Cine-VR

Our nursing and GRID Lab team developed an algorithm for creating and delivering cine-VR, incorporating the best practices for simulation by including a pre-brief, delivery, and a debrief as outlined in Figure 9.3.

ALGORITHM FOR CINE-VR

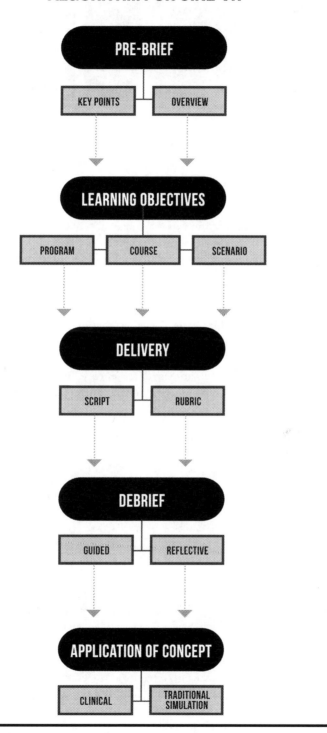

Figure 9.3   Algorithm for cine-VR

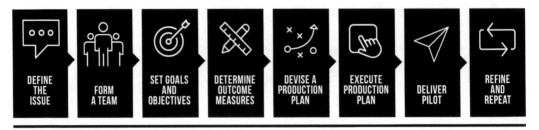

| DEFINE THE ISSUE | FORM A TEAM | SET GOALS AND OBJECTIVES | DETERMINE OUTCOME MEASURES | DEVISE A PRODUCTION PLAN | EXECUTE PRODUCTION PLAN | DELIVER PILOT | REFINE AND REPEAT |

Figure 9.4   Steps for planning cine-VR

How to Plan for Developing Cine-VR

Producing cine-VR in a purposeful, meaningful way requires applying the identified best practices. One must start by clearly defining what educational problems or issues to address. The team should include a subject matter expert, writers, a director, a cinematographer, and audio expert (complete with support crew), as well as dedicated actors (not volunteers) and a team for graphic design during post-production (see Chapters 19 and 20 for details on putting together a reliable team).

The team then determines who will lead the project's development by outlining the specific project goal(s), roles, and responsibilities, setting a production plan that includes a timeline, identifying measurable objectives, and identifying the tools used to measure the outcomes.

Once the plan has been executed, and an initial edit is available, pilot the cine-VR with a small group of consumers representing your intended audience. You may need to refine and produce several iterations to achieve the desired outcome for the intended audience. Figure 9.4 depicts the step-by-step planning process.

What's Next?

Cine-VR has evolved the way that this education team thinks about teaching. The natural evolution for cine-VR began with the team moving forward to create two additional cine-VR opioid scenarios and other projects discussed in Chapters 10 and 11. Due to the global Covid-19 pandemic of 2020–21, educators across all disciplines have had to consider various educational outlets to provide meaningful learning experiences to their student populations. Our GRID Lab team are in the process of converting our cine-VR for streaming services, including YouTube or Vimeo. Audiences may view the streamed content with low-cost "cardboard" HMDs if a higher quality headset is unavailable. Ohio University's School of Nursing has found that cine-VR is a way for educators to provide a consistent, high-quality simulated experience for every student regardless of physical location.

Additionally, there is an opportunity for collaboration among professions to further interprofessional education. The World Health Organization defines interprofessional education as students from two or more disciplines working together to learn from and about each other.[13] By following Kolb's theory, health care interprofessional students who learn new skill sets via cine-VR in an interprofessional environment are more likely to carry those experiences into their future practices in the active experimentation phase.

Financial Implications

The financial impact is undoubtedly something that one needs to consider when planning and creating a cine-VR for healthcare education. Based upon Dr. Buchman's proof-of-concept, she obtained a $10,000 internal grant from the College of Health Sciences and Professions that helped fund her cine-VR project's expansion. Additional noteworthy costs covered by in-kind support made the total budget closer to $11,000.

While this may sound high for creating three seven-to-twelve-minute experiences, one must consider the return on investment. Typically, in a scenario of 100 students in groups of four, an educator would need to deliver a simulation experience at least twenty-five times to allow all students an opportunity to participate, with a faculty member available for each session. For students to experience all three scenarios, that faculty member (and the "actors") would need to be available at more than seventy-five different fifteen-minute intervals. Including a fifteen-minute break, every two hours requires more than twenty hours of work for the faculty member. This effort is equivalent to three full days of work for the faculty member, factoring in lunch breaks and prep times.

Further, the risk of each student group receiving slight variances in the traditional simulation is high because many things can be changed or altered in a seven-to-ten-minute scenario (e.g., different faculty using different words, equipment malfunction, and actor discrepancies). Upon completing a cine-VR production, the cost to deliver the same scenario to every student is minimal.

Viewing

To view and download cine-VR examples mentioned in this chapter, please visit: https://vimeo.com/channels/cinevr4healthcare/ (***password:*** *cineVR4health*).

CONSORTIUM OF INNOVATION IN NURSING EDUCATION - VIRTUAL REALITY

The team that developed this NARCAN cine-VR identified a need in nursing education for a consortium to focus on Innovation and Virtual Reality. Thus, the Consortium of Innovation in Nursing Education - Virtual Reality (or: CINE-VR) was created. If you would be interested in joining this consortium and advancing the use of quality VR in nursing education, please contact the authors.

Notes

1. Centers for Disease Control and Prevention, National Center for Injury Prevention and Control (CDC) (2020, March 19). Drug Overdose Deaths. https://www.cdc.gov/drugoverdose/data/statedeaths.html
2. Scholl, L., Seth, P., Kariisa, M., Wilson, N., Baldwin, G. Drug and Opioid-Involved Overdose Deaths – United States, 2013–2017. *MMWR Morb Mortal Wkly Rep* 2019;67:1419–1427. DOI: http://dx.doi.org/10.15585/mmwr.mm675152e1

3. Centers for Disease Control and Prevention, National Center for Injury Prevention and Control (CDC) (2020, March 19). Drug Overdose Deaths. https://www.cdc.gov/drugoverdose/data/statedeaths.html

4. Wheeler, E., Jones, T.S., Gilbert, M.K., et al. Opioid Overdose Prevention Programs Providing Naloxone to Laypersons: United States, 2014. *Morb Mortal Wkly Rep* 2015;64:631–635. https://www.ncbi.nlm.nih.gov/pmc/articles/PMC4584734/

5. Clark, A. K., Wilder, C. M., & Winstanley, E. L. (2014). A Systematic Review of Community Opioid Overdose Prevention and Naloxone Distribution Programs. *Journal of Addiction Medicine, 8*(3):153–163. doi: 10.1097/ADM.0000000000000034

6. DiGiulio, S. (2017, August 22). *3 ways virtual reality is transforming medical care.* Retrieved from NBC MACH: https://www.nbcnews.com/mach/science/3-ways-virtual-reality-transforming-medical-care-ncna794871

7. Ferguson, C., Davidson, P., Scott, P., Jackson, D., & Hickman, L. (2015). Augmented Reality, Virtual Reality, and Gaming: An Integral Part of Nursing. *Contemporary Nurse, 51*(1), 1–4. https://doi.org/10.1080/10376178.2015.1130360

8. Kolb, D. A., Boyatzis, R. E., & Mainemelis, C. "Experiential learning theory: Previous research and new directions." *Perspectives on Cognitive, Learning, and Thinking Styles.* Sternberg & Zhang (Eds.). NJ: Lawrence Erlbaum; 2000. (pp. 227–248). Routledge.

9. Buchman, S., & Henderson, D. (2019). Interprofessional Empathy and Communication Competency Development in Healthcare Professions' Curriculum through Immersive Virtual Reality Experiences. *Journal of Interprofessional Education & Practice, 15*, 127–130. https://doi.org/10.1016/j.xjep.2019.03.010

10. Fewster-Thente, L., & Batteson, T. (2018). Kolb's Experiential Learning Theory as a Theoretical Underpinning for Interprofessional Education. *Journal of Allied Health, 47*(1), 3–8.

11. Buchman, S., & Henderson, D. (2019). Qualitative Study of Interprofessional Communication through Immersive Virtual Reality 360° Video among Healthcare Students. *International Journal of Nursing and Health Care Research, 3,* 076. https://gavinpublishers.com/articles/research-article/International-Journal-of-Nursing-and-Health-Care-Research-issn-2688-9501/qualitative-study-of-interprofessional-communication-through-immersive-virtual-reality-360°-video-among-healthcare-students

12. Buchman, S., Miller, C., Henderson, D., Williams, E. & Ray, S. (2020). Interprofessional Students Learning to Save a Life through Cine-VR Simulation. *EC Nursing and Healthcare,* 2.11, 04–20. https://www.ecronicon.com/ecnh/pdf/ECNH-02-00120.pdf

13. World Health Organization. (2010). *Framework for Action on Interprofessional Education and Collaborative Practice* (No. WHO/HRH/HPN/10.3). World Health Organization. https://hsc.unm.edu/ipe/resources/who-framework-.pdf

Chapter 10

Nurse Education- Parkinson's Disease Beyond the Shuffle

Char L. Miller, Sherleena Buchman, and Rebecca Bryant

Contents

As faculty in the Ohio University School of Nursing, we posited developing a cine-VR simulation series is an effective teaching strategy to increase undergraduate nursing student knowledge about Parkinson's Disease (PD) and their perceived competence in caring for a patient with PD in the hospital setting. Nursing students' opportunities to gain experience and confidence in patients' care with PD may be inconsistent as these opportunities are dependent upon the specific case mix available on the clinical units during student clinical experiences. Subsequently, in real-world practice settings, nursing faculty have little control over ensuring quality, evidence-based teaching and learning opportunities related to PD in the hospital setting. In addition to these contextual challenges of real-world clinical experiences, it can be problematic in educational settings for

DOI: 10.4324/9781003168683-13

faculty to meaningfully evaluate and assist students in enhancing assessment and management skills for the PD patient population.

Although PD is not often the primary reason for hospitalization, persons with PD are hospitalized 50% more often than peers without PD.[1] These patients are often cared for by hospital staff who are not familiar with PD's complexity, the implications on comorbid conditions, and specialized hospital care required by this population.[2] More than 20% of patients with PD reported a deterioration of their PD symptoms while hospitalized, and 44% reported an inability to return to the pre-hospital level of function following hospital discharge.[3,4,5] Simulation provides opportunities for an improved educational experience for nursing students as more standardized learning opportunities can be delivered and evaluated with constructive feedback in a safe learning environment.

Simulation has been used in nursing education since the early 20th century, with the first simulations being on mannequins used to teach primary care of patients in skills laboratories. Simulation in nursing has since expanded and advanced to the mainstream use of high-fidelity mannequins to effectively simulate bodily functions such as breathing, circulation, and reflexes to teach a myriad of basic to advanced nursing skills.[6] The recent landmark study conducted by the National Council for State Boards of Nursing (NCSBN) suggested that high fidelity simulation could equivalently replace up to one-half of the regular clinical learning hours that nursing students have historically attended in clinical settings.[7]

As healthcare has become more technologically driven, virtual reality (VR) and augmented reality (AR) simulations have become available.[8] One of the significant drawbacks to using digital interactive VR and high-fidelity mannequin simulations is the substantial costs of the equipment – both initially and ongoing (to maintain software, replace hardware, and maintain, repair, and replace mannequins). Video-based, immersive VR simulations, such as that used in cine-VR, offers several benefits over these more traditional platforms:

- Cine-VR is less expensive to develop than digital VR.
- Cine-VR is more accessible for students, requiring less specialized equipment and less space than high fidelity simulation experiences.
- Cine-VR can provide similar learning experiences to multiple users over time.

How Is It Used?

The Parkinson's cine-VR simulations are useful as a teaching strategy for senior-level baccalaureate nursing students to apply concepts of safety, pharmacological management, communication, and assessment for patients with PD within the immersive cine-VR environment. Specific learning objectives related to course objectives were determined for the scenarios and included:

1. Recognizes patient safety measures,
2. Recognizes nursing interventions,
3. Critically analyzes findings to detect changes/variations from normal that may indicate action.

Overviews of the three scenarios presented:

Scenario	Overview
Scenario #1: *Emergency Department* **Key concepts** Falls/Safety	A 68-year old patient presents to the ED following a fall at home. The patient's history and exam rule out head trauma; however, they exhibit resting tremors to both upper extremities and have a shuffling gait. The nurse provides discharge instructions/education that details safety and falls precautions in the home environment.
Scenario #2: *Medical-Surgical Inpatient* **Key concepts** Communication/Hallucinations	A 64-year old patient with an 8-year history of PD is on a medical-surgical unit on day 2 of admission for pneumonia. The patient has had a new onset of visual hallucinations. The nurse provides therapeutic communication and patient/family education.
Scenario #3 *Post-op Elective Surgery* **Key concepts** Pharmacological Management	A 71- year old patient presents to the post-anesthesia care unit following an elective knee replacement surgery. The nurse notes that his speech is slow, mental processing is slow, and swallowing is impaired. The patient has had nothing by mouth for the past 14 hours but typically takes medication every 4 hours to control PD symptoms. The nurse determines that the PD medications' omission is causing the increased symptoms and notifies the provider for new medication orders.

The concepts addressed in the scenarios are critical to developing the knowledge, skills, and attitudes of future nurses as specified in the standards that govern nursing education. As a pre-brief, nursing students complete a web-based training module in which the basic concepts of care of the patient with PD are presented through voice-over lectures, videos, case scenarios, and sample questions with feedback and review before engaging with the Parkinson's cine-VR.

Students view each of three PD cine-VR scenarios using a head-mounted display (HMD) with earbuds during a face-to-face lab session of 15–20 students. Students sit in seats that allow them to rotate in a 360° view, enabling them to turn towards any action that occurs in the room, just as they might respond to an aural or visual cue in an actual patients' room. Students report that this ability to move freely creates a feeling of presence and inclusion, transforming them from a viewer to having the feeling of immersion. Faculty observing the students with their HMDs can see a physical transformation throughout the cine-VR experience as the students move from one direction to the other, vocalize aloud, shake their head, or laugh at specific pivotal points. Once the cine-VR experience ends, we ask the students to refrain from talking; instead, we ask them to *think* about what they just experienced while collecting the HMDs.

Following simulation best practices, a fifteen-minute debriefing session occurs after each approximately 5–7-minute cine-VR experience. In groups of six, a faculty facilitator leads a discussion of what the students saw done well, what they saw that should happen differently, and what needs improvement if they encountered this type of patient situation in the future. Students learn the most through the debriefing stage of simulation as they can reflect on the scenario that they just experienced, which can lead them to new interpretations.[9] During this debriefing

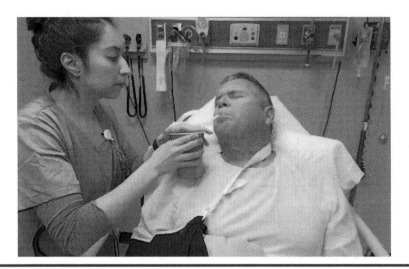

Photo 10.1   Screen grab from the cine-VR experience *Parkinson's Disease Post-op Elective Surgery*

stage, faculty facilitate a self-directed student discussion, gaining a sense of the students' collective knowledge, skills, and attitudes related to any given topic. Students have reported positive and memorable learning from experiencing the realistic scenarios simulated within these cine-VR experiences.

> *I felt like I was in the room, and I got emotional when the patient cried....that really surprised me because I was like, I know it isn't real, but it felt real to me.*

Senior Nursing Student, Ohio University

Production Process/Technical Overview

Realism in the PD cine-VR was a priority. Therefore, casting actual persons with a PD diagnosis highlighted their real-world experiences and added authenticity in the patient's role. A variety of hired actors and volunteers were used in each scenario to complete the nurse, family member, and extras' roles. The authenticity portrayed by the PD actors facilitated a deeper understanding of living with the disease and ignited a passion in the other actors. Due to the nature of the disease, the PD actors tired quickly. Therefore, the crew and other actors were challenged to portray their roles quickly to preserve PD actors' energy and tolerance for the recording.

Production for the three cine-VR scenarios occurred over three separate days, with one scenario recorded per day. The cine-VR video was captured by placing the camera as close to the patient/nurse interaction as possible without interfering with the characters' movement. The audio was recorded with microphones on each actor and an Ambisonic microphone to record the room's environmental sound and provide sonic directionality.

Challenges of working within a multi-departmental group included:

A. Training professional/student actors to be nurses in a way that the intended audience of actual nurses and nursing students would view as authentic,

B. Working with nonprofessional actors (persons with PD) with actual health issues and physical limitations safely and effectively,

C. Balancing the needs of the actors and the crew simultaneously.

Since we worked with a new set of actors (both professional and nonprofessional) for each scenario, addressing these issues was a daily occurrence. Also, cine-VR as a medium requires the actors to perform each scenario from start to finish without stopping, further taxing them to remember their lines and not make mistakes. One mistake required reshooting the entire 5–7 minutes scenario from the beginning. Bringing in new actors was a challenge each day that we recorded.

Lessons Learned

The experience of designing, developing, and then using the final product of a cine-VR experience is an exciting one. The collaborative team approach was integral to the success of this project. The nursing faculty acted as subject matter experts, and the GRID lab faculty and crew provided the production expertise to bring the scenario to life. Having a systematic approach to planning the cine-VR, including the script, the cast, the props, and the backdrop, is critical.

We found the most helpful approach was to first identify both SME and GRID Lab team members, including faculty. This team met on multiple occasions to discuss how to best use cine-VR to develop a focused learning activity for senior-level baccalaureate nursing students. We were able to identify specific learning objectives for the cine-VR experience.

Our team collaborated to cast the actors and choose the real-life "patients." As mentioned before, this involved careful consideration. Using real persons with PD as our PD "patients" in the scenarios added depth and an authenticity that we may not otherwise have created. We recruited these actors through our community PD Education Advisory Council, a group founded by nursing faculty and involving faculty from various units within our College of Health Sciences and Professions. The council members had input into the cine-VR scenario development and added an immeasurable degree of authenticity to the final product.

Perhaps one of the critical lessons that we learned was that, in the future, we plan to use actual nurses/nursing students in our cast whenever possible. We used drama students for our "nurse" in each scenario, and it took quite a bit of time to get the actors to portray the specific behaviors of a nurse realistically (e.g., proper handwashing, donning of personal protective equipment, effective nonverbal communication; as well as the technical skills such as assessment techniques and medication administration processes). Although the actors brought professionalism and acting talents, the process required multiple walk-through rehearsals, teaching, and reshoots due to their lack of understanding of necessary nursing actions. Given the short length of the cine-VR videos and our intended audience noticing every detail that does not adhere to the profession's strict processes and techniques, we believe that casting nursing students or faculty provides better authenticity and credibility with nursing students. Alternatively, we recommend having a pre-production, in-depth training session with the actors to teach the common language, actions, and portrayal of healthcare providers' fundamental roles.

Locating the set and gathering props required careful consideration. It is essential to consider and note every detail on a cine-VR set, including identification badges, specialized equipment, environmental noise, and background activity for realism in healthcare settings.

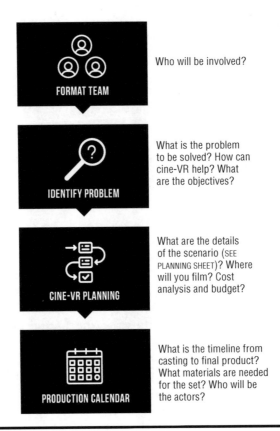

Figure 10.1   Structuring the creative process of cine-VR

We developed a production calendar from preproduction to the final product with all the pieces finally in place. See Figure 10.1 for a step-by-step process of our approach to structure our creative process. We also developed a Healthcare Scenario Planning Sheet through this process (see the two-page addendum at the end of the chapter).

Impact on Learning

Cine-VR technology has opened possibilities for future use in our learning space. It offers a cost-effective alternative to traditional high-fidelity mannequin simulation. It allows the use of the technology in both the bricks and mortar learning labs on campus and the capacity to easily be adapted to an online learning platform using inexpensive cardboard viewers that hold a student's smartphone and enable the students to watch the cine-VR at home. The innovations and rapid-fire transition to virtual learning across higher education, necessitated by the 2020 COVID-19 pandemic, made technology with this capacity for flexibility even more valued, ensuring that cine-VR has a place in the educational space of tomorrow.

Overall, the Parkinson's cine-VR simulation has been well received by students and by faculty. Our use of cine-VR technology in nursing was presented nationally to nurse educators and received a great degree of interest and excitement. Nursing has only recently fully embraced simulation as being equivalent to clinical experiences in meeting specific learning objectives. Most nursing faculty equate simulation with high-fidelity mannequins, and the use of VR (whether through animation or video immersion) is still relatively new. Just as simulation has disrupted traditional nursing education over the past twenty years, we expect VR and cine-VR to disrupt nursing simulation soon; with disruption comes possibility.

Financial Implications

The financial impact is undoubtedly a necessary factor to consider for each institution when evaluating cine-VR as an appropriate tool. Costs versus benefit analyses specifically for cine-VR compared to traditional simulation or digital VR are limited in the literature. There is also the potential for costs being underreported due to the complexity of simulation components. The literature demonstrates a lack of consistency and transparency with specific components of the simulation, including cost.[10] Many academic institutions maintain existing simulation centers, which may be partially or fully subsidized by large health systems, for specific skills and task training to mitigate risk and contribute to reimbursement, making an accurate analysis of the cost and potential return on investment difficult to gauge accurately.[10]

When considering cine-VR, there are several cost elements that we suggest should be examined:

1. **Direct costs**: Hardware and software required for production.
2. **Implementation costs:** Hardware and software required for viewing the experiences, as well as required educator time.
3. **Maintenance costs**: Updating hardware/software components and the possible need to reshoot scenarios as core information changes.

Stakeholders should consider each of these concerning the project goals and the goals of the unit or institution. Further exploration of the return on investment to institutions, patients, providers, governments, payers, and research funding is essential for the future expansion of this technology.

Short-term financial implications include substantial front-end costs of cine-VR related to the development of case scenarios, hiring actors, recording, editing, and creating the cine-VR videos. However, long-term cost implications may be lower as cine-VR technology becomes less expensive and the costs of repetition of the cine-VR videos once produced are minimal. In comparison, traditional simulation has substantially higher maintenance and replacement costs with similar learning acquisition.[11,12]

A final financial consideration when embarking upon cine-VR development is the potential for entrepreneurship through copyright of cine-VR videos and distribution for profit to other academic and healthcare institutions.

What's Next?

The natural evolution of technology going forward is limitless. The use of cine-VR in academic institutions with healthcare professional training remains innovative. Health systems affiliated with academic centers have used various VR styles for innovative and complex surgical procedures to decrease errors and complications.[10] The COVID-19 pandemic demonstrated the value of VR as a viable learning strategy with the capability for real-time feedback from a distance. Healthcare education continues to evolve in academia and has room to grow in clinical education settings as well. The COVID-19 pandemic has given educators a push into seeking out technology-based strategies for providing education to students in a virtual format. Soon, students could have the flexibility of accessing a library of learning content through cine-VR. Accessible from any location with infinite replays, this library is advantageous compared to a long day with limited run-throughs presented by faculty in the simulation lab. Repetition in a virtual environment allows students to make errors in a safe learning space, thus building student confidence.

There is an increasing need to deliver the cine-VR content via web-based and mobile device applications, thereby allowing students to complete cine-VR learning scenarios from anywhere while simultaneously ensuring standardized learning experiences to each student learner without having to purchase expensive viewing equipment. In the future, new hardware, mobile applications, and real-time interactions will promote an enhanced learning experience with improved access to information and learning activities to promote knowledge and skill acquisition.

In conclusion, the lessons learned through creating the Parkinson's Disease cine-VR are immense for nurse educators. Cine-VR has demonstrated a high degree of utility and capacity for flexibility across learning platforms (in person and web-based). Additional research to explore the value of cine-VR in student retention of learning, impact within and across multiple domains of learning, and evolution of the technology is needed.

Viewing

To view and download cine-VR examples mentioned in this chapter, please visit: https://vimeo.com/channels/cinevr4healthcare/ (**password:** *cineVR4health*).

> ### CONSORTIUM OF INNOVATION IN NURSING EDUCATION- VIRTUAL REALITY
>
> The team that developed this cine-VR project identified a consortium's need to focus on innovation and Virtual Reality. Thus, the Consortium of Innovation in Nursing Education - Virtual Reality (or: CINE-VR) was created. If you are interested in joining this consortium and advancing the use of quality VR in nursing education, please contact the authors.

Healthcare Scenario Planning Sheet

Please see the next two pages for the Ohio University's School of Nursing's Healthcare Scenario Planning Sheets.

Ohio University School of Nursing – Cine-VR Planning Sheet

Overview
Enter a basic overview of the scenario to be represented including the critical concepts/skills etc.

- Elderly patient w/ an 8-year history of PD presents to Emergency Department with a history of a fall at home.
- Critical concepts are falls prevention and safety in the home setting for the patient with PD.
- Patient will demonstrate overt physical signs of PD (resting tremor, shuffling gait, bradykinesia, slowed speech and low voice quality)
- Nurse will provide discharge teaching to patient & family regarding safety precautions & falls prevention at home.

Learning Objectives	
General	**Scenario**
Enter program or course level learning objectives.	*Enter the learning objectives specific to the cine-vr.*

General

Enter program or course level learning objectives.

1. Students will be able to distinguish between signs and symptoms of normal aging and those that indicate a potential disease process.
2. Students will be able to integrate information from various assessments to determine client needs.
3. Students will be able to identify safety concerns in nursing and health care.

Scenario

Enter the learning objectives specific to the cine-vr.

1. Identifies physical assessment findings consistent with PD.

Student Information
This is the brief that is provided to students before they enter the scenario; this can be given orally or in written form prior to beginning the cine-vr experience.

- Historically Jo/Joe was diagnosed with Parkinson's disease 8 years ago following complaints of uncontrollable shaking, loss of muscle control and unsteady gait. When he/she would try to ambulate, he/she would have moments of time where he/she could not move his/her body at all. He/she reported increased feelings of weakness although he/she led an active lifestyle and worked out regularly. He/she reported difficulty with daily activities of daily living. He/she decided to seek treatment when his/her daughter questioned him/her about his/her motor function.

- Following diagnosis, a treatment regimen was developed that up until 2 months ago proved to be successful in managing symptoms. However, 6 months ago his levodopa- carbidopa 100/25 mg was increased from 1 and a half pills to two pills q.i.d., and his ropinirole was increased from 3mg to 4 mg t.i.d. He/she was given instruction on the importance of following a strict medication regimen and keeping medications on an every 6-hour rotation even during sleeping hours to provide optimal results.

Additional Information	ED Setting
Patient Data:	BP:
DOB:	HR:
Vital Signs:	Resp:
Prior Medical History:	SPO2:
Past Surgeries:	T:
Allergies:	
Code Status:	

Scenario Details
Enter details of scenario here.

- Pt is having resting tremor to right/left upper extremity
- Speech is slow, voice is soft
- Movements are slow
- Has difficulty swallowing sips of water with overt dysphagia (coughing)

Nursing Interventions:

Example:

1. Administer medications: Dopaminergics, Dopamine agonists, Levodopa-Carbidopa
   a. The goal is to increase the levels of available dopamine within the central nervous system.
2. Provide safety/falls education
   a. The goal is to help patient/family identify fall risks and minimize

Debriefing/ Guided Reflection
1. What do you think went well?
2. Describe the objectives you were able to achieve? Facilitator will point out aspects of objectives met that are not mentioned by students.
3. Which ones were you unable to achieve (if any)? Facilitator will point out aspects of objectives not met that are not mentioned by students.
4. Did you have the knowledge and skills to meet objectives?
5. Were you satisfied with your ability to work through the simulation?
6. How did you feel throughout the simulation experience?
7. What were the key assessments?
8. Were vital signs accurately obtained? What causes/contributes to these vital signs?
9. What concerns do you have for the Parkinson's medication regimen?
10. What will you take away from this experience?
11. Overall, what did you think of this experience?
12. Is there anything else that you would like to discuss?

Notes

1. Aminoff, M., Christine, C., Friedman, J., Chou, K., Lyons, K., Pahwa, R., Bloem, B., Parashos, P., Price, C.,Malaty, I., Iansek, R., Bodis-Wollner, I., Suchowersky, O., Oertel, W., Zamudio, J., Oberdorf, J., Schidt, P., Okun, M. (2011). Management of the hospitalized patient with Parkinson's disease: Current state of the field and need for guidelines. *Parkinsonism and Related Disorders, 17*, 139–145.
2. Ibid.
3. Ibid.
4. Magdalinous, K., Martin, A., & Kessel, B. (2007). Prescribing medications in Parkinson's disease (PD) patients during acute admissions to a district general hospital. *Parkinsonism and Related Disorders, 13*, 539–540.
5. Gerlach, O., Broen, M., van Domburd, P., Vermeij, A., & Weber, W. (2012). Deterioration of Parkinson's disease during hospitalization: Survey of 684 patients. *BMC Neurology, 12*, 1–6. doi.org/10.1186/1471-2377-12-13
6. Simulation-based learning: No longer a novelty in undergraduate education. *The Online Journal of Issues in Nursing, 23*(2), 1-1, 10.3912/OJIN.Vol23No02PPT39
7. Hayden, J., Smiley, M., Alexander, S., Kardong-Edgren, P., Jeffries, P. (2014). The NCSBN national simulation study: A longitudinal, randomized, controlled study replacing clinical hours with simulation in prelicensure nursing education. *Journal of Nursing Regulattion, 5*(2), S3–S40, 10.1016/S2155-8256(15)30062-4
8. Rizzo, A., & Koenig, S. (2017). Is clinical virtual reality ready for primetime? *Neuropsychology, 31*(8), 877.
9. Decker, S., Fey, M., Sideras, S., Caballero, S., Boese, T., Franklin, A. E., ... & Borum, J. C. (2013). Standards of best practice: Simulation standard VI: The debriefing process. *Clinical Simulation in Nursing, 9*(6), S26–S29.
10. Hippe, D. S., Umoren, R. A., McGee, A., Bucher, S. L., Bresnahan, B. W. (2020). A targeted systematic review of cost analyses for implementation of simulation-based education in healthcare. *SAGE Open Medicine, 8*. https://doi.org/10.1177/2050312120913451
11. Farra, S. L., Gneuhs, M., Hodgson, E., Kawosa, B., Miller, E. T., Simon, A, Timm, N, Hausfeld, J., 2019. Comparative cost of virtual reality training and live exercises for training hospital workers for evacuation. *Computers, Informatics Nursing, 37*(9), 446–454. DOI: 10.1097/CIN.0000000000000540
12. Haerling. K. A. (2018). Cost-utility analysis of virtual and mannequin-based simulation. *Simulation Healthcare, 13*, 33–40. DOI: 10.1097/SIH.0000000000000280

Chapter 11

Funding an "Introduction to Workplace Violence" Experience

Melvina Brandau and Sherleena Buchman

Contents

Workplace violence is a pervasive problem in the healthcare sector and is on the rise. In reports from 2002–2013, the Occupational Safety and Health Administration[1] revealed that serious violence incidents were four times more common in healthcare than in the private sector. The National Institute for Occupational Safety and Health[2] (NIOSH) describes four types of workplace violence in healthcare:

Type I violence: perpetrated by a group or individual with criminal intent and no relationship to the employees or facility.
Type II violence: perpetrated by a customer, client, or patient while receiving care.
Type III violence: employee-to-employee violence, also known as horizontal violence.
Type IV violence: perpetrated by a group or individual with a personal relationship to the victim(s), often viewed as a domestic situation.

Nurses are at significant risk of workplace violence in healthcare, particularly Type II or patient-visitor violence, with 24% of registered nurses and nursing students reporting physical assault and

DOI: 10.4324/9781003168683-14

more than 40% reporting verbal abuse.[3] A 2014 study of emergency department nurses found that a shocking 76% of nurse participants had experienced violence in the previous twelve months[4]. Nurses endure a wide range of violence, from verbal aggression and slander to aggravated assault with a weapon. The media has reported workplace violence incidents resulting in bruises, torn muscles, human bites, broken bones, and even death.[5,6,7,8] Perpetrators of this violence are often intoxicated or experiencing an altered mental status or psychosis, but this is not always the case.[9] In the healthcare setting, patients and visitors may react violently to a personal or loved one's injury or diagnosis, a negative interaction with a staff member or healthcare professional, or just because they are having a bad day. Regardless of the precipitating factors, nurses worldwide have decided that they will no longer tolerate violence in the healthcare workplace.

Personal experiences with patient-visitor violence have resulted in the authors' interest in educating nurses about the types and risk factors for workplace violence and prevention and intervention strategies. In collaboration with the Centers for Disease Control and Prevention (CDC), NIOSH offers a comprehensive online course with free continuing education credit for nurses[10]. This course and training in Nonviolent and Verbal Crisis Intervention[11] and Therapeutic Crisis Intervention for intervening with children[12] offer a wealth of information and training on preventing, de-escalating, and responding to hostile and violent situations. However, these programs do not allow for a rich, real-life experience that triggers the senses and heightens emotions, as could be reasonably expected to occur in situations of potential violence. Additionally, it is unreasonable to believe that the ethical implementation of face-to-face training and high-fidelity simulation will immerse the trainee enough to trigger a fight-or-flight response. As Rabinovich describes, "In the absence of emotional regulation, a person is flooded with overwhelming emotions that could hinder his or her ability to cope with and process relevant content." Rabinovich contends that ineffective emotional regulation activates defense mechanisms and impacts occupational and social performance based on Bion's Theory of Thinking.[13] In the case of a hostile or violent situation in the workplace, this could worsen the situation and psychological or physical harm to the perpetrator, the victim(s), or bystanders. Consequently, emotional regulation is necessary, especially in times of high anxiety, to allow the individual to facilitate effective coping and response.[14]

To learn from experience, Bion explains that the individual must have an awareness of the emotional experience that moves thoughts from raw impressions of the experience (as they are occurring) to unconscious stores, reappearing as unconscious waking thinking in the future.[15] These thoughts have evolved into what Bion calls "alpha-function" and require conscious thinking and reasoning.[16] Thus, to facilitate learning from experience and emotional regulation, education may be best approached in a manner that elicits an emotional response. Virtual reality (VR) allows for immersion and presence in education in a safe environment[17] and is the best approach for eliciting an emotional, visceral response[18].

> **Note:** The term "Virtual Reality" historically described an experience created digitally. Many VR experiences allow the audience to walk around in an environment created through digital animation and motion capture. Cinematic VR (cine-VR) also creates an experience with digitally captured environments but limits the audience's ability to move around within the environment or interact with objects.

VR is gaining a reputation in education with evidence to support learning, improve self-efficacy, and offer a strong emotional and behavioral response compared with other simulated or clinical experiences.[19,20,21,22] However, due to the equipment and expertise needed to create VR, it is not always financially feasible to develop and implement. Therefore, we have found that a multi-tiered financial approach to funding such projects – one including internal and external grant funding opportunities – must be considered.

At the time of this writing, we are in the middle of a three-tiered approach to ultimately creating what we hope to be an internationally viable cine-VR project called "Introduction to Workplace Violence in Healthcare".

Tier 1: Less than $2,500.00 (Proof of Concept)

When moving toward the development and implementation of VR for education, it is crucial to define needed digital VR or cine-VR requirements. For some projects, it may be practical to "start small." A small project can utilize modest internal grants to support an introduction to the project and prove whether cine-VR is viable. While working with the GRID Lab, we call this the Proof-of-Concept stage.

The authors began their cine-VR project on workplace violence with a small internal grant, set initially at $1500. The project's goal was to educate students on the four types of workplace violence, signs of pending hostility or violence, and tips for defusing and mitigating those situations (see Photo 11.1). The initial project was limited to:

A. Traditional still images,
B. 360° still images,
C. Traditional video.

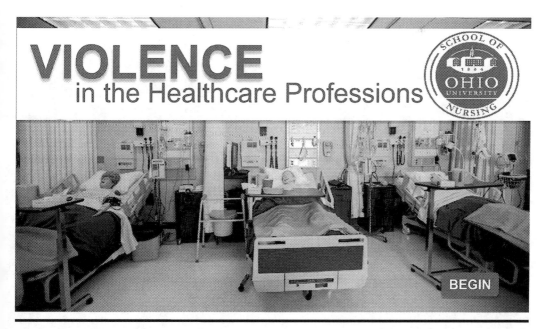

Photo 11.1 Title page of the *Workplace Violence I* project highlighting Ohio University's College of Health Sciences' Simulation Suite

Personnel was provided in addition to the allotted funds. The project was supported by:

- Nursing students for script development and acting,
- Nursing faculty for the overall design, script development, directing, content expertise, and integrating best practices for instructional delivery via technology,
- Instructional design and technology staff members (and students) to assist with the integration of the video and 360° still images into the Adobe Articulate software,
- Students from the schools of Visual Communications and Media Arts and Studies handled video production and photography.

As this particular project had a small scope, the most considerable costs were A) supporting personnel to create the cine-VR, B) developing the educational module, and C) implementing the research component. Undergraduate and graduate students from the Schools of Visual Communications and Media Arts and Studies were valuable resources. The project also benefitted these students by providing a hands-on learning experience.

With internal personnel and student support, the project cost less than $700.00:

- Access to the e-learning authoring application: Free
- Stipend for student actors: $90.00
- Articulate 360° software: $600.00 annual subscription

We created the articulate-based *Workplace Violence I* project (WV1) with the intent of providing low-fidelity simulation that also incorporated components of traditional content delivery. The 360° still images of the emergency department patient room allowed for the placement of interactive hot spots over items that the learner is encouraged to identify as potential weapons for violence (see Photo 11.2). Upon clicking each hot spot, the learner is provided with text and audio explaining how each commonplace healthcare item might become a weapon.

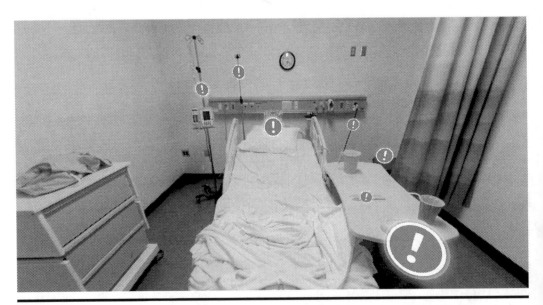

Photo 11.2   Screengrab of the *Workplace Violence I* project with interactive hot spots

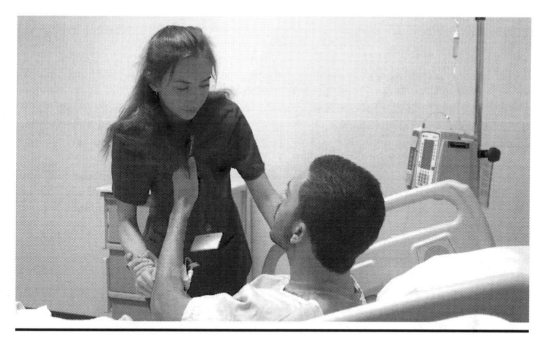

Photo 11.3 Screen grab from the *Workplace Violence I* project dramatizing the workplace violence of nurses

Production occurred in the College of Health Sciences' Simulation Suite during a three-hour block of time (refer back to Photo 11.1). Subsequently, the project took two-months for editing, graphic design, and use of the Articulate 360° software to create interactive hotspots for the 360° still images.

The ultimate design of the workplace violence module focused on pre-nursing students. Students complete a short pre- and post-quiz, receive a brief lecture on the content, complete the Articulate module, and ultimately complete a post-quiz – all of which is accomplished online. Analysis of the pre- and post-quiz scores demonstrates statistical significance in the immersive, interactive approach increasing students' knowledge of workplace violence. Additionally, the module receives positive feedback from students. This project, though low-fidelity and brief, offers promising results and drives the authors' motivation to continue to develop, implement, and evaluate interactive and engaging forms of content delivery (see Photo 11.3).

Since the creation (and during the implementation) of the WV1 module, the authors moved to secure larger funding sources for the creation of VR and cine-VR. The first step in securing external funding is identifying an appropriate funding source: "Exploratory grants" do not offer a substantial amount of funding but leave room for detailed development of the project. "Seed Grants" (e.g., $2,500–$25,000) can be challenging to find and secure, but ultimately provide support for larger proposals.

Tier 2: $2,500.00-$25,000.00 (Seed Grant)

The authors, in collaboration with the GRID lab, recently submitted a proposal for $10,000 in funding from a private, external organization. The goals of the proposal were to create and implement an educational simulation using cine-VR, to evaluate its effectiveness, and to identify "best practices in simulation" in the delivery of its educational components.

The authors have both received internal and external grant funding to develop a wide variety of interactive educational VR projects (e.g., see Chapters 9 and 10). Based on the success of WV1, the authors and the GRID Lab team proposed a cine-VR experience with more advanced content, including escalation of patient aggression and the augmentation of the Articulate module for pre-nursing students. This project was to be implemented to first-year nursing students who had already completed the previous module, further exposing them to the risks of workplace violence in healthcare.

In this case, we decided to focus on a scenario that presented an escalation in patient aggression, beyond the wrist grab and verbal escalation presented in the first Articulate scenario. This scenario was designed to reinforce previously reviewed content and best practices in managing patient aggression, while including more content on de-escalation and basic physical maneuverability. The authors found through previous research that realism and presence are a key priority when preparing learning content to deliver to healthcare students[23]. The team needs to understand that healthcare students are astute learners; they look at every aspect of a final product with a keen eye.

Cine-VR has to be weighed out with the risks and benefits. The benefits of delivering learning content through cine-VR include:

A. Using real people instead of avatars to increase realism,
B. Consistency in the delivery of what each student experiences,
C. Students report a feeling of immersion and being present in cine-VR scenarios,
D. Having a closed system deliverable to learners via a headset or a simple cardboard delivery method.

Challenges, as expected, include:

A. Lack of financial resources,
B. Lack of personnel resources,
C. More advanced projects require more time.

This project was expected to cost more than the WV1 project, primarily due to the use of 360° video. Paid actors would also account for some of the increased costs. Theater students should be considered as volunteers and amateur actors often require additional production time and re-shoots that may hinder the development of more advanced projects. Learning from previous experiences, the authors suggest hiring professional actors and delegating funds to obtain needed equipment, such as authoring applications for learning modules, cameras, and equipment accessories. The project would also benefit from the purchase of props and costumes; food and drinks for the cast and crew; the purchase of high-quality memory cards and storage devices for all digital content; and stipends for GRID Lab student who have advanced knowledge of cine-VR development (e.g. as opposed to the unpaid services provided by ad hoc students selected from a volunteer board). Furthermore, the project would take longer to plan and implement.

We expect the production process of this project to be similar to the projects described in Chapters 9 and 10, as both projects fall within a similar budget. It is important to note that each of these projects is copyrighted prior to use. The copyright allows for the distribution of the cine-VR product without fear of someone else claiming the product as their own or altering the product to be something the team did not intend it to be.

Ultimately, the delivery of this pilot product allows for a small group of potential users to view the cine-VR as part of the overall learning modules, and for the team to receive valuable feedback, helping us to shape the next tier: a major project spanning multiple years. The last step for the team is to apply for a copyright.

Tier 2: $100,000.00-$500,000.00 (Major Project)

In education, project ideas are endless! Smaller projects allow for creation of a track record that highlights successes, acknowledges lessons learned, and fosters creativity in the development of the content that students want and need. Creating and implementing smaller projects in the world of VR will lead to bigger ideas and confidence in being able to develop and successfully employ additional VR projects.

As was an expected and exciting development, the authors moved even further after submission of the $10,000 grant proposal and have submitted an extensive R21 proposal to support the development and evaluation of an advanced VR simulation in healthcare education. A proposal at this level requires commitment from a number of collaborators including content experts, clinical practitioners, researchers, instructional technologists and designers, statisticians, and others. Bringing all of these individuals together to form a cohesive team can be challenging due to varied schedules and time commitments, but with good planning, it can be achieved. It is important, however, to begin with smaller projects.

The R21 proposal was guided by successes and challenges faced in previous collaborations with the GRID Lab. Based on previous experiences, the authors wanted to propose the development of an advanced cine-VR to immerse learners (both nursing students and practicing healthcare workers) into a scenario with a physically and emotionally aggressive patient. Through contacts with the GRID Lab, the authors were connected with clinical providers and a research team at a large pediatric hospital who wanted to create something similar, but with a unique twist. This added an element of innovativeness to the proposal and after months of collaboration with the clinical research team, the proposal was developed.

As would be expected, this proposal supports the development of an innovative project with advanced content. The GRID Lab team suggested the use of haptics to add to the overall presence and immersion of the cine-VR. The creative approach of haptic integration requires additional cost and equipment. To truly develop a one-of-a-kind product, the team proposed to hire professional actors who could study these types of incidents and delve fully into their roles. The authors had to consider costs associated with production, cast and crew support, locations/props/costumes, and travel, as would be expected in any type of more advanced project. Additional equipment was requested for the research testing associated with this project.

Financial Implications

The return on investment to the grant agencies and to the academic institution and recipients of the grants are numerous. Short term return on the grantor's investment includes:

- A cine-VR product that delivers a consistent product to every user,
- The ability to educate a large number of learners in a quick time frame, and
- Knowledge that can be assessed quickly in a pre/posttest delivery session.

Long term return on investments includes being able to continue meeting short-term goals but over time, by continuing to deliver the cine-VR in a consistent, quick, and educational format. This can be done in a safe environment that can be further developed with future iterations. Each iteration can go greater depth via additional story details, emotional reactions, and through differing physical intensity. For example, a cine-VR experience that was originally developed for a seasoned registered nursing student, might be modified to a nurse practitioner student by adjusting the story, emotions, and physical intensity while still using the same learning objectives.

By starting small and growing bigger with each iteration of the project, the authors were able to start with a product that worked well with a small budget but had a large impact on the target population (in this case: undergraduate nursing students). The delivery of the new concept was well received by these students; therefore, the financial implication was seen as worthwhile. Through trial and error of a lower-cost project, the authors were able to recognize the need to increase the level of realism to make the experiences as real to life as possible for the more experienced nursing student.

Conclusion

Cine-VR is an exciting and innovative method of providing education on workplace violence. It allows for consistent, replicable training in a safe environment. One of the biggest challenges associated with using cine-VR is the costs associated with development and implementation; however, the authors have demonstrated that elements of cine-VR can be included in small projects with progression into larger, more impactful projects through grant writing. The keys, the authors believe, are to identify the need and compile the right team to bring the project to life. With a little creativity, a vision, and a plan, as well as some generous grant funding, the project can be brought to fruition!

CONSORTIUM OF INNOVATION IN NURSING EDUCATION- VIRTUAL REALITY

The team that wrote this chapter identified a need in nursing education for a consortium to focus on innovation and Virtual Reality, thus the Consortium of Innovation in Nursing Education - Virtual Reality (or: CINE-VR) was created. If you would be interested in joining this consortium and advancing the use of quality VR in nursing education, please contact the authors.

Notes

1 Occupational Safety and Health Administration. (2015). *Workplace violence in healthcare: Understanding the challenge.* https://www.osha.gov/Publications/OSHA3826.pdf
2. National Institute for Occupational Safety and Health. (2020). *Workplace violence prevention for nurses.* https://www.cdc.gov/niosh/topics/violence/training_nurses.html
3. American Nurses Association. (2015). *Incivility, bullying, and workplace violence.* https://www.nursingworld.org/~49d6e3/globalassets/practiceandpolicy/nursing-excellence/incivility-bullying-and-workplace-violence--ana-position-statement.pdf
4. Speroni, K. G., Fitch, T., Dawson, E., Dugan, L., & Atherton, M. (2014). Incidence and cost of nurse workplace violence perpetrated by hospital patients or patient visitors. *Journal of Emergency Nursing, 40*(3), 218–228. https://doi.org/10.1016/j.jen.2013.05.014
5. Brusie, C. (2019, Apr 18). Nurse dies after being attacked by mental health patient-Manslaughter charges. *Nurse Organisation.* https://nurse.org/articles/nurse-attacked-by-patient-dies-manslaughter/

6. Landers, K. (2020, January 30). *"It's getting worse every year": Workplace violence inside hospitals on the rise.* https://www.10tv.com/article/news/local/its-getting-worse-every-year-workplace-violence-inside-hospitals-rise-2020-jan/530-48241b6c-b6f7-43a6-bb4b-00836ac5cbe9

7. McCarthy, C. (2020, October 16). ER nurse attacked on the job: "We're just human punching bags." *Boston25news.com.* https://www.boston25news.com/news/local/er-nurse-attacked-job-were-just-human-punching-bags/JOZXOYERGFAQRF7DTGFYQFZIIM/

8. WCVB Channel 5 Boston. (2019). *Nurse assaulted by patient at hospital, police say* [Video]. https://www.youtube.com/watch?v=XDcoMGtE-Ps

9. Gillespie, G. L., Pekar, B., Byczkowski, T. L., & Fisher, B. S. (2017). Worker, workplace, and community/environmental risk factors for workplace violence in emergency departments. *Archives of Environmental & Occupational Health, 72*(2), 79–86. https://doi.org/10.1080/19338244.2016.1160861

10. National Institute for Occupational Safety and Health. (2020). *Workplace violence prevention for nurses.* https://www.cdc.gov/niosh/topics/violence/training_nurses.html

11. Crisis Prevention Institute. (2020). *Nonviolent crisis intervention.* https://www.crisisprevention.com/Our-Programs/Nonviolent-Crisis-Intervention

12. Cornell.edu. (2016). *Therapeutic crisis intervention system.* https://rccp.cornell.edu/tci/tci-1_system.html

13. Pallavicini, F., Pepe, A., Ferrari, A., Garcea, G., Zanacchi, A., & Mantovani, F. (2020). What is the relationship among positive emotions, sense of presence, and ease of interaction in virtual reality systems? An on-site evaluation of a commercial virtual experience. *PRESENCE: Virtual and Augmented Reality, 27*(2), 183–201. https://doi.org/10.1162/pres_a_00325

14. Ibid

15. Bion, W. R. (1962). *Bion: Chapters three and four* [PDF]. http://dravni.co.il/wp-content/uploads/2016/10/Bion-W.R.-1962.-Ch-3-4-.-Learning-from-Experience.pdf

16. Ibid.

17. Buchman, S., & Henderson, D. (2019). Interprofessional empathy and communication competency development in healthcare professions' curriculum through immersive virtual reality experiences. *Journal of Interprofessional Education & Practice, 15,* 127–130.

18. Pallavicini, F., Pepe, A., Ferrari, A., Garcea, G., Zanacchi, A., & Mantovani, F. (2020). What is the relationship among positive emotions, sense of presence, and ease of interaction in virtual reality systems? An on-site evaluation of a commercial virtual experience. *PRESENCE: Virtual and Augmented Reality, 27*(2), 183–201. https://doi.org/10.1162/pres_a_00325

19. Beverly, D. A., Love, C., Love, M. Williams, E. R. & Bowditch, J. (2021). Using virtual reality to improve healthcare providers' cultural self-efficacy and diabetes attitudes: A pilot study. *Journal of Medical Internet Research (JMIR),* 23.1, 01–21.

20. Buchman, S., & Henderson, D. (2019). Interprofessional empathy and communication competency development in healthcare professions' curriculum through immersive virtual reality experiences. *Journal of Interprofessional Education & Practice, 15,* 127–130.

21. Lee, Y., Kim, S. K., & Eom, M-R. (2020). Usability of mental illness simulation involving scenarios with patients with schizophrenia via immersive virtual reality: A mixed methods study. *PLoS ONE, 15*(9), e0238437. https://doi.org/10.1371/journal.pone.0238437

22. O'Rourke, S. R., Branford, K. R., Brooks, T. L., Ives, L. T., Nagendran, A., & Compton, S. N. (2020). The emotional and behavioral impact of delivering bad news to virtual versus real standardized patients: A pilot study. *Teaching and Learning in Medicine, 32*(2), 139–149. https://doi.org/10.1080/10401334.2019.1652180

23. Buchman, S., Miller, C., Henderson, D., Williams, E. & Ray, S. (2020). Interprofessional students learning to save a life through cine-VR simulation. *EC Nursing and Healthcare, 2.11,* 04–20. https://www.ecronicon.com/ecnh/pdf/ECNH-02-00120.pdf

Chapter 12

Audio Considerations for Cine-VR

Charles "Chip" Linscott

Contents

While adept in their areas, many media production professionals may have little audio production experience with cine-VR. In addition, many audio production experts are unfamiliar with Ambisonics and other immersive formats and techniques commonplace in virtual reality workflows. By detailing some of the technology and practices used in this type of audio production, we can illustrate the role that sound plays in cine-VR and its importance to the user experience of immersion. To unpack these audio considerations, I will employ brief examples from cine-VR work undertaken by the GRID Lab.

DOI: 10.4324/9781003168683-15

Achieving Realism

As discussed in Chapter 2, combining audio and video in cine-VR elicits a sense of presence so that users feel that they are "inside" the recorded world. In cine-VR, users (or audiences) can look all around a 360° field. What they see will change as they glance about, and spatial audio allows sounds to shift as well. There are a diverse variety of ways to achieve immersive sonic effects, but this chapter focuses chiefly on cine-VR production methods with examples drawn from GRID Lab work. Remember, one of the principal goals is to make audiences *feel* that their experiences are real. This sensation requires believable images and sounds, but these images and sounds *do not* have to be precisely the same as those encountered in the real world. For example, most cine-VR images are two-dimensional rather than three-dimensional, and users are seldom able to touch the objects they see in the cine-VR world.

Similarly, the sounds that users hear need to impart a sense of presence in the virtual world, but those sounds do not have to mimic what's heard in "real life" precisely. The sounds can be exaggerated, understated, highly ambient, or precisely placed in space, but overall, the sound design should make the virtual experience more authentic. This sort of realism is achievable by combining Ambisonic recordings of environments with dialogue captured through a "spot mic" (usually a lavalier) along with added sound effects generated through foley work.

Understanding Ambisonics

Ambisonics, as renowned audio designer Simon Goodwin concisely puts it, "is a generalized way of representing a sound field – the distribution of sounds from all directions around a listener[1]." The key here is the phrase *all directions*. Ambisonic audio recreates the sound field spherically. Other spatial audio and surround sound formats usually do not include height information and are locked to a specific number and order of outputs (like speakers). As stated in Chapter 2, Ambisonic audio is uniquely suited for VR applications because it provides motion-tracked variations of audio signals and enables sounds to be positioned anywhere around a user – up/down, front/back, left/right, and so on. Properly implemented, Ambisonic audio allows users to move their heads and bodies around in the sound field just as they might turn to look for the source of a sound in real life. As users glance around, the headset uses motion tracking to alter sound direction and quality. Ambisonic audio ultimately requires some physics and math for a complete understanding of its properties. This chapter largely avoids the more technical aspects of Ambisonics and instead focuses on the process's practical aspects. Readers can find a list of more technical texts at the end of the chapter.

Most of the Ambisonic microphones we use at the GRID Lab produce first-order Ambisonic audio. Simply put, such audio has four channels of spatial and audio information contained within a single track. As the Ambisonic orders go up (to say, second- or third-order), the channel amount goes up. Any Ambisonic audio above first order is considered higher order Ambisonics (HOA). Higher orders provide more precise spatial information but can be more challenging to work with both on set and in post-production. Also, higher order Ambisonic audio is currently very limited in terms of distribution platforms. First-order mics are easy to use on set because they are either self-contained mic/recorder combinations (like the Zoom H3-VR) or are readily compatible with field recorders (such as the Zoom F8n or Zoom F6). There are second- and third-order (and beyond) microphones that record HOA natively. Ambisonic software applications can convert lower-order Ambisonic audio by extrapolating data not captured initially. Generally speaking, first-order Ambisonic workflows provide excellent ambiance and environmental sounds to surround the listener, but higher orders can offer a more precise spatial location of particular sounds.

Appreciating Lavalier Microphones

Ordinarily, you should avoid Ambisonics when recording dialogue. Combining environmental sounds and spoken lines on a single track can make it challenging to discern speaking parts. Further, any post-production edits or processing will affect both dialogue and ambient sounds at once since they would all be on the same Ambisonic track. This combination improves by using spot microphone techniques, wherein lavalier microphones (lavs) are generally needed. In short, spot microphone techniques involve the placement of an additional tiny microphone on or near an actor to ensure that her dialogue is discernable. This audio is mixable as a separate track in post-production. Thus, if the Ambisonic mic records chaotic emergency room sounds, a doctor's dialogue can be processed and edited separately from the hospital's ambient sounds, keeping key spoken lines upfront in the mix. (As mentioned in Chapter 2, dialogue of this sort is usually a mono recording.) Generally, the use of lavalier microphones for dialogue is wise. Lavs are tiny and can be clipped to a collar or surreptitiously taped underneath clothing. However, these lav mics are quite susceptible to noise and interference generated by bodily movement or the rustling of clothes, so proper placement is crucial.

Lavs vary in both price and quality. The most straightforward system runs about $10 and records directly into a smartphone concealed in a pocket. There are numerous self-contained lav mic/recorder combos that are very affordable. However, professional-grade systems usually employ separate wireless transmitters and receivers connected to a field recorder like the Zoom F8n. The GRID Lab favors this approach. High-quality wireless systems can run into the many thousands of dollars, to say nothing of the higher quality mics themselves. Production teams must take great care to understand how many transmitters and receivers can be in operation at once without interference. Most countries have legally reserved large swaths of wireless frequency bands for first responders, wireless broadband, television/radio transmission, and so on. Your team must be aware of which frequencies are legally available in your production area and what bands operate on the wireless systems you're using. Transmission frequency bands vary by model, manufacturer, and country. If possible, teams should always scan for usable frequencies on location well before production starts.

Like many things in life, there are always exceptions to norms. A good rule of thumb is to do what is best for each project. For example, when using cine-VR projects such as the DPT library to train physical therapists to observe hospitalized patients (see Chapter 3), the actor's movements and vocalizations form the soundtrack's bulk, but he really doesn't speak. Without extensive dialogue, Ambisonic recording works wonderfully on its own to convey the sonic action in the room, and the use of spot microphones is not necessary at all. All vital sounds are recorded clearly on the Ambisonic track alone.

The Need for Foley

So, now that we understand the rationale behind Ambisonic recording and the separate capture of dialogue with lavalier mics, there is at least one more broad audio production technique that can contribute to the immersive realism of your cine-VR projects. Foley is the art of post-production sound effects design whereby foley artists (those who perform the foley) and producers/engineers (those who record and process the foley) make realistic facsimiles of sounds needed in production. In other words, imagine the production team requires the sound of a bone saw opening a patient's rib cage during emergency surgery. What to do? This is where foley shines. A trip to the butcher shop for some beef ribs and a visit to the hardware store for a circular saw could be fun (if messy and expensive), but there are usually easier ways. Foley work might allow the sound of dry twigs cracking to stand in for real rib bones breaking. Foley is extremely useful for cine-VR projects and has the added benefit of often being rather fun to create. Such post-production effects may be recorded in stereo, mono, or Ambisonically, depending on the project's requirements. Engineers will often process the foley sounds with effects and plug-ins. Audio professionals will have to make such determinations based on the specific foley sounds required and the audio mix's overall needs. The importance and advantage of foley come from several areas: ease/utility and naturalism/realism. Sometimes, foley is as easy as jiggling a bottle of pills to stand in for what might be a shaking pill bottle sound that is too low to capture on-set. Other times, the actual source of the sounds itself is prohibitive – say, an exploding car tire or a rabid dog growling. Atypical sound needs are where foley comes in. Don't have a fire-breathing dragon? Foley! Using advanced Ambisonic post-production techniques, spatial audio engineers might tie a specific foley sound to an object in the cine-VR recording itself. In this way, the sound (of a jiggling pill bottle, for instance) will remain tethered to the object throughout the viewer's movements. The way the sound is *heard* will change with movement, just as it does in real life, but the sound will remain precisely tethered to the object's discrete position.

Further Production Considerations

Following, you will find some precise practices, possibilities, and cine-VR audio production problems that address the topics above.

Ambisonic Microphone Placement

One key thing to keep in mind on-set is that Ambisonic microphones – by design – pick up all the sounds in the broader environment. Microphone placement is crucial, and loud sounds too close to your mic will cause your audio to peak (clip or distort). That said, placing the microphone too far away from essential sound sources – an operating table, for example – will result in portions of the audio that are too quiet. Raising an Ambisonic track's overall level raises all the sounds on that track and the inherent noise. (Not to get too complicated, but each microphone has something called self-noise, which is just what it seems: sound generated by the microphone. You want this noise to be as low as possible, and different mics have different levels of noise. Turning the whole track up also turns up the noise.)

Further, Ambisonic microphones will pick up overlapping dialogue in conversations. This undesirable effect can lead to a somewhat chaotic soundtrack, and lavs may be necessary for crucial speaking parts. Sometimes, this chaos is appropriate since conversations are often cacophonous in real life. At other times, ADR (automated dialogue replacement, where actors re-record their lines in post-production) may be necessary for clarity. If possible, location sound recordists should arrive early to the set, test equipment and levels, and ideally get actors to run through some test shoots to perfect mic placement and recording levels.

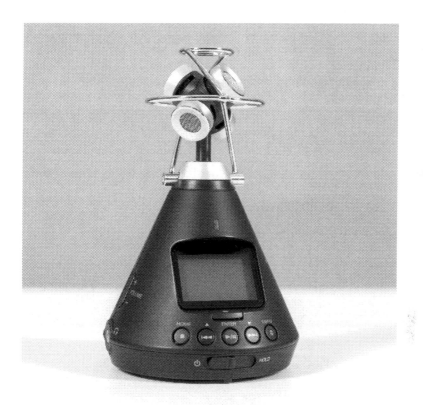

Photo 12.1   The Zoom H3-VR is an all-in-one first-order Ambisonic microphone and recording device. It includes a mounting bracket to connect it to a 360° camera.

To adequately capture spatial audio, Ambisonic microphones must be carefully placed relative to the camera as well. Because such mics record both spatial information and audio, arranging the microphone upside down or skewed from the camera can mean a lot of work in post-production to make sure the image and sound match each other spatially. Some Ambisonic recorders (like the Zoom H3-VR) have built-in gyroscopes that let the device know how the mic is placed and automatically adjust the recording in real-time. Alternately, the device can warn the recordists to recenter the microphone themselves before shooting/recording.

Another consideration is that a 360° camera will capture the image of your microphone – that is, the device will be visible in the video recording, which is not very realistic. Other chapters of this book discuss how to eliminate images of mics, tripods, and so on in video post-production, but it is good to minimize the appearance of microphones in the original image when possible. Devices like the Zoom H3-VR include a special bracket that attaches the 360° camera and the Ambisonic recorder together, one atop the other. (See Photo 12.1)

A Note on Room Tone

Room tone is what it sounds like, if you pardon the pun. It is the natural sound of a space – like a doctor's office, a front porch, a kitchen, a pharmacy waiting room, or an ambulance's interior. On-set audio recordists need to capture a moment or two (times will vary, but usually less than a minute) of room tone because pure silence in production sounds odd. Thus, if no one is speaking and there are no sound effects or music in an audio mix, room tone is added in post-production. Room tone might include sonic reflections, the sound of HVAC equipment, wind, the creaking of floors and walls, and so on. Room tone is easy to overlook until it is needed, and then nothing else will do. Neglecting to record room tone on-set, thus necessitating room tone recreation during post-production, can produce serious challenges and delays. If possible, production crews should record room tone with all microphone types used on set and in various positions and locations throughout the space.

Choosing the Right Equipment

All-in-one cine-VR Cameras and Ambisonic Recorders

The GRID Lab has tested several of these, and the audio quality is always poor. Therefore, we do not recommend their use.

Ambisonic Microphones, Field Recorders, and Laptop Computers

The Zoom H3-VR mentioned above is a self-contained, first-order Ambisonic microphone and recorder. This configuration means that it can do all of the recording and Ambisonic format decoding necessary for spatial production. It is tiny (see Photo 12.1), affordable, and relatively easy to use. That said, the microphone capsules on this device are not high quality, and it has a good deal of self-noise. (There are always trade-offs.) Other higher-quality, first-order microphones like the Sennheiser AMBEO, Rode SoundField, and Core Sound TetraMic are microphones *only*. Thus, plugging them into compatible field recorders such as the Zoom F8n (Photo 12.2), Zoom F6 (Photo 12.3), or Sound Devices MixPre-6 and MixPre-10 is required. For first-order Ambisonics, field recorders need to contain at least four separate XLR inputs and high-quality preamplifiers that allow for the recording of four channels simultaneously. All of the field recorders mentioned above include excellent preamps that reduce noise and capture pristine audio signals. Yet, these

Photo 12.2   The Zoom F8n field recorder is optimized for first-order Ambisonic recording but can do much more, such as record lavs.

Photo 12.3   The Zoom F6 field recorder is also optimized for Ambisonic recording but features "32-bit floating technology," which virtually eliminates the problem of clipping/distortion.

set-ups are somewhat bulky, harder to hide, complicated to use, and draw a great deal of power relative to the H3-VR. They are also the professional choice for first-order Ambisonic recording. When using such a workflow, it is essential to ensure the gain levels are set equally on each channel (most of these devices facilitate this by design). Again, trade-offs.

As mentioned earlier, higher order Ambisonics allows for a greater degree of spatial accuracy. Suppose one recorded an ambulance siren blaring in second or third-order Ambisonics and compared it to a first-order recording. The sense of spatiality, or *precisely* where the siren is coming from, may enhance with increasing Ambisonic orders. Higher orders do not necessarily guarantee an increase in overall audio quality, though. Audio quality has a great deal to do with microphone and recorder choice, set conditions, and the skills of recordists and post-production engineers. There are a variety of HOA microphones available today. Some of these are expensive and require proprietary hardware set-ups and software (the Core Sound OctoMic, the Eigenmike). Others plug directly into a computer or smartphone via USB (Voyage Spatial Mic, Zylia ZM-1). Mics like the Voyage (second-order and Zylia (third-order, Photo 12.4) do not require field recorders and therefore have potentially higher self-noise. Yet, these microphones offer a tremendous variety of processing and configuration options since they record directly to a computer or mobile device. Yet again, laptops are more challenging to hide in 360° images and more delicate than field recorders, while phones and tablets have limited processing power and storage. Trade-offs. (When choosing a laptop, production teams should be aware that Apple computers currently do not support HMDs, though this does not necessarily matter for the audio production side. You should strive for fast processors, lots of RAM, and solid state drives (SSDs) for audio production laptops. Better still are two drives: one to run the software and another for storage.)

Photo 12.4 **The Zylia ZM-1 is a third-order Ambisonic mic that plugs directly into a computer or smartphone.**

Batteries, Tripods, Shock Mounts, Wind Screens, Recording Media

Some scattered practical considerations: devices like the Zoom H3-VR and (especially) Zoom F8n suck batteries at an astonishing rate. Always bring extra sets of batteries to the location, and use portable battery packs whenever possible. Bring additional sets of those battery packs too! (These portable battery packs may be captured in the 360° images, though, so creative techniques to hide or "plate out" the batteries – along with the recording devices themselves – may be needed.) Ambisonic microphones are, by nature, susceptible to wind noise and vibrations. Be sure to always place them on a tripod, bespoke bracket, or shock mount. Appropriate windscreens should be on hand at all times. Most of the field recorders described here record directly to SD cards. Many of them will also record straight to computers or external drives, and some (like the Zoom F8n) can record to SD cards and external drives simultaneously. Always bring extra SD cards; they are not sturdy and fail regularly. Always back up everything!

Quick Takes on Post-production Processes and Distribution Formats

While it is possible to simply combine cine-VR video footage and Ambisonic audio in a program like Adobe Premiere Pro, professional productions use a DAW. A digital audio workstation, or DAW, simply means a software application that allows for recording, mixing, processing, and mastering audio (and often MIDI). DAWs are essential for most contemporary audio production because they allow for versatile workflows and nonlinear and nondestructive editing. However, when undertaking spatial audio production, selecting a DAW requires careful consideration, especially when working with Ambisonic audio. Production teams must carefully consider DAWs simply because many DAWs do not adequately support Ambisonic audio production. This lack of support is changing. While this chapter does not endeavor to recommend specific software post-production workflows, AVID's Pro Tools, Cockos's REAPER, and Steinberg's Nuendo have features explicitly designed to handle Ambisonic audio. The chief concern with Ambisonic audio post-production is routing. First-order Ambisonic audio requires a single track with four channels. Second-order Ambisonic audio requires a single track with *nine* channels. Third-order needs a single track with *sixteen* channels, and so on. As Ambisonic audio becomes increasingly popular and gains broad acceptance, more DAWs will undoubtedly incorporate these capabilities. For now, teams should do their homework before settling on a post-production workflow and should proceed with caution before hiring audio engineers. Spatial audio software and Ambisonic hardware are rapidly evolving, but DAW and computer operating system updates can change workflows significantly. Lack of experience with compatible DAWs and Ambisonic workflows can lead to significant production delays and yield potentially shoddy results.

When it comes to post-production, there are a dizzying variety of Ambisonic converters, spatial audio plug-ins, studio software, 360° video players, and virtual microphone programs. Chief among them is the Facebook 360° Spatial Workstation. It is free, simple to learn, extremely feature-rich, and regularly updated. It is also glitchy and difficult to install correctly. Unfortunately, I am unaware of any other free options that compare to this program in terms of its versatility and power. The Ambisonic Toolkit is also free and quite robust, if a little oblique and less frequently updated than the Facebook tools (but it is much easier to install). Finally, a set of paid Ambisonic software tools from dearVR shows excellent promise. Of particular note is the company's software, dearVR Spatial Connect, which allows Ambisonic mixing *inside* an HMD. In other words, with Spatial Connect, spatial audio engineers can use a Windows computer and a head-mounted display to arrange their Ambisonic audio while immersed in the VR project itself. It is this sort of innovation that makes the future of spatial audio feel very bright indeed.

A Final Note on Distribution Platforms and Hardware

If distributing content online, YouTube, Facebook, and Vimeo support cine-VR image content and have a vast global audience. However, as of early 2021, Vimeo *does not* support Ambisonic audio at all. YouTube supports first-order Ambisonic audio in the AmbiX format and features simultaneous head-locked stereo tracking. Facebook supports higher-order Ambisonic audio such as second-order. Each platform will have its standards, and these will change with time. Production teams might want to distribute on all platforms, which may require multiple different edits and mixes. Yet, sound designers and audio engineers will undoubtedly be dismayed to find that their hard work creating immersive Ambisonic audio experiences was for naught when posting projects to incompatible platforms. More importantly, the lack of Ambisonic support diminishes the sense of presence in users.

Finally, crafting a convincing stereo mix and an Ambisonic mix are two very different processes. Experienced engineers can accommodate these diverse mixing environments, but it will take extra time and is not as simple as clicking a few buttons. Yet again, different hardware distribution methods (HMD brands such as Oculus, HTC Vive, Valve Index, etc.) may support divergent audio and video standards. These devices have the advantage of being able to accept large cine-VR files loaded directly onto their internal drives (if self-contained) or the drives of their attached computers (if tethered). Directly loading cine-VR projects onto VR systems can increase quality (and thus presence) compared to online streaming. Still, many users do not own such headsets, and yet again, trade-offs are a factor.

Despite some audiences and even many industry professionals' unfamiliarity, it is hard to ignore the strides made in spatial audio production in just a few short years. The technologies and practices detailed here are certainly not limited to cine-VR – or even to VR more generally – but cine-VR is a highly germane application of such production processes. The emerging possibilities are staggering. Nowadays, some smartphones have spatial and Ambisonic audio capabilities, as do video game systems, site-specific art installations, museums, concert facilities, live streams, and even everyday headphones. (A reminder: users should generally wear headphones when listening to spatial audio of any sort. Sound quality is paramount if you want to feel a sense of presence. Also remember that Ambisonic audio will be decoded to binaural sound for headphone listening.) All of which is to say that sound recording and audio production are arts all their own, and immersive audio is flourishing. With the rise of podcasts and the ubiquity of earbuds/headphones, people today seem to be *listening* to media more than ever. Immersive audio will no doubt play a significant role in the future of audible media. It's a fascinating time to be working in this space.

Note

1. Goodwin, Simon N. *Beep to Boom: The Development of Advanced Runtime Sound Systems for Games and Extended Reality.* New York: Routledge, 2019.

References and Suggestions for Further Reading

Garner, T. (2018). *Echoes of Other Worlds: Sound in Virtual Reality.* Cham, Switzerland: Palgrave MacMillan, 2018.

Jerald, Jason. *The VR Book: Human-Centered Design for Virtual Reality.* Williston, VT: Morgan & Claypool, 2015.

Schütze, Stephan and Anna Irwin-Schütze. *New Realities in Audio: A Practical Guide for VR, AR, MR, and 360° Video.* Boca Raton: CRC Press, 2018.

Sinclair, Jean-Luc. *Principles of Game Audio and Sound Design: Sound Design and Audio Implementation for Interactive and Immersive Media.* New York: Routledge, 2020.

Zotter, Franz and Matthias Frank. *Ambisonics: A Practical 3D Audio Theory for Recording, Studio Production, Sound Reinforcement, and Virtual Reality.* Cham, Switzerland: Springer, 2019.

Chapter 13

Emotion vs. Information in Cine-VR

Eric R. Williams

Contents

In our book, "Virtual Reality Cinema Narrative Tips and Techniques," my colleagues and I go to great lengths to explain how cine-VR differs from other media – specifically film/video, theater/ simulation, and video games/interactive storytelling. Cine-VR is its own medium. A song and a movie can both make you cry, but they do it in different ways. Similarly, cine-VR has its own tools – tools that need to be considered, examined, and perfected if we, as storytellers, are going to harness the impressive power that it contains.

One of the most intriguing aspects of this emerging medium is how the audience processes emotion and information. This aspect may seem obvious: *Of course, emotion and information are processed by the audience. That's the point of using stories for educational purposes.* I agree. Yes, those are complementary purposes of narrative training pieces. However, it is becoming apparent to us at the GRID Lab that the way emotion and information are "ingested" by the audience may be very different in cine-VR than in other media. Very different indeed. In fact, it seems as if emotion and information are processed at the exclusion of one another. If a cine-VR audience is picking up emotional cues … they may be shunning informational cues. And vice versa.

We believe that this phenomenon comes from the fact that the audience is building a cine-VR story for themselves. You see, in traditional media, the story is *delivered* to the audience. You sit back in your seat or on your sofa, and you *receive* the story. It's given to you, didactically, through shot selection and editing. The director guides you, making you see what she wants you to see.

DOI: 10.4324/9781003168683-16

Cine-VR, on the other hand, is much more active. You have to build the story for yourself – actively. There are no shots to guide you. Edits are a rarity. You are there. You exist in a location, and you have to make sense of the story around you. You have to construct the story for yourself. Yes, there may be voiceover and instructions to guide you, but you – the audience – still get to choose what to pay attention to and for how long, and how much weight (emotional weight and intellectual weight) you want to give to each object and each character. It can be exhausting having to make all of these decisions. Or, at least, it can be overwhelming – which is what we have observed.

Constructing vs. Receiving a Story

To explain these observations and their uses, I will excerpt a large section from our previous book about narrative storytelling in cine-VR:

> The idea of audiences in cine-VR either receiving a story or constructing a story isn't new. Charles Dickens seems to have understood the layered potential for cine-VR way back in the 1840s[1]. In *A Christmas Carol*, three ghosts visit Ebenezer Scrooge, who take him backward, sideways, and forward in time. At each stop, Scrooge sees a scene as if he were invisibly present. And yes, the audience may be "invisibly present" in cine-VR, but Dicken's parallel goes deeper than that. Consider the ghosts. They are not the storytellers. No, they simply guide Scrooge to each scene. Scrooge gathers the story details himself – he has a directorial agency as well as an emotional agency. There is no story in these scenes, per se, until Scrooge constructs the meaning and the emotion himself. The settings mean something *to Scrooge* – not to the ghosts.

The Christmas Carol Continuum

Nearly eighty years later, we can use Dickens' approach to reconsider stories in cine-VR. When we write books and short stories, films and plays and webisodes, we want to be like Dickens. We want to tell the story. We want people to catch the stories we are throwing their way. We want them to listen to our words, enjoy the images, think about the messages, meanings, morals, and emotions we so carefully crafted. We want to be like Dickens, writing *A Christmas Carol*. But in cine-VR, we're more like the ghosts than we are like Dickens. Our new role is more of a shepherd than a narrator, introducing rather than explaining. Asking rather than telling – at least theoretically.

Practically speaking, the role of cine-VR storytelling can best be visualized as a continuum between two approaches. We call this the Christmas Carol Continuum. On one end of the spectrum is the audience *constructing* a story based upon personal observations (the Scrooge approach). On the other end is the audience *receiving* a story delivered by the author (the Dickens approach) – see Figure 13.1.

The continuum illustrates a fundamental balance between *meaning* and *understanding*. When the audience is invited to construct a story, they are encouraged to find meaning through what is observed. When the audience is invited to receive a story, they are asked to understand what is being delivered. Constructing a story may lead to various interpretations. Receiving a story inevitably leads to similar – if not identical – interpretations.

CONSTRUCTING   **RECEIVING**

Figure 13.1   Christmas Carol Continuum

Directorial Agency vs. Emotional Agency

Storytellers can add additional complexity to the Christmas Carol Continuum by considering how the audience mentally and emotionally absorbs their cine-VR worlds. Theater worlds strike us differently from literary worlds, just as a music video strikes us differently from a radio song: different medium, different mindset. The audience's ability (or inability) to absorb various aspects of a cine-VR story turns our continuum into a matrix.

In 2016, three women collaborated with the National Film Board of Canada and Stanford's d.school Media Experiments to conduct a series of important cine-VR experiments. Katy Newton, Karin Soukup, and Paisley Smith – each with backgrounds in filmmaking and experience design – teamed up to explore some of the boundaries of storytelling in this new medium.[2]

Many people, when first experiencing cine-VR believe that the medium is somewhat passive – especially when compared to Virtual Reality, where you can walk around inside of the environment and interact with people and objects. But Newton, Soukup, and Smith discovered that this isn't exactly true. The process of visually exploring an environment is extremely active. So much so that we have to be careful not to overload the cine-VR audience with extraneous information.

In essence, they discovered that audiences would constantly try to make meaning from their environment. Perhaps more so in cine-VR than in real life because a cine-VR audience expects some sort of show or story. Newton, Soukup, and Smith hypothesize that an audience can either pick up story details or they can pick up the emotions of a story, but rarely can they pick up both at the same time. If the cine-VR environment feels complete to the audience, and everything "makes sense," then the audience settles into the story and starts to relate emotionally with the characters. However, if there is a lot of information to absorb, or if details distract the audience, then the audience goes into "detective mode" and tries to find meaning in the details.

Neither reaction is "right" or "wrong." But instead, they are at either end of a continuum. For instance, you may want to craft a cine-VR experience that emphasizes informational detail and observation. That's great – but just realize that if your audience is paying attention to these intellectual aspects, they will be less likely to feel the experience's emotions. On the flip side, if emotion is a vital part of the experience, the audience will most likely lose some of the informational details.

Newton, Soukup, and Smith expanded on their idea by investigating how the production process can influence whether the audience is more influenced by story details or the story's emotions. Their findings showed that when the narrative provides potential information in every direction (360°), then the audience is less likely to absorb information (especially information delivered via audio). Therefore, they are more likely to absorb the emotions of the scene. The team theorized that "perhaps there was too much information in 360° for the audience to process."

However, if the audience's area of view is limited, then the slider seems to slide in the other direction. This limitation isn't to say that you would "black out" areas of the screen as they did in the experiment. Instead, you could use camera placement for a similar effect. As an example, if the camera were placed against a wall (limiting the view to 180°), then the audience tends to be able to "hold more details in their head." Therefore, their ability to engage emotionally decreases. Further, if the camera were placed more into a corner (essentially limiting the view to 90°), the audience is even more primed for story detail and less likely to engage emotionally.

Christmas Carol Continuum in Practice

Consider that you are developing three scenarios to educate nursing students about the use of Narcan in the community (as discussed in Chapter 9). How does the Christmas Carol Continuum apply to these projects? Well, we started by shooting our proof-of-concept experience with action surrounding the camera in full 360° (see Figure 13.2). This scene was highly emotional – two women discover their friend who has overdosed. Neighbors come by to ogle and post the chaos online as the women struggle to administer Narcan.

In hindsight, we realize that we were setting ourselves up for disaster. We utilized the full 360° to tell a story to increase the audience's emotions and decrease their ability to recall intellectual detail. Adding to that, we created a highly charged event: a man overdosing. The audience members came out of the experience highly emotional, but with very little else. They couldn't explain the physical actions required to administer Narcan, nor could they repeat the necessary steps to make sure that it was working. The experience was practical emotionally, but not intellectually.

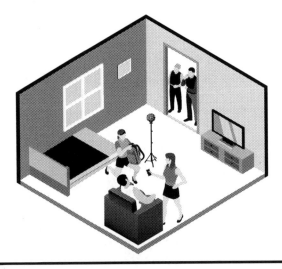

Figure 13.2   Camera placement for Narcan proof-of-concept project

Figure 13.3   Example camera placement for a 90° experience

However, this was at the time when we were unpacking the work that Newton, Soukup, and Smith had done, and we came back to the project with a different – and subsequently much more effective – approach:

90° Experience: We knew that we wanted the audience to learn all of the basic steps and procedures in the first experience, so we staged the experience so that all of the vital information was within a 90° segment of the room (see Figure 13.2). We knew that the scene's emotion would be intense on its own, so we didn't want a 360° set to intensify it any further.

180° Experience: The second experience in the series repeated the same intellectual information but in a new setting: a skilled nursing facility where a nurse discovers a patient who has overdosed. We decided to raise the emotion by placing the camera, so the story was told in the 180° segment of the room (see Figure 13.3).

360° Experience: By the third experience, we felt that the students should have a pretty good understanding of the Narcan processes and procedures, so we chose to increase the emotion and decrease the intellectual aspect. This choice is not to say that the students couldn't pick up the information – just that they would have to work harder to do so. We thought that his extra mental strain would mimic a person's mental pressure in this sort of situation. By their third cine-VR experience, we thought they would be ready for this emotional/intellectual combination. Notice that this set up is identical to the camera placement in the proof of-concept. The main difference is that this is the third experience in a series. We are using this scene as part of an "Arc of Engagement" (see next page).

In the Parkinson's project (see Chapter 10), we chose to shoot all three scenes primarily within 180° because we wanted a balance of emotion and information in each scene.

Emotion We wanted the nursing students to connect with the patients. During the scriptwriting, we added visual elements, verbal elements, and story elements that would hopefully create an emotional bond with the patient. This bond was necessary because the students have to balance their own emotional and intellectual demands on the job.

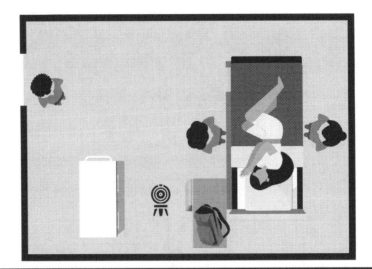

Figure 13.4   Example camera placement for a 180° experience

Information Students had to make some careful observations in these experiences. They had to pay attention to visual and verbal cues. They had to pay attention to physical behaviors and cognitive behaviors – and we wanted them to work at it. We didn't wish to just hand them the information on a platter.

For this reason, all three experiences were shot in the same way – from the center of the Christmas Carol Continuum.

Arc of Engagement

In the previous examples, each cine-VR experience was designed as a single scene in a single location with single camera placement. Therefore, we can place the experience on a specific point on

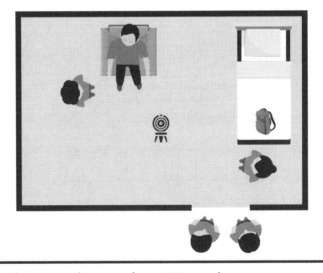

Figure 13.5   Example camera placement for a 360° experience

the Christmas Carol Continuum. However, it's also possible (and sometimes preferable) to have multiple scenes within a cine-VR experience. If you have a variety of settings within a piece, then you have the opportunity to mix and match your camera placement, and if you are specific in your choices, then your story is designed to have what we call an "Arc of Engagement."

As an example, you might imagine a story with three scenes:

■ The first scene is shot within 90° – emphasizing the intellectual content and deemphasizing the emotional. Perhaps we want to ensure that the audience understands a lifesaving technique.

■ The second scene might then occur within 180° by design – equalizing the intellectual and emotional content. Maybe this scene is a scenario where the audience assesses a situation and decides whether the lifesaving technique is required. The emotional balance may be used as a slight detractor from the intellectual question at hand.

■ The third and final scene might end the story staged in full 360° – increasing the emotional impact of the moment and decreasing the audience's ability to comprehend intellectual content. As with the third Narcan scene we discussed earlier, this scene might be the height of a lifesaving experience where the audience is being asked to "push through" the moment's emotion and focus on remembering the steps from the first scene.

Using the Arc of Engagement in this way, we've designed the cine-VR experience to put the audience through an emotional and intellectual obstacle course in a unique way to the medium and – if properly implemented – can affect the purpose and results of the educational experience. I believe that these concepts warrant further study and will potentially open up new aspects of immersive storytelling in ways we can't yet comprehend.

Viewing

There are no cine-VR examples to view for this chapter. Images are from a project detailed in Chapter 9.

Notes

1. Dickens, Charles. A Christmas Carol. (England: Chapman & Hall, 1843).
2. Weedon, Georgie. "Tech: The Storyteller's Guide to the Virtual Reality Audience." Ministry of Counterculture, May 5, 2016. https://moc.media/en/487.

Chapter 14

Graphic Overlay in Cine-VR

Adonis Durado

Contents

Giving viewers control over what they want to see in a 360° environment poses a tremendous challenge for cine-VR content producers. The absence of traditional editing techniques or simple camera tricks makes it harder for a storyteller to indicate what is important about a scene. For example, the ability to zoom in or to create a montage (from an establishing shot to an extreme close-up) is no longer possible. Cine-VR breaks the fourth wall. Instead of using traditional frames, we now work with an entire field of view (FOV). Editing within a 360° location has to be done with a light-hand. Employ too many cuts, and the scene will feel too jarring, giving your audience a headache.

The viewer's wandering gaze has produced deep-seated anxiety about whether a 360° spherical canvas proves to be more or less advantageous for telling stories, even setting aside the limitation of what the human eyes can see. The uneasy feeling is mutual for both the content producer and the viewer. If cine-VR producers worry too much that essential details and elements might be missed, viewers could also suffer from this same fear of missing out (or FOMO). Therefore, since the onset of cine-VR, one technique that has proven helpful in drawing the viewer's attention is a graphical overlay. Adding textual elements or graphical layers not only enhances and provides context, but graphics also cogently function as a unique set of visual cues.

This chapter will explain how I arrived at constructing a spherical grid to map various safe areas for graphic overlay placement.

DOI: 10.4324/9781003168683-17

Field of View

In *The VR Book: Human-Centered Design*, author Jason Jerald defines the field of view as the angular measure of what can be seen at a single point in time[1]. This definition, by the way, applies both to the human eyes and the VR headsets. To understand the significance of FOV, we first need to know how a pair of human eyes work.

Physiologically, a pair of human eyes can see 220° with a straight-ahead fixation in the horizontal axis. Each eye (or monocular sight) is capable of perceiving 175°. The area where our left eyesight and our right eyesight overlap defines our central vision (also known as binocular FOV), which measures between 114° and 120° (see Figure 14.1). Beyond our central vision is the field of regard or peripheral vision, which we use when we sense motion or do sideways glances without turning our head. The problem of inserting text in a spherical video is the tendency to warp when it reaches a certain angle, height, and direction. This is known as distortion and can be seen as either vertical or horizontal distortion (see Figure 14.2).

Our binocular FOV brings about stereoscopic vision, which is responsible for judging distance and grasping depth perception. At best, our stereoscopic vision can discern shapes and symbols within a 60° angle, but only at 30° for text.

Our eyes cannot see nearly as much due to our forehead and torso on the vertical axis. Again, if we look straight ahead, we could perceive a total of 135° – that's 60° above and 75° below (see Figure 14.3). Like in the horizontal axis, symbol and text recognition is within 30°.

By the way, FOV specs for VR headsets vary considerably. For example, Google Cardboard has 80° while top-of-the-line headsets like the Oculus Rift have a standard of at least 110°. A narrow range of FOV means users will be deprived of their peripheral visions. Think of a horse wearing a blinder.

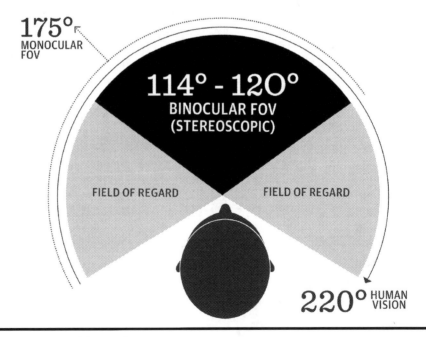

Figure 14.1 Human vision and FOV

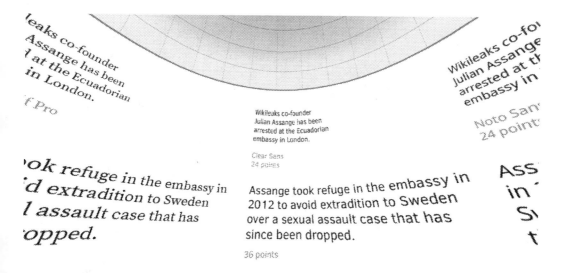

Figure 14.2   Vertical distortion

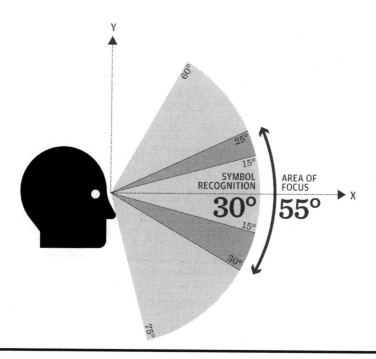

Figure 14.3   Vertical FOV

Spherical Grid and Safe Zone

Perhaps the most important takeaway from my research on FOV is that humans can quickly recognize text within a 30° angle in both horizontal and vertical axis. Theoretically, the graphics overlay within that range can be perceived with ease and comfort.

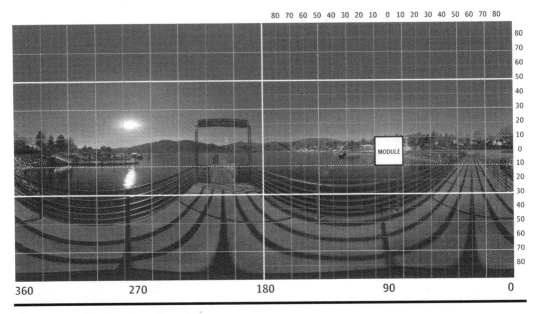

Figure 14.4 Equirectangular grid

However, during various experiments, I was surprised by what I found. When I placed a title sequence in Adobe Premiere using the "VR Plane to Sphere" effect with a length exceeding the 30° limit, the warping becomes quite noticeable. Readability also becomes an issue. When I adjusted the size of the title sequence down to 20°, the result was perfectly fit for the human gaze. When projected into a plane view mode, the equirectangular grid consists of an 18 × 9 division, with each module consisting of a 20° × 20° angle (see Figure 14.4).

While conducting these same experiments, I also discovered the sweet spot for placing objects and overlays in the vertical axis. If an object is fixed not far away from the gaze line – just within 40° above and 30° below – you'll avoid extreme foreshortening and shape distortion (see Figure 14.5).

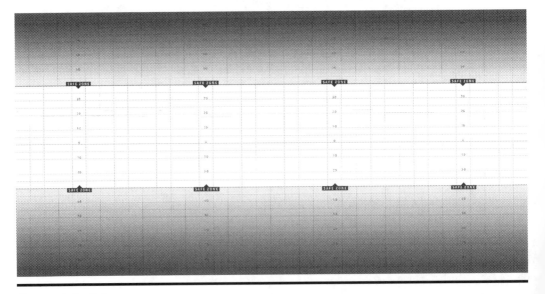

Figure 14.5 Safe zone

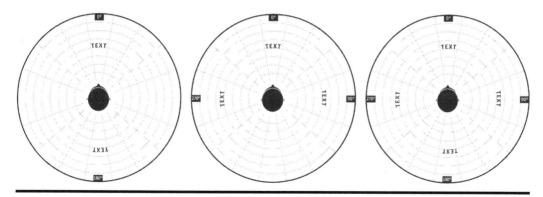

Figure 14.6   Types of orientation points

As we fondly call it, the safe zone turns out to be very handy when working with greenscreen imagery. We shot our subject in front of a green screen (we captured him traditionally with a DSLR camera) and then dropped the image into the post-production video sphere. Once correctly scaled, we could drop the image into the safe zone without any concern about vertical or horizontal distortion.

Orientation Points

I've seen numerous VR shorts (narrative, documentaries, and nonfiction) and noticed that content producers are pretty nonchalant about stabilizing their orientation points, whether to split the spherical grid into halves, thirds, and quadrants (see Figure 14.6). In placing text overlay (intertitles or subtitles), The New York Times seems to prefer the latter, but I reckon it doesn't really matter as long as they are constant.

Orientation points serve as spatial markers, enabling the viewer to situate oneself in the virtual space. Establishing these orientation points is a way of negotiating with your viewers to fix their gaze or anticipate where essential elements are placed in the spherical grid.

In VR documentaries where intertitles (or subtitles) are an integral part of the narrative, three orientation points work best, especially if the viewers are watching in a sitting position. So even if the viewer is looking sideways, it ensures that the text will not be missed.

It is crucial to establish these orientation points right away, which can quickly be done by placing the opening credit simultaneously on these fixed angles shown in Figure 14.6.

Type Fit for Cine-VR

"What would be the best fonts to use for VR?" the most common question is often asked by VR practitioners. My short answer: web fonts. This is true when we specifically consider a typeface that is best for subtitling.

Web fonts are specifically designed for the screen and are optimized for screen viewing. These typefaces have the following properties: taller x-height, wider characters, spacious tracking, and basically designed around the natural properties of pixels (see Figure 14.7). Some of the most popular web fonts are Roboto Sans, Titillium, Avenir, Cormorant, and Source Sans.

Figure 14.7   Web font

Some traditional classic print typefaces underwent a facelift to include web font versions in the family, such as Helvetica, Gotham, and Sentinel. You may find a good selection of free, downloadable web fonts from the Google Fonts website.

While the ideal text size for reading in print is between ten and twelve points, in VR, the safest minimum body text size is twenty-four points. We all know that not all fonts are created equal, but to find the sweet spot for a body text size is to fit thirty characters within the 20° angle (see Figure 14.8).

Modular Treatment

Be it in traditional media or in VR, using a grid helps organize space, text, and other elements on a given canvas. The equirectangular grid that I created above will ensure that all text is displayed correctly, but each module can be used as a building block in arranging the elements. For example,

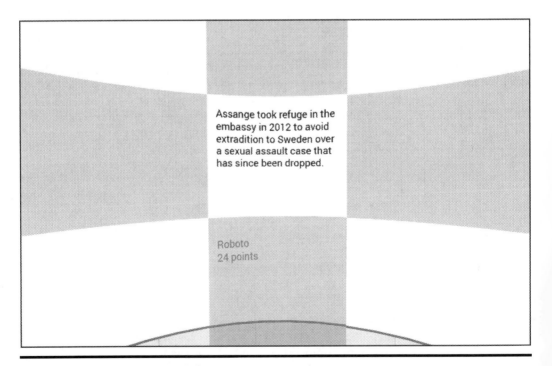

Figure 14.8   Font size in 20° angle

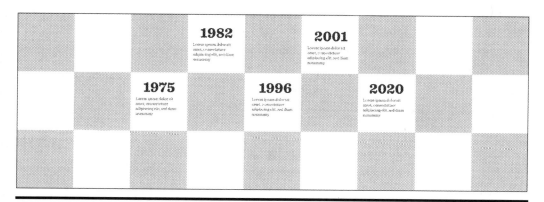

Figure 14.9   Modular treatment

if you plan to create a timeline, you can display the sequence of information either linearly or in a zigzag fashion, with each entry occupying one module (see Figure 14.9).

Another important takeaway that I learned from this research is to consider the viewing limitations. If one uses a tethered headset while sitting on a fixed chair, the viewer's head can only turn so much on both sides. Even if we have the 360° canvas at our disposal, we must consider the said limitation when presenting sequential information in a rotational fashion. We must avoid text placement that utilizes the entire 360° space, or viewers would wind up entangled by the headset cable. Employing a modular treatment within the orientation points will fix this issue. If I have ten entries in my timeline, I will do the same thing in Figure 14.9 but repeat it twice in a similar sequence.

Resources

1. If you want to know how to add text in a 360° video in Adobe Premiere, here's a short, easy-to-follow tutorial: https://bit.ly/2m7mW51. It specifically talks about using "Plane to Sphere" effect, as well as how to adjust and control "stereo disparity."[2]
2. Want to know the hottest – and best of all, free! – web fonts available online[3]? Check this top 20 typefaces: https://bit.ly/2t9di37
3. Without using any editing tool or VR viewer, you can quickly transform an equirectangular image into a sphere using this JavaScript web application tool – https://bit.ly/2g8graO. You

can use this to swiftly test the legibility and size of a font when displayed in a 360° sphere by merely following a couple of steps. Open any rectangular image in Photoshop and add text to it and save it as a jpeg. Go to the link above and then drag and drop the jpeg file into the browser[4].

4. What's the best way to add motion graphics and visual effects to VR composition during post-prod? This Adobe After Effects tutorial will not only show you the way but help you understand how a cube map works when you're editing, by turning the spherical video canvas into six flat planes as you add graphical elements or VFX: https://adobe.ly/34d03Bx.[5]

5. And finally, I have curated a YouTube channel containing examples of graphic overlay for cine-VR that I find especially interesting (including some of my own nonfiction work that didn't meet the book's narrative criteria Vimeo page). https://bit.ly/2FwgFtH

Notes

1. Jerald, Jason. The VR Book: Human-Centered Design (United States: Morgan & Claypool Publishers, 2015).

2. Redohl, Sarah. "How to Add Text to 360 Videos." Immersive Shooter. Travel Channel and National Public Radio, January 16, 2019. http://www.immersiveshooter.com/2019/01/11/how-to-add-titles-to-360-video/.

3. AWWWARDS in Resources & Tools. "20 Best Google Web Fonts." 20 Best Google Web Fonts. AWWWARDS, May 1, 1970. https://www.awwwards.com/20-best-web-fonts-from-google-web-fonts-and-font-face.html.

4. "Equirectangular Panorama Demo." three.js webgl - equirectangular panorama. Accessed May 22, 2020. https://threejs.org/examples/webgl_panorama_equirectangular.html.

5. Adobe.com. "Construct VR environments in After Effects" https://helpx.adobe.com/after-effects/using/immersive-video-VR.html

SECTION IV

Collaboration is Essential

Complex problems are best solved by creative thinkers working together. The more diverse the thinkers, the better. It's easy to find examples of historically significant problems achieving success due to a team's assortment of specialists. For instance, successfully landing astronauts on the moon took tens of thousands of individuals from hundreds of disciplines, all working toward a common goal. Can you imagine if one profession tried to solve all of the problems related to walking on the moon? It's silly to even contemplate. Would mechanical engineers be your first choice to research the psychological impacts of space travel? You wouldn't want naval aviators determining the best practices for collecting geological samples, or telecommunication specialists designing the reentry parachutes.

With reflection, we realize that all great projects require a diverse mix of individuals. This has been true for all GRID Lab projects, regardless of size. The quality of completed projects was not determined by budget or gear, but rather by the unique composition of experts working together.

Some of our projects have only had four team members, while others have had close to two hundred contributors. From our experience, the more bizarre a team composition seems, the more potential there is to create something truly innovative. In Chapter 17, you'll see how an administrator from student affairs, a police detective, a filmmaker, and a game developer came together to develop training that helps individuals experiencing emotional distress. This project ran head first into production challenges. In fact, the first attempt was so bad, we had to start over. If you can build a team of individuals willing to do that, eventually, you will achieve success, as this team did.

The production for two of the projects featured in this section employed nearly two hundred individuals (Chapters 15 and 16). The number of researchers, actors, and production crew was challenging to manage. Still, it was terrific seeing so many different disciplines working together toward a common goal. Many of the crew were students from Ohio University and Hocking College (a community college near Ohio University). All of our student staff were paid. Employment on this project was an incredible learning opportunity for these students. They were able to apply the knowledge learned in the classroom to a socially-impactful production. If you're creating cine-VR at a university, adding students to your crew will be mutually advantageous.

Lessons Learned

I wanted to share some of our lessons learned relating to the nuances of creative collaborations. These lessons will be expanded upon in this section's chapters, but the challenges faced are common to most cine-VR projects. Therefore, these lessons are worth highlighting.

DOI: 10.4324/9781003168683-18

Lesson 1: Learn to Compromise

I feel confident declaring that no one likes to work with jerks. Egos need to be checked at the door. Just because your team is formed, it doesn't mean chemistry naturally happens. This relates back to the point about what you may not know about a particular subject. For example, filmmakers working on a healthcare project don't know everything there is to know about healthcare. Likewise, healthcare professionals know little to nothing about filmmaking. This is perfectly normal yet sometimes difficult for collaborators to grasp. There is nothing wrong with you if you don't know everything about every subject. That's why we collaborate. However, you must be willing to admit you don't know everything. Trust those who have studied the subject matter for years or decades.

Everyone brings different talents to a project. Each may have strong opinions about what should be included or excluded. Be reasonable and communicate the importance of not pursuing every idea suggested. Your project will never end if every individual is unwilling to compromise – this can lead to feature creep. Only the ideas that contribute to the project's success, both in production and research, should move forward. Making decisions about what works can be done effectively if every team member is willing to compromise (partially at least). Having a unified vision before the start of any creative project is required.

There will be several elements that may force some sort of compromise. From a production standpoint, speed, quality, and expense can all be factors driving the project. There is an old adage in media production. Paraphrasing, media productions can be:

1. Created quickly
2. Budgeted reasonably
3. Produced at excellent quality

However, you can only pick two of these. Fast, cheap, or good? For example, a project can be developed quickly with high quality, but it certainly will not be cheap. A project can be inexpensive and quickly produced, but the quality will likely suffer. These three considerations are constantly juggled on every project.

Lesson 2: Pre-production is Crucial

A team needs to commit to making as many detailed production decisions as possible before actually starting production. If pre-production is shortened or skipped entirely, each step of production will not go smoothly. If you have a funded project, make pre-production a significant part of your proposed timeline. You may need to spend a month of planning for only two days of production.

Pre-production is more than discussing the production and research objectives. Pre-producing cine-VR requires scriptwriting, gear procurement, location scouting, set design, actor and crew hiring, and constant iteration.

Scriptwriting will likely be the most iterative process. A script written about healthcare without such professionals' input will result in being too "Hollywood-like." The dialogue, settings, and actions are usually absurd when reviewed by a topical expert. Great acting and a visually appealing final product cannot make up for nonsensical dialogue.

The scriptwriting phase has to be iterative. Have your team outline the story's broad strokes, theme, and desired results before a scriptwriter begins. Once the scriptwriter has completed a draft, start iterating. Scripts should bounce back and forth regularly from the scriptwriters to subject experts. It is not uncommon to have 8–10 drafts before you have a production-ready script.

In summary, don't rush pre-production. Detailed decisions made before production will pay dividends once production begins.

Lesson 3: Create a Distribution Plan Early

Distribution plans are necessary and should be planned as early in the project as possible. Whether you're sharing your cine-VR through a single headset or broadcasting it to the world, it is helpful to sufficiently plan. Details about distribution are covered in Chapter 21.

Regardless of which distribution method you select, there is one thing you should avoid at all costs. Avoid making the user troubleshoot your project. If a project is difficult to launch or configure, frustration will occur. Starting your experience with a frustrating task may tarnish everything. Make sure your directions for playback are clear and have several different individuals test the process. VR can be overwhelming to individuals new to the platform, so don't add stress with unclear experience instructions.

Lesson 4: Don't Lie to Yourself

If you don't think your project is good, neither will anyone else. Cine-VR production requires a significant financial and mental investment. That investment may require you to publish, regardless of the overall quality. While seeming obvious, don't post lousy content. Most of the time, you do not need to wait until the end of a project to determine whether it's working or not. If the production is not going well, sometimes it may be necessary to pump the brakes and make changes. Replace actors if needed, rewrite scripts, or find new locations. If the content is terrible in production, no amount of post-production or wishful thinking will fix that.

It's difficult to admit that something you've invested a significant amount of time in is awful. The GRID Lab continually struggles with this. Our first production of a cine-VR series to train first responders about dealing with persons experiencing emotional distress was not good at all. So many things went wrong on that production that it was apparent the overall quality would be insufficient and poorly received. We had to throw the production out and go back to the drawing board. Those costs were sunk, and new funds needed to be raised for another production attempt. It was worth it. The next production avoided repeating mistakes from the last effort, and the finished project was significantly better. If you can make changes early in production, do so. Don't lie to yourself that it might turn out alright.

The Formula

GRID Lab team members are often asked what our recipe for project success is. Frankly, we've struggled to answer that question on more than one occasion. If there is a recipe or formula, it absolutely requires multidiscipline collaborations. There is nothing supernatural about what we do. We have genuinely loved doing significant projects with people from different backgrounds. If we had to create a formula, it would look pretty simplistic. Maybe something like this:

subject experts + creative media producers + good stories = cine-VR success

This formula is not fool-proof. It doesn't always work out this way, but this has been a good starting point for GRID Lab projects over the last five years. Find individuals you like working with. Not only will the quality of the projects increase, but the likelihood of future collaborations will also be high. Try out our formula and let us know if it works for you.

In the following chapters, you will learn about some of our creative collaborations. All of them have led to more collaborations. You will be introduced to a concept we call guided simulation in Chapter 18, maintaining medical accuracy on set in Chapter 19, and advanced production considerations in Chapters 20 and 21.

Chapter 15

Empathy Training: Diabetes and Poverty

Carrie Love and Elizabeth A. Beverly

Contents

Empathy is the ability to sense what another person is thinking and feeling. In medicine, empathy is key to developing a successful patient-provider relationship and improving patient outcomes. Increasing evidence shows that patients seek out empathy from their providers and value this quality equally, if not more, than clinical expertise.[1,2] For this reason, medical educators recognize the importance of integrating empathy in training for healthcare providers and students.[3,4] Cine-VR is a digital platform that increases understanding and empathy from the patient perspective.

In early 2019, the GRID Lab partnered with the Ohio University Heritage College of Osteopathic Medicine (OU-HCOM) to create a twelve-part cine-VR series depicting the diabetes epidemic in southeastern Appalachian Ohio. In this region, diabetes rates are more than double the national average (19.9% vs. 10.5%[5,6]), and people with diabetes are more likely to experience complications, lower limb amputations, and depression.[7,8] Before this partnership, OU-HCOM delivered presentations emphasizing the disproportionate rates of diabetes in the region without cine-VR. OU-HCOM diabetes researchers presented statistics and facts via traditional didactic

DOI: 10.4324/9781003168683-19

lecture and PowerPoint presentation. Our team hypothesized that two factors contribute to the higher rates of diabetes in the region:

1. People in Appalachian Ohio encounter more social determinants of health, including financial insecurity, lack of access to providers, lack of access to specialists, lack of access to transportation, food insecurity, housing insecurity, lower educational achievement, and lower health literacy, compared to people in other regions of the country. These factors are associated with an increased risk for diabetes.
2. People in southeastern Ohio are often recipients of implicit bias or stereotyping of Appalachian culture. Providers with higher levels of implicit bias are less patient-centered, and patients who perceived implicit bias from providers are less likely to follow treatment recommendations, both of which can lead to adverse health outcomes.

Question

The partnership between the GRID Lab and OU-HCOM facilitated a coalescence between digital storytelling and medicine. Specifically, cine-VR inclusion allowed the team to develop a protagonist to command an audience's emotional investment. Within the twelve-part cine-VR series, we portrayed examples of social determinants of health and dispelled stereotypes about Appalachian culture through Lula Mae's character, a seventy-two-year-old woman with type 2 diabetes. The team designed every detail of the Lula Mae character. Lula Mae has had type 2 diabetes for twenty-two years. She is a widow, her husband died twenty-seven years ago from a heart attack, and she has three adult children and seven grandchildren. She cares full-time for her adult son, Junior, who suffered a traumatic brain injury while serving in the military. Lula Mae and Junior live in a house originally belonging to her grandparents. Her two adult daughters and grandchildren live on the same family land in their separate homes making Lula Mae a source of care and support for her entire family. In doing so, her own healthcare needs often become secondary to the daily needs of the people she loves. Despite Lula Mae's struggles, the audience learns about Appalachian culture's strengths and the resiliency one person can have if providers invest the time to connect with her one-on-one. The primary audience for the series was healthcare providers; the secondary audience was healthcare students.

When placed in the headset, the design of these cine-VR experiences allowed the audience to feel as if they were in Lula Mae's situation – whether at the medical appointment with her primary care physician or stuck on the side of the road where the family car broke down. Cine-VR offered healthcare providers a rarely seen glimpse into the history and home life of Lula Mae outside of the patient room. Providers and students could observe each social determinant of health that interfered with Lula Mae's diabetes self-care, and they received information about the Appalachian culture that could help empower Lula Mae in her diabetes management.

This cine-VR project utilized a new technique developed by the GRID Lab called guided simulation (see Chapter 18). The cine-VR series began with a background video, an example of a "sub-optimal" interaction with a healthcare provider. At the end of each series, we offered providers and students an opportunity to participate in the guided simulations, where the providers and students received text-based prompts designed to coach them through a better verbal interaction related to patient care. The guided simulation was a distinctive feature of the training designed to incorporate experiential learning to facilitate understanding and cultivate empathy.

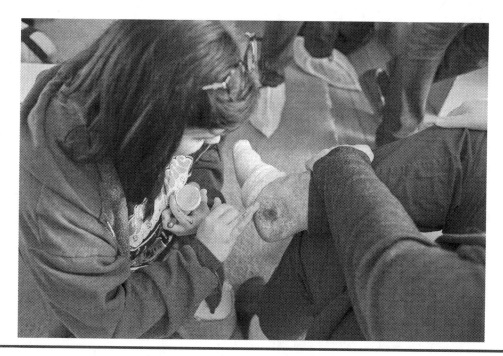

Photo 15.1   Makeup artist Chloee Griffith creates a fake foot ulcer on actor Rita Preston, who plays Lula Mae. Throughout the series, the audience watches as Lula Mae repeatedly prioritizes her family's well-being over herself, resulting in worsening health issues.

Production Approach

The increasing use of cine-VR as a buzzword is proof that an organization is on the cutting edge in its methods; however, there are a few examples where this media successfully elevates a user's experience to new levels. The *Lula Mae* cine-VR series is an example of a successful breakthrough.

It is necessary to understand the benefits that cine-VR offers to intelligently integrate the medium as a tool within an existing educational program. While cine-VR can be an exciting and valuable asset, it must still successfully speak to real needs within the organization if it is to be of value.

To leverage cine-VR's strengths, our team realized that we needed to combine the educational needs of the presentation with the artistic possibilities of digital storytelling.

The Lula Mae project's creation was in response to Ohio's Department of Medicaid's invitation to create and test virtual reality experiences to reduce implicit biases in medical providers. The first step in building an outline for the project was to piece together insights offered by various partnering departments at Ohio University.

Medical experts compiled researched talking points they wanted to cover through the narrative (i.e., social determinants of health as they relate to the Medicaid population in southeast Ohio) as well as the needs and values of the audience for the final product – which would be a two-hour presentation comprised of live (or online) presentation combined with twelve cine-VR vignettes. Digital storytelling experts from the GRID Lab offered suggestions on how image composition, lighting, audio, and editing can engage viewers and convey ideas. Scriptwriters, directors, actors, and the art department gave insights on the power of worldbuilding through script development, nuanced performances, and production design to create meaningful experiences that transport viewers and open minds. The Visual Communications (VisCom) team shared how intelligent web design can broaden the project's audience and utilize data analytics.

While time-consuming, these early conversations were essential to setting the project up for success by establishing earned buy-in with critical advocates and building team rapport across many disciplines.

Eventually, this diverse team concluded that we should build out two six-part series that mirrored each other. Each series would follow a representative character of our desired patient population. The series would start with a traditionally shot film introducing Lula Mae's character, her world, and a problematic visit with her provider. Then we created three slice-of-life cine-VR videos highlighting how social determinants of health stood in the way of Lula Mae's medical treatment. The series would culminate with two interactive guided simulations: a private conversation with the provider and a redo of Lula Mae's problematic visit at the beginning of the series. The formula repeats with Lula Mae meeting a second provider on her healthcare team: a traditional film setting up the story, three cine-VR slice of life scenes, and two interactive guided simulations.

Each of the six segments are designed for specific educational and artistic purposes:

- Traditional filming was leveraged for the introduction because traditional film techniques can easily manipulate the audience's attention and emotions. The medium more easily allows for jumping through time and locations in a familiar manner, which allowed the storytellers to compress more information into a shorter duration.
- The slice of life vignettes leveraged cine-VR's strength in observational storytelling, giving the viewer privileged, unaltered access to a patient's environment, social interactions, and daily obstacles.

Photo 15.2 Directors Carrie Love (left), and Eric R. Williams (right) watch a take with production designer Nick Gardin (center).

■ The guided simulations can leverage calls-to-action where viewers suggest more positive decision-making from a fellow provider and the patient through virtual conversations within the narrative. These conversation simulations are low stress and low stakes as they occur with a prerecorded character instead of a live person.

Each of the twelve segments is augmented with informational interludes (either live or online). If you would like to see the entire project in its online format, please visit https://mesp.ohio.edu/. Each six-part storyline takes approximately forty-five minutes to experience.

Distribution

When beginning an endeavor like this, it is wise to plan the project's distribution approach. In this project, we knew the videos would be shared via in-person presentations using headsets (e.g., at medical conferences or scheduled group presentations) or via the web on a personal device (as the website is available for free to anyone wishing to use it). This understanding allowed our team to make specific decisions that would help make each viewing experience successful.

The first step was to have the content experts (who will also be the in-person presenters) identify the necessary supplementary content covered after each of the six segments. Our VisCom team, led by professors Becky Sell and Juan Thomassie, developed strategies for adapting the style, interactivity, and level of detail of the desired live content into a digital format. The VisCom team presented the plan to the content experts, who provided feedback during a months-long iterative process.

In larger projects like this one, visual consistency is crucial. Font and color guides were developed and used throughout the project. We encouraged all new materials (e.g., teaching guides and fliers) to be developed in collaboration with one of our design experts (graduate students in Ohio University's VisCom program) under Sell's and Thomassie's tutelage to maintain this consistency.

Results

The purpose of this project was to call attention to social determinants of health and Appalachian culture and delineate their relationship to diabetes in southeastern Appalachian Ohio via a twelve-part cine-VR series. To evaluate this project's effectiveness, healthcare providers and administrators completed pre- and post-surveys that assessed cultural self-efficacy changes diabetes attitudes and presence in virtual reality. Also, a subset of providers and administrators participated in in-depth interviews about their experience with cine-VR.

We observed positive improvements in all four of the cultural self-efficacy subscales (see Figure 15.1): "Knowledge and Understanding," "Interview," "Awareness, Acceptance, & Appreciation," and "Recognition." In other words, providers and students improved their confidence in 1) knowing how healthcare is influenced by cultural factors, 2) learning about the values and beliefs of diverse patients, 3) increasing awareness and self-awareness of culturally different patients. The most significant change was observed with the "Interview" subscale (Cohen's d=1.27), which assessed factors analogous to social determinants of health (see Figure 15.1).

Also, we observed positive improvements in all five of the diabetes attitudes subscales (see Figure 15.2): "Need for special training," "Seriousness of type 2 diabetes," "Value of tight glucose control," "Psychosocial impact of diabetes," and "Attitude toward patient autonomy." Thus, providers and students recognized the following: (1) diabetes care required special training, (2) type 2

	Pre-Survey	Post-Survey	p-value	Cohen's *d*
Knowledge and Understanding (n=66)	6.77±1.63	8.06±1.30	<0.001	0.87
Interview (n=66)	6.15±1.78	8.00±1.38	<0.001	1.16
Awareness, Acceptance, & Appreciation (n=67)	8.58±1.04	9.07±0.85	<0.001	0.51
Recognition (n=58)	7.96±1.54	8.81±1.24	<0.001	0.61

Figure 15.1   Mean Differences between Transcultural Self-Efficacy Tool Subscale Scores Pre- and Post-Conference

	Pre-Survey	Post-Survey	p-value	Cohen's *d*
Need for special training	4.59±0.38	4.81±0.27	<0.001	0.65
Seriousness of type 2 diabetes	4.23±0.49	4.57±0.39	<0.001	0.78
Value of tight glucose control	4.10±0.40	4.24±0.43	0.001	0.32
Psychosocial impact of diabetes	4.43±0.43	4.75±0.31	<0.001	0.87
Attitude toward patient autonomy	4.09±0.46	4.26±0.48	<0.001	0.38

Figure 15.2   Mean Differences between Diabetes Attitude Scale Subscale Scores Pre- and Post-Conference (n=68)

diabetes was a serious condition, (3) keeping blood glucose levels at target was critical, (4) diabetes took an emotional toll on people with the condition, and (5) people with diabetes should take an active role their diabetes care. We observed the most considerable change with the "Psychosocial impact of diabetes" subscale (Cohen's d=0.87), meaning providers and students understood the emotional impact of managing type 2 diabetes (see Figure 15.2).

Finally, we observed high scores of cine-VR presence in all of the subscales: Involvement, Sensory Fidelity, Adaptation/Immersion, and Interface Quality. All of the subscales achieved means above 5.0 (out of a 7-point scale). These results reflect favorable perceptions of the technology and strength of presence in our cine-VR.

	Post-Survey
Involvement	6.22±0.59
Sensory Fidelity	5.90±0.81
Adaptation/Immersion	6.22±0.61
Interface Quality	5.92±1.31

Figure 15.3   Mean Subscale Scores of Virtual Reality Presence Post-Conference (n=65)

A smaller group of healthcare providers and administrators performed content analysis by independently marking and categorizing keywords, phrases, and texts to identify themes. The qualitative analysis revealed three themes. The first theme, "Feeling Immersed in the Experience," reflected participants' comments on cine-VR realism. Seeing a 360° sphere allowed participants to immerse themselves in the simulations, feeling the disarray and chaos of Lula Mae's home and the panic when her car broke down:

> *The first time I watched it, I was just in awe. I felt like I was a fly on the wall. I can look all around. I can look at the unfinished walls. I can look at the clutter. I can look at the unwashed dishes that might be two or three days, maybe an overflowed trashcan. Kids in and out. The chaos, the child with the traumatic brain injury that's just kind of part of the wallpaper. I mean, they're existing in there, and we're all working our lives around them. I think that happens all the time in rural Appalachia. But to be inside someone's home and inside their life, it's almost like being invisible and seeing all the things that people want to hide, either purposely or indirectly, that affect their lives. It's like a glimpse inside someone's personal life and why things are the way they are.*

The second theme, "Empathizing with People's Stories," showed that participants identified with the content in the cine-VR – the dress, vehicles, housing, barriers, health conditions, and the notion of "taking care of everyone else but yourself." They felt Lula Mae's frustrations, her disappointments, and being torn between competing responsibilities:

> *I identified with the video. I identified with the dress. The vehicles. The scenarios and problems that those families face. The coexisting disorders. The housing. How things are undone and unfinished. Raising grandchildren. You know, taking care of everyone else but yourself, and being viewed and stereotyped as someone who is heavy and lazy, and maybe just doesn't care when really that is not the case in impoverished areas such as southeast Ohio.*

The third theme, "Contextualizing Barriers in Appalachia," conveyed the participants' views that Appalachian culture is frequently portrayed as a caricature in the media. Importantly, they felt that the cine-VR captured the true essence of Appalachian culture. Participants noted the program's emphasis on family, caregiving, loyalty, and generosity, and how the cine-VR properly contextualized these values concerning Lula Mae's behaviors:

> *I learned a lot more about the labor of love when it comes to the land component of it and just the way that people showcase their love and care. And then I also thought it was really interesting learning about how it's kind of shifted to this maternal-centered community. And it makes sense from the story that I heard, too, growing up, just because my – both of my grandparents lost their parents really early on in life, and they would stay with their aunts and uncles – well, aunts primarily, and maybe their grandmother, and kind of that component of like, oh, yeah, it is very maternally driven as far as care for one another.*

In sum, cine-VR is an effective training method for cultivating empathy via increased cultural self-efficacy, improved diabetes attitudes, and presence in the virtual environment. This cine-VR program's strength was the realism afforded by providing participants access to the whole environment to learn about Appalachian culture.

Personal Reactions

To date, we have screened *Lula Mae* in front of hundreds of providers, and we have watched numerous "Aha"! moments. People get mad at providers misbehaving, cry with the characters, and talk for hours and hours about their personal experiences with helping patients to manage their health. There was a Medicaid administrator who, after watching a simulation on provider burnout, said, "That cold doctor, that was me. That is why I left medicine and am now an Administrator." Or a crew member's grandmother who took off the headset, and with tears in her eyes, said, "Are you going to show this to doctors? They need to see it, so they can get it."

For us, however, the most meaningful feedback came from an administrator who found us outside the building after a presentation. She shared how she had grown up in a very rural space, much like the environment we created in the series. Now, as an administrator, she has a foot in both worlds. She is both a suit-wearing, highly educated professional who works in the big city, but she is also the young girl whose grandparents' house was cluttered with items they refused to throw away because it could possibly be used again. It was not hoarding but rather resourcefulness. It was a way of having more when your economics would point to having less. It was a small-town cohesiveness where individuals are proud and private but would help one another at the drop of a hat. She thanked us for capturing the nuances of what is commonly portrayed as cultural flaws but could also be seen as cultural strengths if you understood them as an insider.

This testimony affirms to us, on a personal level, that the project was a success. Hundreds of people have collaborated to combine science, technology, and art to create an experience that explored how social determinants of health affected access to healthcare. The result was the fantastic *Lula Mae* cine-VR series, which provokes thought, understanding, and, often, tears.

Photo 15.3 Actor Lawrence Green (left) entertains child actors Averi, Taelin, and Aurora Richardson between takes. Production designer Nick Gardin did a fantastic job of building a lived-in, chaotic looking set to point to how Lula Mae was struggling to take care of both her family and her health.

Lessons Learned

Collaboration is Key

Early in our meetings, it became evident that we had a team of talented individuals who desired to contribute their areas of expertise. As project leads, we needed to aid in interdepartmental communication, clarify the goals, and secure resources.

Successfully melding science, technology, and art was a high priority for the project. In the *Lula Mae* series, we had two lead medical professionals who offered their expertise, often leaning on a half dozen others to make sure the content was accurate. The four scriptwriters held dozens of meetings where the plot points and dialog were written, shown to the medical experts, and then rewritten so that the project resulted in a teaching experience that would be both compelling and educational. In the end, it took five to seven drafts of each script before the content experts approved the project to move into production.

This same dedication to the craft applied to the camera department, lighting, sound, costuming, props, casting, location scouting, web design, scheduling, finances, editing, sound design, and so forth. A small group of talented individuals can cover all the roles on such a project, making it faster and cheaper to produce (possibly for internal or proof of concept purposes). However, something will inevitably need sacrificing, likely the production quality or the medical accuracy. This project amounted to a feature film's worth of medically accurate, beautifully performed, and expertly recorded cine-VR narrative training videos. The secret to our success was deeply respecting the discrete needs in each production area and creating an environment where our talented team could offer us their best.

Art Elevates the Medium

Cine-VR is a 360° medium that requires intelligent use of the whole space. When scouting for locations, choose settings that artistically add to the story. In the *Lula Mae* series, we recorded in a medical clinic, a pharmacy, a food pantry, a home that we dressed to look chaotic and cluttered, and on the side of the road with a tow truck. Our set designer then elevated the spaces with specific prop choices that brought the spaces to life. In cine-VR, the viewer can look in any direction, so well-dressed locations can help tell the story we want viewers to absorb.

Further, the Lula Mae project focused our artistic attention on four specific cine-VR production areas: (1) Character blocking and movement, (2) Actor performances, (3) Lighting and sound, and (4) Editing techniques. In particular, we have found that cine-VR is a medium with one foot in traditional filmmaking and one foot in theater, – but, paradoxically, cine-VR is something completely new that stands on its own. Here are some specific "discoveries" we made while working on the Lula Mae project:

- Choose locations that allow your actors to move around. Cine-VR currently works better in long takes and with less pinching of time. Block your actors to move and gesticulate more broadly than they would for a film. Actors positioned closer to the camera will generally read to the audience as more important; actors further away are better suited for less necessary action or subtle hints. Locations with various entryways are helpful since actor entrances and exits are an excellent way to redirect attention.
- Like any performance, actors need a director to harmonize their performances and push them toward emotional truth. It can be difficult for a director to successfully monitor

Photo 15.4   In this 360° split-screen, Lula Mae appears three times simultaneously, which both shows the many roles she plays in her family, but also causes the viewer to feel overwhelmed.

everything going on in a 360° scene because so much is happening simultaneously in each direction. Consider hiring two directors: the lead director focuses on a 90° section where the main action occurs, while the second director watches the supporting action taking place in the other 270° section.

■ Our director of photography, Matt Love, developed some innovative techniques that elevated the production value of the images created. Good cinematography requires strategic lighting. Many times, Matt recorded our scenes in slices (think three slices of 120°) and then stitched the separate images together in the post-production process. This approach allowed us to light the scene and observe actors inside the room rather than around a corner. Read more about how to successfully hide stitch lines and 360° lighting in Chapter 20.

■ It is best practice to record audio with 360° microphones in addition to traditional lavalier and shotgun microphones. This method takes more time and requires more equipment but offers the opportunity of using directional sound cues, which can elevate a story, such as if someone starts talking from behind where the viewer is looking. See Chapter 12 for details.

Photo 15.5   In this Lovrick montage, the crossfading ghosting images show a passage of time and point to the volume of people that come through the food pantry.

- Editing in cine-VR is still in its infancy, but we developed a few interesting (and artistic) techniques on this project.
  - **360° split-screen:** When the 360° space is divided into more than one, simultaneously playing scenes that require the viewer to choose a storyline to follow.
  - **Lovrick montage:** A passage of time shown through ghosting images that crossfade into each other and then solidify.

In the Lula Mae series, we also successfully experimented with flashbacks that leaned on color shifts and sound design to help hide the edits in time.

Viewing

To view and download cine-VR examples mentioned in this chapter, please visit: https://vimeo.com/channels/cinevr4healthcare/ (password: cineVR4health).

Final Note

One crucial element that aided in this project's cultural setting was the GRID Lab's philosophy of open generosity and their desire to pay things forward. Leadership in the GRID Lab firmly believes that reciprocity is the key to healthy growth and collaboration. If we can openly help another department, they will in return, openly help us or others. This practice invites some crazy requests but also exciting new relationships and resources in unpredictable ways. We are honored to count so many departments and individuals as co-collaborators and colleagues. With this as a priority, we always share credit with those who have helped, and we give lots of free press to these entities when we see opportunities to connect them with potential partners.

Notes

1. Halpern J. What is clinical empathy? *Journal of General Internal Medicine.* 2003;18(8):670–674.
2. Hirsch EM. The role of empathy in medicine: A medical student's perspective. *Virtual Mentor.* 2007;9(6):423–427.
3. Batt-Rawden SA, Chisolm MS, Anton B, Flickinger TE. Teaching empathy to medical students: An updated, systematic review. *Academic Medicine: Journal of the Association of American Medical Colleges.* 2013;88(8):1171–1177.
4. Kelm Z, Womer J, Walter JK, Feudtner C. Interventions to cultivate physician empathy: A systematic review. *BMC Medical Education.* 2014;14:219.
5. Ruhil A, Johnson L, Cook K, et al. What does diabetes look like in our region: A summary of the regional diabetes needs assessment study. In. Athens, OH: Ohio University's Diabetes Institute; 2017:1–8.
6. National Diabetes Statistics Report 2020: Estimates of diabetes and its burden in the United States. In. Atlanta, GA: Centers for Diabetes Control and Prevention; 2020.
7. de Groot M, Doyle T, Hockman E, et al. Depression among type 2 diabetes rural Appalachian clinic attendees. *Diabetes Care.* 2007;30(6):1602–1604.
8. Schwartz F, Ruhil AV, Denham S, Shubrook J, Simpson C, Boyd SL. High self-reported prevalence of diabetes mellitus, heart disease, and stroke in 11 counties of rural Appalachian Ohio. *Journal of Rural Health.* 2009;25(2):226–230.

Chapter 16

Empathy Training: Drug Addiction

Kerri A. Shaw

Contents

> Empathy isn't just listening, it's asking the questions whose answers need to be listened to. Empathy requires inquiry as much as imagination. Empathy requires knowing you know nothing. Empathy means acknowledging a horizon of context that extends perpetually beyond what you can see.
>
> **Leslie Jamison, The Empathy Exams**

It is no secret that rural communities in Appalachia have been ravaged by the opioid epidemic recently. Between methamphetamines, prescription pain pills, and heroin, addiction and overdose rates have devastated small towns across southeast Ohio. Access to healthcare is a challenge, and substance use treatment facilities have struggled to keep up with the need. According to the National Institute on Drug Abuse, the most recent data for infants in Ohio born with Neonatal Abstinence Syndrome (NAS)/Neonatal Opioid Withdrawal Syndrome (NOWS) reported 11.6 cases per 1,000 hospital births, above the national average of seven cases per 1,000 in 2016. With healthcare professionals facing burnout as they watch their community members suffer and die

DOI: 10.4324/9781003168683-20

from substance abuse disorders, the *Destiny Empathy Training* cine-VR project seeks to decrease bias and grow empathy with twelve cine-VR experiences.

Empathy is, by definition, the ability to understand and share the feelings of another. In his book, *The Gift of Therapy, An Open Letter to a New Generation of Therapists and Their Patients*, Irvin D. Yalom describes empathy as "looking out the patient's window." The *Destiny Empathy Training* allows the audience to look out the window of a pregnant woman from Appalachia who struggles with drug addiction. The woman's name is Destiny.

My background is in social work. Emphasizing empathy in social work education is crucial. It is, in fact, a part of the social work core competencies. That said, how often are we, or any healthcare professionals, genuinely able to see out a patient's window? How do we understand someone's feelings when we see them in a professional office for an appointment? How do we understand the role of addiction and trauma in a client's life if we have never walked in their shoes? While home visits can enhance one's perspective, most healthcare professionals see clients and patients for a limited amount of time in a healthcare facility's controlled environment. Furthermore, regardless of where we engage with clients, we are limited in *what* we see; we see what they allow us to see at the moment.

Virtual reality (VR) technology is being used in educational settings more often than ever before. In many healthcare professions, though, community-based training uses traditional classroom methods such as lectures, videos, and discussion-based lessons. The *Destiny Empathy Training* project bridges the gap between lecture-based delivery and personalized home visits by training community healthcare providers serving Medicaid patients using cinematic VR (or: cine-VR) technology. This training has been made available at no cost in Ohio through grant funding from the Medicaid Equity Simulation Project (MESP). The majority of our audiences (or: viewers) have been social workers, nurses, or community health workers, as well as students of those disciplines.

When I joined the Ohio University's MESP team, I was skeptical that we could create a product that would move the needle on viewers' empathy scale. Indeed, my lack of familiarity with the technology itself played a part in my hesitation. However, I also wondered how healthcare professionals would make significant gains from another training about empathy and bias. Not only is developing empathy an aspect of social work core competencies, we, along with most healthcare professionals, must maintain our licensure through continuing education, and the focus on substance use disorders is a popular content area these days. Didactic training commonly addresses empathy and bias. *Besides, don't social workers eat, sleep, and breathe this stuff?* I thought. What could be "new" about cine-VR? Yes, I had a lot to learn. This new concept was not going to be just another slide presentation and surely not *another* self-assessment of biases. No, this project would be a real needle-mover.

Editor's note: As with the *Lula Mae* project, discussed in the previous chapter, the *Destiny Empathy Training* project also responded to the state of Ohio's Department of Medicaid's invitation to create and test VR experiences to reduce implicit biases in medical providers. The *Destiny Empathy Training* project focused on the implicit biases toward unmarried, opioid-dependent women. The final project consisted of two six-part stories; each story utilizing different media approaches:

Part 1: A traditional short film designed to introduce Destiny and her world using a medium more familiar to the audience – allowing the production to use standard filmmaking techniques to engineer emotions and story detail specifically.

Parts 2–4: Three slice-of-life vignettes leveraging cine-VR's strength in observational storytelling, giving the viewer privileged, unaltered access to a patient's environment, social interactions, and daily obstacles.

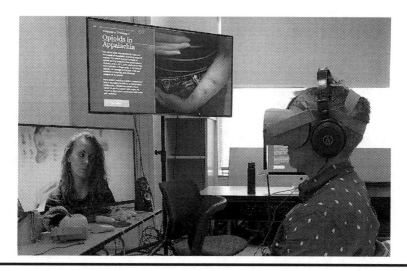

Photo 16.1   Healthcare professional participates in the *Destiny Empathy Training* experience

Parts 5–6: Two cine-VR guided simulations designed to be calls-to-action, prompting the audience to suggest more positive courses of action to fellow healthcare providers (Part 5) and then to Destiny herself (Part 6) through scripted, virtual conversations.

For more detail on the design decisions for each of these six parts, see Chapter 15. For further explanation of guided simulation, please see Chapter 18. As with the *Lula Mae* project, each six-part storyline augments informational interludes experienced during a live presentation or online (see Photo 16.1). If you would like to see the entire project in its online format, please visit https:// mesp.ohio.edu/.

Production Process/Technical Overview

The use of cine-VR allowed the team to create a relatable and believable protagonist, Destiny, a twenty-three-year-old woman who struggled with an addiction to opioids. Illicit drug use during pregnancy leads to poor maternal and infant outcomes, yet women who use substances during pregnancy tend to have lower attendance rates to prenatal appointments. People with opioid use disorder are "often stereotyped as criminals, lousy employees, and lacking a moral."[1] The fear of this stigma is a reported reason patients do not attend appointments and withhold substance abuse information from their providers.[2] Destiny begins her prenatal care at twenty weeks into her pregnancy.

During the project's character development phase, the medical team and media professionals discussed the importance of balancing the harsh reality of living in poverty, substance abuse, childhood trauma, and domestic violence with personal relatability. We wanted healthcare workers to connect with her. While we started with a generic profile of a "typical" pregnant patient with an addiction seen at a women and children's center in southeast Ohio, we filled in Destiny's character by envisioning her as a strong, sassy, determined young woman. We wanted viewers to be in her corner by the end of the twelve cine-VR videos that told her story.

Photo 16.2   Destiny and her grandmother fight while shopping for maternity clothes

In the segment "Destiny and Grandma Prepare," Destiny and her grandmother argue about who will take care of the baby after she is born (see Photo 16.2). The relationships in Destiny's life are complicated. For example, she seems to have a loving relationship with her grandmother initially; they are shopping together for maternity and baby clothes, and her grandmother often calls her "sweetie." However, the tone quickly changes when Destiny realizes that her grandmother thinks the baby will live with her. Destiny feels betrayed by yet another family member and yells, "You are supposed to be on MY side. SOMEBODY is supposed to be on my side in this STUPID family." Viewers realize how alone Destiny is in this battle against her addiction and her desire to be a "good" mother. Even her more supportive relationships involve judgment and abuse.

Destiny's flashbacks triggered in this segment by her grandmother's assumption that she will take custody of the baby because Destiny is a "junkie" gives us a direct window into how trauma affects substance use. Viewers watch Destiny be verbally attacked in public by her grandmother and have a flashback to her mother choosing someone else over her (see Photo 16.3). We can hear her internal messages that remind her of a lifetime of rejection, and we naturally want her to escape to safety. Unfortunately, using heroin is the only escape for Destiny. While we may not empathize with her behavior, we can certainly empathize with her desire to end the flashbacks and cope with this intense stress.

Childhood trauma, especially sexual trauma, and substance abuse disorders are strongly correlated. The National Institutes of Health (NIH) report that more than a third of adolescents with a report of abuse or neglect will have a substance use disorder before they reach their eighteenth birthday. Addressing underlying trauma when providing treatment for substance use disorders is critical to recovery. Cine-VR allows us to travel across time and location while also hearing Destiny's internal messages, to connect the dots between her childhood and her current behavior. While conventional training curricula may tell a story from a client's perspective, cine-VR allows us to see and hear what Destiny sees and hears. Because we are sometimes even engaging with the content as Destiny, as is the case in the scene where she is fired from her job, we experience these encounters in first-person, which is quite powerful. We also created scenes that were not unfamiliar to the general public. Most of us have experienced a curt, distracted doctor or nurse who

Photo 16.3   Destiny's flashback of childhood events underly her history of abuse

did not fully attend to us as patients, and many parents have been in prenatal classes with excited parents. These shared connections helped make Destiny real to viewers.

We had similar discussions about portraying Nurse Kate and Olivia, her social worker, in a light that showed their human compassion while also showing their professional shortcomings and bias (see Photo 16.4). If we painted them with too broad a brush, healthcare participants might not see themselves in their actions or words. Not only did we want viewers to connect with Destiny, but we also wanted them to connect with the healthcare professionals in the videos. Seeing the nurse and social worker change and grow created opportunities for the viewers to reflect on personal barriers to serving clients and patients, including burnout, high productivity requirements, and limited time allotted to meet with clients. These themes surfaced in our processing discussions.

In the video *Communicating with Nurse Kate*, the viewers see both Nurse Kate's frustration and compassion. We can engage with the character by reading a script presented on the screen. We support Nurse Kate and encourage her to see herself as being on Destiny's team. Nurse Kate shifts from being cynical about her recovery and generalizing her as being "just like all of them" to having hope that Destiny can change. Nurse Kate's disclosure that she has known Destiny since she was a child also gives us insight into her perspective. She has a personal connection to Destiny, as many healthcare providers in small communities do.

Destiny's story also presents information about how social determinants of health affect treatment and recovery. In addition to experiencing Destiny's interactions with her family members, healthcare providers, and other pregnant women, we also experience her living space, struggles related to poverty and employment, and how being a young, pregnant woman factor into her situation. There is so much to unpack that discussion can continue beyond the classroom, as communicated by a Community Health Worker who participated with her team, "We are still talking about the virtual reality presentation. It was a fantastic training tool for us!"

If a typical healthcare provider is part of an educated middle class, some of these issues related to class may be foreign to them. Exploring Destiny's substandard housing visually, and having an opportunity to then debrief with peers and the trainer, is a unique method of training. It offers

Photo 16.4 Destiny and her social worker, Olivia, discuss prenatal care

both a private experience to participants while experiencing cine-VR and a chance to share observations with the group. Exploring various spaces through technology allows facilitators to connect social determinants of health with Destiny in a visual and meaningful way. Destiny's house, for example, has a broken heater, leaky roof, and gaps around the door. While not an actual home visit, it presents much information. One community health worker noted, "The virtual reality training was by far the best training we had. It was so immersive, and it did help us feel that we were about to become community health workers!"

Not everyone will notice all of the issues presented that may affect Destiny's well-being and safety and that of her soon-to-be-born baby. However, most viewers notice the substandard conditions (see Photo 16.5). The technology is, as the community health worker shared, immersive. While participants all have the same information in front of them, they each experience it uniquely and learn from each other during the discussion.

Photo 16.5   Exploring Destiny's living space allows facilitators to discuss social determinants of health in a visual and meaningful way

Capturing Growth of Empathy Through Word Clouds

After facilitating just a few sessions, we noticed a pattern in the shift in participants' attitudes. The way they were talking about Destiny even after just a few videos was evident; they were aligned with her and rooting for her success. While wearing the Oculus Go headsets, participants often reacted physically and verbally to what they were watching. When they removed the HMDs for discussion, participants were animated and invested in Destiny's story. We decided to attempt to capture this shift through a word association activity. The first time we collected words from participants, we spontaneously reacted to what we noticed in the classroom. The results were revelatory and, when we shared them with the team, we unanimously decided to revise the IRB proposal to include this activity.[3] We were already collecting pre- and post-data on participants through various instruments, but now this exercise became a teaching tool and part of the research plan.

Methodology

Before participants have any information about the storyline or characters, the facilitator reads the following profile to participants:

> *Destiny is a 23-year-old pregnant woman attempting to overcome her struggle with addiction to opioids. The opioid crisis has significantly impacted the people of Appalachia, including pregnant women. The rate of women addicted to opioids during pregnancy has quadrupled in 15 years, and in 2017, over 5,040 mothers in Ohio were addicted to illegal drugs at the time of delivery. An average of 6 infants a day are admitted to hospitals with Neonatal Abstinence Syndrome.*

After reading this to the participants, participants write down the first three words that came to mind when they think of Destiny and then set the paper aside.

After participants viewed the full twelve videos, they again write down the first three words that came to mind when they think of Destiny. The words from each list (pre-experience and post-experience) are compiled and used to create "word clouds." According to the Google definition, a word cloud is "an image composed of words used in a particular text or subject, in which the size of each word indicates its frequency or importance." We focused on the most powerful 6–10 words as the most prominent in the following images.

This exercise serves two purposes: it allows participants to reflect on their own bias and shift in attitude immediately, and it provides qualitative pre- and post-data about what participants think about a young, pregnant woman with an addiction to opioids.

At the end of the training session, participants reflected on the differences between their two lists of words. Notably, the participants were reluctant to share their actual lists aloud to the group, indicating a heightened degree of self-awareness about their own bias. They would, however, share that their first list was more pessimistic and hopeless than their second; after learning about Destiny's story, though, they had more hope and focused on her strengths. The words they listed were more optimistic about her ability to be a mother. To illustrate the results, compare Figure 16.1a (pre-experience) with Figure 16.1b (post-experience) from the same group (Group A). Figures 16.2a and 16.2b illustrate the same process with a different group (Group B). Figures 16.3a and 16.3b again illustrate the same process with a third group (Group C).

Word clouds provide a visual representation of identified words. The words commonly repeated by multiple subjects appear more prominent in the word cloud; fewer mentions appear smaller. Upon completing the word cloud, we identify and categorize the "tone" of each cloud's most prominent words. Traditionally speaking, tone words are literary devices used by authors to convey tone through diction, viewpoint, and syntax. For example, they can connote a character's positive, negative or neutral attitudes about a subject matter in writing fiction. In fiction, they can be used to set up a mood. Here, we applied the tone word model to the word association activity to identify a shift in attitude before and after the presentation.

The tone words are noticeable when comparing the pre- and post-word clouds from each group. The most prominent tone words in the pre-test from Group A (Figure 16.1a):

■ pregnancy
■ opioids
■ struggle

The most prominent tone words in the pre-test from Group B (Figure 16.2a):

■ treatment
■ support
■ struggle
■ strong
■ dangerous

The most prominent tone words in the pre-test from Group C (Figure 16.3a):

■ struggle
■ dangerous

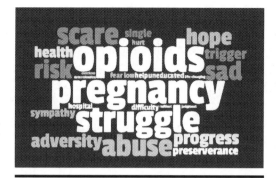

Figure 16.1a Group A pre-experience word cloud

Figure 16.1b Group A post-experience word cloud

Figure 16.2a Group B pre-experience word cloud

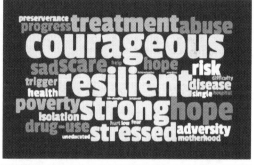

Figure 16.2b Group B post-experience word cloud

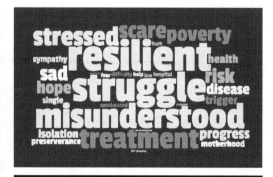

Figure 16.3a Group C pre-experience word cloud

Figure 16.3b Group C post-experience word cloud

As stated, tone words can be positive, negative, or neutral, and their connotation can change depending on the context. We identified five out of these ten words that have a negative tone, or 50% ("dangerous" [used twice], and "struggle" [used three times]). The prominent tone of post-collection words was more favorable.

The most prominent tone words in the post-test from Group A (Figure 16.1b):

- addiction
- aid
- support
- hope
- stress

The most prominent tone words in the post-test from Group B (Figure 16.2b):

- hope
- courageous
- determined
- strong
- resilient

The most prominent tone words in the post-test from Group C (Figure 16.3b):

- help
- strong
- resilient
- determined
- hope

Out of these fifteen words, we assessed thirteen to have a positive tone, or 87% (we identified all of the words except "addiction" and "aid" as positive). When comparing these images side-by-side, it is apparent that the participants were feeling more optimistic and positive toward Destiny and her situation as a young, pregnant woman struggling with opioid use disorder after learning more about her family history, trauma, and challenges.

While word clouds may not represent long-term change, we find them powerful visual representations of how using cine-VR can help reduce bias and increase empathy. They give us information about the importance of knowing someone's story and background when providing health care services. They also provide a collaborative tool that demonstrates how we might believe that we are operating from a strengths-based perspective. Nevertheless, our biases are present without us even realizing it.

Conclusion

Discussing the word association lists at the end of delivering the Destiny training emphasizes the importance of recognizing bias when working with patients and clients with substance abuse disorder. It personalizes the message that we all carry biases, even with training, and we need to be aware of them and not allow them to affect our services. When participants leave the *Destiny*

Empathy Training, they take with them the story of Destiny, as well as an increased awareness of their preconceptions about clients.

As healthcare providers, we have the privilege of hearing the stories of our clients. Doing so is not just part of the job; it is part of the *work* that helps clients to heal. Childhood trauma, abuse, and neglect connect inextricably to maladaptive behaviors of adults. The use of cine-VR technology to make these connections is powerful and versatile. Integrating technology, such as what we used to create Destiny, into child welfare, behavioral health, and medical training centers stand to benefit professionals, patients, and clients.

In implementing word clouds to capture a shift in attitude for individuals struggling with substance use disorder, we stumbled upon a simple yet useful tool that illuminated our work. It bridged the explicit goal of telling Destiny's story with that of growing empathy. We found that it is beneficial to process the exercise before the session ends collectively and, if possible, to share word clouds compiled from previous groups to illustrate the change visually.

Cine-VR allowed users to personally explore details in Destiny's life, including her workplace and living environments. If seeing out a patient's window cultivates empathy, this project comes very close to making this happen, albeit briefly, through the use of cine-VR technology.

Viewing

To view and download cine-VR examples mentioned in this chapter, please visit: https://vimeo.com/channels/cinevr4healthcare/ (***password:** cineVR4health*).

Notes

1. Brener L, von Hippel W, von Hippel C, Resnick I, Treloar C. Perceptions of discriminatory treatment by staff as predictors of drug treatment completion: Utility of a mixed methods approach. Drug Alcohol Rev. 2010 Sep;29(5):491–7. https://doi.org/10.1111/j.1465-3362.2010.00173.x
2. Fonti, S., Davis, D. & Ferguson, S. (2016). The attitudes of healthcare professionals toward women using illicit substances in pregnancy: A cross-sectional study. *Women and Birth, 29(4)* 330–335. https://doi.org/10.1016/j.wombi.2016.01.001
3. Author's note: initial results are not published.

Additional References

DePaolo, C. & Wilkinson, K. (2014). Get your head into the clouds: Using word clouds for analyzing qualitative assessment data. *TechTrends: Linking Research and Practice to Improve Learning, 58(3)*, 38–44. https://doi.org/10.1007/s11528-014-0750-9

Milliman, H. 2019, March 2. *SAT/ACT prep online guides and tips: 122 tone words to set the mood in your story.* https://blog.prepscholar.com/list-of-tone-words

NIDA. 2020, April 3. Ohio: Opioid-involved deaths and related arms. Retrieved on December 19, 2020, from https://www.drugabuse.gov/drug-topics/opioids/opioid-summaries-by-state/ohio-opioid-involved-deaths-related-harms

Odhayani, A.A., Watson, W.J., & Watson, L. (2013). Behavioural consequences of child abuse. *Canadian Family Physician*, 59(8), 831–836. https://www.ncbi.nlm.nih.gov/pmc/articles/PMC3743691/#__ffn_sectitle

Phillips, E.S., Wood, G.J., Yoo, J., Ward, K., Hsiao, S.C., Singh, M.I., & Morris, B. (2018). A virtual field practicum: Building core competencies prior to agency placement. *Journal of Social Work Education*, 54(4), 620–640. http://dx.doi.org.proxy.library.ohio.edu/10.1080/10437797.2018.1486651

Van Boekel, L.C., Brouweres, E.P.M., van Weeghel, J., & Garretsen, H.F.L. (2013). Stigma among health professionals toward patients with substance use disorders and its consequences for healthcare delivery: Systematic review. *Drug and Alcohol Dependence, 131(1–2)*, 22–35. https://doi.org/10.1016/j.drugalcdep.2013.02.018

Yalom, I.D. (2017). *The gift of therapy: An open letter to a new generation of therapists and their patients.* Harper Perennial.

Chapter 17

Preparation for Emotional Disturbances

Patricia McSteen and Rick Sargent

Contents

Picture the following situation:

> *You are a student on campus in the waning days of summer before your Junior year. You have accepted a position as a resident assistant (RA) to help defray the cost of attending school. As an engineering major, you have a considerable course load staring you in the face, mounting debt, and a desire to have comfortable on-campus housing. A friend tells you that all you have to do is sit through a couple of training sessions. You walk out a freshly-minted RA, ready to tackle mediation of roommate disputes, policy violations, and the occasional alcohol incident. You spend the better part of two days in a room with others like yourself, discussing how to fill out the appropriate documentation about obtaining replacements for lost residence hall room keys and how to make a creative, educational bulletin board.*
>
> *After lunch on the final day, you will run through mock scenarios to know what to do when the rest of the students arrive on campus. Each of you receives a half-dozen index cards numbered 1–6. On one side are a few words describing the scenario; homesick student, noise complaint, and guest policy violation. RA veterans from last year are staged in*

DOI: 10.4324/9781003168683-21

different small rooms down the hall from you. Their job is to read from their scripted index card and act out the scenario with as much realism as they can muster. Your response will be based on the combined total of 12 hours of training received in the last two days. You are as prepared as you will get and hope that your future engineering firm appreciates the rigorous training you have just endured. You wait your turn for what seems like an hour, then enter the room with a sticky note marked, "Scenario 1."

The age-old "index card scenario" training method is the standard for instruction in many study and training fields. It occupies space in our training programs because those who prepare the curriculum see it as an established norm. We recognize that budget, time, and a dearth of creativity play a role in maintaining the status quo. Nevertheless, does this scenario prepare the participant to handle the situation effectively? Perhaps – but is this the most effective way to present the material? Are we putting people in a position to succeed and giving them the best tool to build effective habits?

Based upon an informal pilot study at Ohio University, we argue that cine-VR can create a more potent and versatile tool for building effective habits in people preparing to deal with an individual with a mental health crisis. The result is a trainee who is in a better position to succeed.

Our Modern Landscape

Since the tragic shooting at Virginia Tech in 2007, the landscape in higher education has dramatically changed. Best practices dictate that all campuses have behavioral intervention and threat assessment teams to address potentially dangerous people and situations. Multidisciplinary teams often include higher education professionals in student affairs, campus law enforcement, student conduct, counseling centers, housing and residence life, academic affairs, and legal counsel. The primary focus of behavioral intervention is to provide support and resources to community members experiencing a behavioral or mental health crisis while assessing the greater community's threat risk. In short, these processes attempt to assess harm to self versus others, both while balancing the rights of a person and the community's safety.

One goal of an effective behavioral intervention team (BIT) is to educate the campus community on the concept of "see something – say something." The goal of this type of training is to understand the classroom management to threat assessment continuum. University administrators, faculty members, and law enforcement professionals help the campus community understand a person's trajectory on the continuum through a collaborative process. Often a student will first demonstrate concerning behavior in the classroom or their residence hall, and without early intervention, the behavior can escalate to a more severe crisis or threat. Over the past fourteen years on the Ohio University campus, the two most common referral sources have consistently been faculty and residence life staff – demonstrating a need to adequately train these populations to understand how to work with people in crisis. Simultaneously, there is an evident and continued need to train law enforcement officers as well.

On a fundamental level, we realized that housing and residence life staff and law enforcement officers (LEO) required training to encounter a person in crisis in their living space (i.e., dorm room). In contrast, other BIT members (such as administrators or faculty) would not require such training. Therefore, the audience for this project focuses on housing and residence life staff and LEO. Despite their similarities, however, these two audiences are significantly different. Therefore, designing a training scenario to meet the needs of both housing and residence life staff (our primary audience) and LEO (our secondary audience) was crucial.

Similarities and Differences

Drawing from the traditional methods of training for people in danger or crises, a collaboration of content experts and technical experts created a checklist of five desired outcomes:

1. Build confidence through repetition, as repetition encourages confidence and resonates with the subject.
2. Immerse the participant in a dangerous situation without exposing them to danger.
3. Provide consistent (and consistently repeatable) training experiences.
4. Provide a unique, high-quality experience for every participant.
5. Find a cost-effective approach by decreasing the perpetual need for actors, props, and on-site locations.

These outcomes applied to both audiences, yet there are differences in content:

- **Housing and residence life staff (especially students) may be new to interacting with people in crisis.** While they may feel comfortable with a college dorm environment, personal interaction with a concerning student is probably entirely foreign. Staff training, therefore, will likely focus on "the big picture" of the initial interaction.
- **Law enforcement officers are well-trained to work with people in crisis.** More likely than not, their training needs might focus on practice rather than obtaining new skills. LEO also might benefit from being updated on current student culture and slang. LEO training, therefore, requires a deeper layer of instruction – one that moves beyond initially interacting with the person of concern and focuses instead on more careful observation and assessment of the situation.

Fortuitously, we discovered that cine-VR was able to not only provide a state-of-the-art approach that achieved our initial five outcomes but was also able to take the traditional (index card) method to a more sophisticated level. Depending upon the audience, cine-VR allows training facilitators to uncover multiple layers of meaning. Each facilitator can use an approach that combines traditional techniques (group discussion) with new technologies (cine-VR) to address predetermined learning outcomes for each particular audience.

Project Genesis

This project started simple enough, a chance meeting of individuals with vastly different education, training, and experience. In early 2017, the GRID Lab held an exhibition to highlight various virtual reality, augmented reality, and immersive design projects. After this demonstration, Rick Sargent with the Ohio University Police Department (OUPD) approached the GRID Lab to discuss utilizing some of their technologies to create an updated training path for first responders. Explaining the first-hand experience with the traditional approach in entry-level law enforcement training concerning interactions with dangerous or emotionally disturbed individuals, Sargent conveyed that this type of training relies heavily on stale role-playing scenarios acted out by peers or instructors. Similarly, this is the same observation when discussing residence hall first responders (student RAs or professional residence hall directors). The role-playing technique was outdated and not adequate for many reasons, including:

- The scenarios were inconsistent from one person to the next.
- The scenarios were often not believable or mentally/emotionally immersive.
- The scenarios were time-consuming and labor-intensive to execute.
- What might work for one audience (RAs) might not work for a different audience (OUPD), and vice versa.

In law enforcement, implementing a new curriculum or best practices takes a considerable amount of time, even at the state level. Training budgets are low, time is a premium, and even with the student's best intentions and enthusiastic participation, no accurate realism level is achievable. Participants receive vastly different experiences from their peers, as the presentation of the material is, at best, inconsistent, and at worst, a mailed-in pantomime of what should be a stress-inducing or intellectually stimulating experience. Piloting a new approach seemed like a practical way to better prepare both RAs and OUPD audiences.

Patti McSteen, from the Ohio University Office of the Dean of Students, joined the team. It quickly became apparent that there was an opportunity to broaden the collaboration's focus and serve a larger demographic within the university setting. Through collaboration with our BIT and OUPD, McSteen reinforced the need to train those in the university community that may find themselves thrust into a situation with a distressed or disruptive individual. The obvious audiences who would benefit most from this type of training are residence life staff and faculty teaching assistants. Behavioral intervention is a campus-wide concern, but the individuals on the front line do not always have the proper training to adequately prepare them for these scenarios.

As we brainstormed with John Bowditch and Eric Williams, from the GRID Lab, we began to realize that cine-VR may be able to address all of our primary objectives:

- Since cine-VR is a recorded medium, the experiences are consistent, repeatable, and consistently repeatable.
- By creating high-quality experiences, participants can feel immersed in a dangerous situation without being exposed to danger.
- As cine-VR is (ideally) experienced within a personal headset that allows each participant to explore their surroundings as they choose, it creates a unique experience.
- Cine-VR can provide experiences that eliminate the perpetual need for actors, props, and on-site locations.

Furthermore, the GRID Lab had recently conducted a pilot project where they recorded live emergency room traumas to train medical interns. During the process, they made an unusual discovery. While the cine-VR experiences achieved their desired effect with their primary audience, other emergency room staff members also found the experiences useful for separate training. Because each participant controls what to observe within cine-VR, each experience is unique. The experience is different from watching a film or video – where the images have a more restricted field of view.

In cine-VR, the participant becomes "the director." A medical intern can watch what the doctor does, but a nursing student can watch what the head nurse does instead. In essence, there are various ways to view each cine-VR experience uniquely. This potential was intriguing, and we began thinking of how one cine-VR experience could simultaneously train novice RAs and first responders.

First Draft

Our first iteration in December of 2017 involved multiple scenarios recorded in unoccupied residence hall rooms during the semester break. The production team consisted of graduate and undergraduate students, faculty, and content expert administrative staff. The diversity in this team production approach worked well in drawing upon individual expertise and resources. Differing viewpoints contributed to the authenticity of the scenario while incorporating the most current technology. For example, current trends in distressing or self-harm behaviors such as ingesting laundry detergent pods and drug and alcohol abuse popularized by social media provided valuable insight into realistic residence hall behavior.

The collaborative approach allowed the production team to brainstorm innovative ways to experiment with the cine-VR capabilities, which initiated creative uses of the technology not seen before. Content experts were on hand to ensure continuity and content accuracy. The recording of the scripted scenes happened in a room that two student residents typically occupy. It was shot with 360° cameras and wireless microphones hidden on the actors for audio capture. The student actors performed in a prescribed area of the set that was relatively tight.

Unfortunately, the project was not successful. Everything looked good while we were shooting. However, when we saw the experience in a headset, we noted a wide variety of issues:

A. Frankly, the experience was boring. There was no real "story" other than the fact that the student was in crisis. Yes, the room's objects were "warning signs," but there was no real connection (no story) between the objects and the student.

B. We tried various ways to move the camera from the hallway into the dorm room. Initially, the idea was to physically move the camera from one location to the next on a small, rolling platform as if the audience member was "walking" from the hallway into the room. However, if the audience was not looking "forward" as the camera moved, the audience member immediately felt nauseous. Their vestibular system was out of synch with the visual information that the body was receiving[1]. We also tried a special effect to make the audience feel like they were transporting from one room to the next. This approach felt hokey.

C. We brightly lit the scene so that everything was visible. While this allowed the viewer to see all objects in the room, it did not create any atmosphere. This lack of atmosphere, we believe, diminished the performance and did not evoke an emotional response in the audience.

D. We attempted to record all noises "naturally" from the position of the camera. We needed to hear actors easily, so we decided not to add additional sound to the room. The recordings were "authentic," and it was easy to hear the actor, but the environment did not seem realistic.

E. With limited space available in the residence hall rooms, the cine-VR camera placement was in the background. Viewers could observe all the action without adjusting their perspective, and we could have recorded the scenes with a standard camera configuration and achieved the same effect. The footage lacked depth and resulted in something that simply looked like a fly-on-the-wall perspective.

F. The viewer played no role in the scenario. It was a completely passive experience.

Second Draft

After a well-intended but ultimately scrapped first run, we again decided to mock up an unoccupied residence hall room in the off-season and presented a student in crisis. Our second attempt
was during the summer months of 2018, again focused on a student experiencing a mental health
crisis. However, this time we addressed our five previous mistakes:

The set dressing emulated a residence hall room belonging to a traditionally aged college
student: unkempt and complete with an array of empty food containers, scattered laundry, and
frankly, overtly dangerous props (see Figure 17.1). This time we distinctly crafted the experience to
utilize the immersive aspect of the cine-VR:

A. We chose to craft a specific story, thereby allowing the audience to recognize multiple items
   of concern: weapons, indicators of a lack of personal care, drug abuse, and alcohol abuse. All
   combined, these items told a consistent and convincing story about the student of concern,
   why she was behaving the way she was, and possible outcomes of the scenario.

B. Lacking the ability to move the viewer/camera between spaces effectively, we elected to edit
   the two scenes together. In retrospect, this seems like a simple solution, but believe it or not,
   it took trial and error to find the solution. Although the cine-VR had a fixed-perspective, a
   quick fade transition transports the audience from the hallway to a point within the dorm
   room – a location that was within their earlier line of sight. This simple solution kept the
   storyline consistent for the audience and effectively eliminated the need for "teleporting"
   or moving the camera. We chose to use visually limiting stimuli. In our second scenario,
   we set a tone to invoke sensory deprivation by purposely recording in a dimly lit space

**Figure 17.1 Proposed set decorations and camera placement for the second draft *Emotional
Disturbance* experience**

using soft and indirect lighting. The lighting created a more foreboding mood. Secondarily, it enhanced the performance of the actor in the scene. The low lighting also forced the audience to pay more careful attention to their surroundings; they had to find the objects because they were less apparent. Aggressive thrasher metal music was added during post-production to amplify the scene's tension, creating a compelling sensory experience. We felt that this added to the ambiance and helped to tell the story better.

C. The converted room typically would have been a three-occupant space, but we staged it as a two-person room. The project team included staff who were able to provide professional staging of the space. The increased space and intentional placement of props were critical for camera location options. We moved the camera to represent the person having the conversation – rather than observing like a fly-on-the-wall.

D. With the inability to directly interact with the student actor, we designed the scenario to provide the viewer with talking points to guide the interaction. We applied a technique involving on-screen dialogue called guided simulation. Internally, we call this "Karaoke VR": the process of encouraging the audience to read lines of dialogue as if they are having a conversation with a character in the cine-VR experience. This karaoke approach used in other projects provided the participant with the confidence to say correct responses at the right moment. The actor provided appropriate lags in dialogue and responded to what the viewer *should* have read on the screen. (See Chapter 18 for more detail about guided simulation techniques).

Preliminary Results

When we presented our second version to test audiences, participants remarked how powerful the experience was, raising heart rates in some, eliciting a fight-or-flight response in others, while causing some to become emotional regarding the urge to comfort or parent the student. Viewers noted that the piece set a clear tone and created the intended distraction and anxiety.

The viewer had the opportunity to observe the disturbing dialog of the trained student actor and soak in the confined space's ambiance. While designed to agitate the viewer, care was taken to present the student actor as upsetting, based on the context of their words, but refrained from being overtly menacing or directly threatening to the viewer.

The first cine-VR project's intended audience was first responder roles, specifically, residence life staff (professional and para-professional) and law enforcement professionals. The final product was piloted with a graduate-level behavioral intervention class of aspiring student affairs professionals and professionals in behavioral intervention through a professional conference presentation.

At the professional conference, participants at the session (Campus Collaboration to Train First Responders Using Virtual Reality Technology, National Behavioral Intervention Association, 2018, San Antonio, TX) provided positive feedback. It enhanced the challenge commonly faced in training the campus community to better "see something – say something." In addition to using cine-VR as a practical training approach, there was a deeper appreciation for the collaboration amongst content experts across campus to solve a university-wide problem.

Similarly, graduate students received a brief overview of the scenario, engaged in the cine-VR, and then processed the experience with the project creators. Analogous to the feedback from the conference presentation, the graduate students similarly shared a positive reaction. The students were very engaged with the technology and felt that this training approach would benefit first responders. Putting the trainee in a stressful environment with prompts on responding to a

Photo 17.1   The staged room contained concerning items such as weapons and empty alcohol containers

person in crisis seemed to create exposure and repetition. Those who worked in a residential setting affirmed that the scenario was realistic and would help train new student staff to engage with a person in crisis while also learning to be aware of their surroundings. The staged room contained many concerning items (prescription bottles, empty alcohol containers, and weapons – (see Photo 17.1) that prompt meaningful follow-up discussions about what to do in this kind of situation.

Others working outside of the residential housing area expressed excitement in the possibilities of training staff in their different content areas (for example, student workers in campus recreation and student union/event management). The graduate students' reactions seemed to reinforce the transferable nature of cine-VR related to student affairs and higher education. The pilot group asserted that traditional-aged college students would respond positively to training using this modality. Another outcome from this pilot group was the importance of developing a facilitator's guide to processing the cine-VR experience. One of the most notable things discovered when discussing the scenario with viewers is their failure to notice the dangerous items staged in the room. Perhaps tunnel vision, adjusting to the new technology and presentation, or personal experience played a role. Nearly 85% of viewers failed to recognize the handgun placed within reach of the actor and the viewer. Those in law enforcement immediately noticed the weapons in the room, while others focused solely on the individual and were oblivious to their surroundings.

Lessons Learned

Our first draft project was important for many reasons. We spent a significant amount of time in the planning phase, including scriptwriting, staging the space, and anticipating the challenges. While the first project did not yield a usable product, the lessons learned significantly impacted the second production's success.

■ It is apparent now how powerful post-production audio can be. We were able to create a mood of our choosing after the production was complete.

- Similarly, lighting choices directly affect the viewer's mood. "Seeing everything" is not always the best choice to make.
- Adjustments in both audio and image allow us to tailor the experience while maintaining the clarity of the actor's performance.
- It is crucial to have plenty of physical space in which to operate. The space's actual look is less important than how it can "feel" by altering the lighting and adding claustrophobic music.
- We learned that camera placement within the action is critical to making the audience feel as if they are part of the story.

Additionally, there was one other significant realization that we made during production. Initially, we scripted (and recorded) interactions with a student in crisis and a resident advisor who responded to the same situation positively or negatively. GRID Lab research suggests that the use of cine-VR can create neuropathways that the viewer remembers[2]. We reconsidered the idea of showing the negative response and ultimately decided to delete those scenes based upon research that has suggested the unintended consequence of the viewer "reverting to training" and that training being negative[3],[4]. We concluded that all training should be presented as a best-practice and desired response.

- Looking back, when we showed this to our pilot audience, they did not say the words out loud but instead merely read along in their heads. This act would increasingly become a challenge because some participants read quicker than others, and some may feel embarrassed and possibly self-conscious about mistakes as they read. We identified another concern through feedback because the dialogue may trigger a personal or emotional response in an unintended individual. Also, non-native English speakers and people with visual impairments might find the pace of the program challenging.

In conclusion, our preliminary results found that using cine-VR technology to immerse a training participant in a real-life scenario improves the learning outcomes identified for responding to challenging situations. It allows for a safe environment where an individual can experience the sensory stressors of lighting, sound, and space while connecting users and providing a consistent experience that promotes critical discussion necessary to process training experiences that are uncomfortable and challenging.

For the last twenty years, using available technology to best train first responders is a cost-effective means to deliver consistent content and facilitate a meaningful discussion that promotes learning[5].

Developing a facilitation guide to accompany the modules will be a critical supplement to using the cine-VR technology. The pilot training conducted shows that the cine-VR technology provided a rich experience. However, without critical discussion and processing immediately afterward, the viewer would be left with many unanswered questions. We believe that the combination of technology and face-to-face discussion will become the best practice in training for response to people in crisis.

Viewing

To view and download cine-VR examples mentioned in this chapter, please visit: https://vimeo.com/channels/cinevr4healthcare/ (***password:** cineVR4health).*

Notes

1. Maeda, T., H. Ando and M. Sugimoto, "Virtual Acceleration With Galvanic Vestibular Stimulation in a Virtual Reality Environment," IEEE Proceedings. Virtual Reality, Bonn, 2005, pp. 289–290, doi: 10.1109/VR.2005.1492799.
2. Williams, E. R., M. Love and C. Love. Virtual Reality Cinema: Narrative Tips and Techniques. Focal Press/Routledge. February 2021.
3. Gage, William. "Four Fresh Ideas." Law Officer, November 30, 2016. https://www.lawofficer.com/four-fresh-ideas/.
4. Raunak M. Pillai, Abbey M. Loehr, Darren J. Yeo, Min Kyung Hong, and Lisa K. Fazio, (2020) "Are There Costs to Using Incorrect Worked Examples in Mathematics Education?", Journal of Applied Research in Memory and Cognition, 9, 4, pp. 519–531.
5. Baños, Rosa & Botella, Cristina & Alcañiz Raya, Mariano & Liaño, V & Guerrero, B & Rey, B. (2005). Immersion and Emotion: Their Impact on the Sense of Presence. Cyberpsychology & Behavior: The impact of the Internet, Multimedia and Virtual Reality on Behavior and Society, 7, pp. 734–741. 10.1089/cpb.2004.7.734.

Chapter 18

Guided Simulations

Matt Love

Contents

Guided Simulations are cine-VR experiences developed by the GRID Lab where a viewer is "guided" through a simulation via text prompts. These prompts help create the perception of being part of a conversation instead of idly viewing a conversation.

What we now call Guided Simulations began as a concept called "Karaoke VR" in 2018. Students of Eric R. Williams' VR Storytelling class were tasked with exploring practical uses of VR. One group had heard of Nationwide Children's Hospital's difficulty training providers to deliver bad news to patients. The skill needed was difficult to attain without practice but, for obvious reasons, practicing on actual patients was an unattractive proposition.

DOI: 10.4324/9781003168683-22

One group of graduate students (of which I was a member) found examples of hospitals using professional actors to train for these scenarios. The challenge of such an approach included finding/training appropriate actors, refining their emotional responses, scheduling issues, reserving proper locations, and, not least, the cost of synthesizing these elements into a high caliber performance. Such training could be practical but was resource-intensive.

The students realized that each of these shortcomings could be addressed by cine-VR's strengths. Actors could work with a director to refine their performance, and the location only needed to be meticulously set once. Once recorded, the same simulation could benefit countless trainees at any hour of the day or night. Given the training's scalability, we theorized that Guided Simulations could be used to accommodate a variety of challenging topics or patients.

Our main sticking point was how the viewer would interact with the actor while still meeting one very critical objective: the project needed to work on readily available, low-cost HMDs. The solution was to embed text within the video file that the viewer would read as if they were reading subtitles for a foreign film. However, in this case, the character whose lines they were reading would be their own.

With this concept in place, the team moved forward with implementation. They selected scenarios that covered two types of experiences:

1. The trainee would be taking on the role of a medical professional sharing difficult news with parents regarding their children (see Photo 18.1);
2. The trainee would take on the role of a police offer sharing difficult news with family members during a visit to their home.

The approach surpassed expectations as person after person took the headset off, saying they felt as if they had been in the room with the patient. One simulation, in particular, was so emotional that we felt compelled to provide disclaimers before viewing. We entered the project in the Ohio University Student Research and Creativity Expo and claimed the first-place prize. That early prototype has since been refined, maturing into what we now call Guided Simulations.

Photo 18.1   Screengrab from the 2018 Breaking Bad News project that initiated "Karaoke VR"

Basic Tenets of Guided Simulations

The goal of Guided Simulations is to prepare individuals for similar conversations in real life. As such, several basic tenets have coalesced from our experience.

1. Space must seem authentic: If the simulation is to train front desk staff to interact with hotel guests, the viewer must have experience set in a hotel. The setting (furniture, lighting, background noise, and art on the wall) must all say, "you're in a hotel."
2. The actors must seem authentic: Each individual present within the simulation must fit the role they are playing. For instance, a simulation where the viewer is delivering bad news to parents will require exceptional actors who can convince us that they are genuinely experiencing the emotion of loss. Just like realistic blocking, casting is essential to maintain the illusion that this scenario is unfolding naturally in front of the viewer. Content experts help with this process during recording (see Chapter 19).
3. The written scenario must seem authentic: An authentic location and actors will be for naught if the scenario introduces cracks in the experience's façade. For this reason, subject matter experts (SMEs) must play a central role in the development of the Guided Simulation scripts. Compelling experiences require an interdisciplinary approach where the scripting, set design, cinematography, and directing are all informed by the SMEs to maximize the likelihood that the viewer will become fully immersed in the experience. Professionals will be pulled out of an inauthentic experience.
4. Unlike PREality experiences (see Chapters 3–5), Guided Simulations should be a singular event. Whereas PREality leverages repetition to create familiarity with routines or locations, such understanding is detrimental to Guided Simulation. If a series of Guided Simulations aims to help a medical professional break the terrible news to a parent, the actors and responses should vary with each simulation. No two people will respond the exact same way. Therefore, neither should any two Guided Simulation experiences.

Project Examples

Once refined, Guided Simulations were adopted by other projects. For example, the Dean of Students' office, along with the Ohio University Police Department, incorporate Guided Simulation to train people to navigate interactions with emotionally disturbed students (see Chapter 17). In fact, one Guided Simulation was so powerful that the Dean of Students questioned whether we had gone too far. Content experts McSteen and Sargent were quick to assure her that it was an actor playing the student's role and that this was not an interaction with an actual emotionally disturbed student.

The GRID Lab's most significant application of Guided Simulations has been with the Medicaid Equity Simulation Project. This state-funded project was created to explore VR simulations' capability to reduce implicit bias among healthcare providers. Our project explored the lives of two fictional characters: Lula Mae and Destiny.

In exploring Lula Mae, a seventy-two-year old grandmother struggling to cope with her diabetes, we follow her interaction with both a primary care physician and her pharmacist (see Chapter 15). For Destiny, a twenty-three-year old pregnant woman with a history of an opioid use disorder, we follow her interactions with a nurse and a social worker (see Chapter 16). Each of the four series culminates with two Guided Simulations. The first is an opportunity for the viewer to

Photo 18.2 Screengrab from the *Destiny* project illustrating the development of Guided Simulation

have a conversation with the respective provider (physician, pharmacist, nurse, or social worker). The second is an opportunity for the viewer to have a discussion with Lula Mae or Destiny (see Photo 18.2).

Moving forward, the GRID Lab is researching (and encourages others to explore) the effectiveness of Guided Simulations in three distinct areas:

Timing of the Conversation

As a result of our earlier work, we note the importance of timing conversations so that the viewer is given ample time to read and process the text. The average rate of speed for conversations in English is between 120 and 150 words per minute[1]. However, this rate is based on speaking ones' own thoughts, not reading what someone else has written. Anecdotally, we have found that reading aloud from a printed text with which one is familiar (for instance, a screenwriter reading their own material) is similar to the average speed for conversations. We have found that reading someone else's text takes approximately 1.25 times as long to read aloud for the first time. Therefore, what a person familiar with the text can read aloud in ten seconds, someone new to the material will often take 12–13 seconds to read comfortably.

To account for this, we typically have the "reader" on set to read the text slowly (at "about 75% speed") as if they were reading it for the first time, leaving a slight additional pause for each paragraph. Care must be taken to ensure that the actor usually responds (at 100% speed) even though the reader progresses slowly. With rehearsal, this is a simple matter for any seasoned actor, and a conversation delivered in this manner provides optimal results.

Value of Viewing in a Headset

Early indicators suggest that viewing Guided Simulations in a headset is more likely to produce the desired results than via other methods (i.e., handheld device or flatscreen monitor) because distractions are minimized, and engagement is maximized. This will come as no surprise to those who have read studies that show that students who take notes during lectures are more likely to retain the information. Isolating the viewer within a headset focuses their attention.

Studies in this area are ongoing. Influenced in part by Peper and Meyer's work in the late 1970s[2], two key ideas are suggested: (1) increasing the general attention process within a student may lead to better concentration; and (2) "notetaking" may encourage students to process material at a deeper level[3]. Both suggest that the degree of effort required of a task (e.g., through engagement in a Guided Simulation) may result in a more robust learning experience.

Significance of the Viewer Reading Text Aloud

The physical act of speaking the words in Guided Simulation (as opposed to reading them silently) appears to affect the participant. We postulate that this process may be similar to the act of "affect labeling" (the act of putting your emotions into words). Affect labeling has been used to manage negative emotional responses, with neuroimaging studies suggesting a possible neurocognitive pathway for this process[4]. Further, studies at both Hiroshima University and Doshisha University in Japan illustrate that affect labeling may reduce uncertainty feelings[5]. The GRID Lab speculates that Guided Simulation may act similarly to affect labeling by mitigating negative emotional responses and reducing feelings of uncertainty during times of stressful conversation. Perhaps the ability to "practice" highly dynamic conversations in a safe environment has a different physiological effect (and is more effective) than silently reading the exact words. We propose this as a direction for future research.

The Effects of Guided Simulations

Our work with Guided Simulations has subjectively demonstrated that participants benefit from the experience. Participants have expressed that they felt a stronger connection to the character they interacted with, particularly those who complete the exercise aloud. Further, completing multiple simulations on a particular topic creates familiarity with vernacular of the subject matter, resulting in a feeling similar to the "on the job" experience.

Entities that employ Guided Simulations as an integral element of the training process enjoy the following effects:

Increased Variety

When training an individual for interpersonal interaction, it is likely vital for them to be prepared to interact with individuals from different ethnic, socioeconomic, and gender identity backgrounds. Having the trainee complete live interactions with a diverse group of simulated patients could prove challenging, while having a library of Guided Simulations at hand which includes the desired subset of individuals is less problematic.

Location Specificity

As with several of the effects of leveraging Guided Simulations, higher production value can be obtained by capturing real locations and atmosphere. Suppose a simulation requires the trainee to be in an emergency room while speaking to a frantic family member where chaos abounds. In that case, the ability to replicate the scene in an actual ER with any sort of frequency is nearly impossible. However, with a Guided Simulation, the experience can be created once (during a slow time in an actual ER using actors to simulate chaos).

Schedule Independence

Because Guided Simulations are experienced within an HMD, they are time and location independent. A trainee could be in their office, at home, or elsewhere, and when they put on the HMD, they are transported to the training location. This eliminates the struggle of scheduling actors, locations, and the trainees themselves. Nevertheless, it must be noted that many scenarios do benefit from post-viewing debriefing sessions.

Increased Consistency

Once the "perfect scene" has been captured with Guided Simulations, it is consistently repeatable any number of times. If multiple individuals on different occasions view the training, they will experience the same performance. Providing this level of consistency allows organizations to fine-tune a Guided Simulation at a granular level and reap the benefit of that effort.

Lower Cost per Experience Over Time

While high-quality cine-VR production can be expensive at its outset, it is difficult to overstate the value economies of scale bring to Guided Simulations. The cost of a simulated patient experience is confined to the small handful of people who participated. For each new group of individuals, the fee must be incurred again. Through Guided Simulations, that cost can be spread across all participants over time. For organizations with multiple locations or large numbers of individuals to train, the savings grow exponentially. A simulation costing tens of thousands of dollars per participant could quickly be reduced to pennies per trainee over time.

Best Practices

Since Guided Simulation's effectiveness comes from the participants' suspension of disbelief, it is essential to craft the most convincing simulation possible. Bearing in mind the resources that will be invested, it's best to consider how many times the simulation will be viewed. The time or money spent has less significance when considered in light of the total number of viewings.

Script Development

The process of creating a compelling Guided Simulation begins long before the camera is turned on. The development of a clear, realistic, and accurate script is crucial to a successful project. It is recommended to consider three perspectives when developing your script: (1) SME, (2) the scriptwriter, and (3) the cine-VR cinematographer or storyteller. Work to find a balance among these voices to find a story that will have enough drama to pull the viewer in, play well to cine-VR's strengths, and remain faithful to the subject matter.

Pre-Production

With a strong script in hand, you'll want to turn your attention to cast and locations. Finding the right actor to embody your character may very well be the most challenging part of crafting a first-class simulation. The temptation is to use a subject matter expert since they know the material, pronunciations of terms, and particulars of using specialized equipment. However, in most cases, this is an ill-advised approach. Acting is a craft. It is much easier to teach an actor to model a piece of equipment or to rehearse with them to pronounce a difficult word than to teach an SME to act professionally. At the end of the project, you'll be glad you went the extra mile to get the right performer.

Likewise, the location, set decorations, and props are essential to get right. If your simulation occurs in a hospital waiting room, then your site, background noises, and people in the background all need to feel like that of an actual waiting room. In fact, if at all possible, record in a hospital waiting room! To achieve this level of detail, be prepared to shoot at odd times (when real locations may be more available), and create detailed plans for how to handle the following:

- Real-world passersby
- Space for the crew to hide while the camera is rolling
- Restrooms for cast and crew
- An area to stage equipment
- Parking
- And every other detail you can think of, no matter how small.

Last but not least, take the amount of time you anticipate for recording and double it. It's much better to let everyone go home early with a round of applause for a job well done than to run out of time and have to re-schedule actors, crew, equipment, and location for another day. For more details on preparing a team to work in a hospital, see Chapter 6.

Production: Camera Placement

For Guided Simulations to be effective, be sure the camera team places the camera at an appropriate height. We recommend a few inches below the average eye height of your target audience or a little below the actor's eye level with whom your viewer will be communicating. The actor should speak directly into the lens of the camera (see Photo 18.3). To make this easier, have the reader who your actor is playing off stand directly behind the camera with their head at camera height if possible. Regarding distance from the camera, place the camera slightly closer to your actor than a person would typically stand to have a one-on-one conversation. It is common for objects to appear farther away than what you might expect when viewed in an HMD. See Chapter 20 for more information on this topic.

Post-Production: Adding the Text

Adding the text to the video for your viewer to read is critical for Guided Simulations' current state. To properly place your text, you will need to know the target HMD you're preparing for. Different displays have different fields of view, which affects the amount of text you will want to display at any given moment and how large that text can be. The majority of mass-market HMDs have a field of view that is around 70°. Once you've determined that target, be sure to match your

Photo 18.3 Guided simulation camera set up for the *Lula Mae* project

preview window to that setting in your nonlinear editor of choice. The text should span no more than 70–80% of the view, and a maximum of three rows of text is recommended. Where possible, arrange your text such that it forms a pyramid shape, with the longest row being the last read. For additional information, please see Chapter 14.

In summary, Guided Simulation benefits have been enjoyed for years by the medical profession through the employment of actors as standardized patients[6]. While effective, this practice has complex scheduling requirements, lacks consistency, and is resource-intensive. When comparing Guided Simulations to the method of simulated patients, Guided Simulations' strengths become apparent and certainly worth consideration as a replacement of or (more likely) a complement to the use of standardized patients in healthcare training.

Viewing

To view and download cine-VR examples mentioned in this chapter, please visit: https://vimeo. com/channels/cinevr4healthcare/ (**password:** *cineVR4health).*

Notes

1. Barnard, Dom. *Average Speaking Rate and Words per Minute.* Virtual Speech January 28, 2018. https://virtualspeech.com/blog/average-speaking-rate-words-per-minute
2. Shrager L, & Mayer RE. Note-Taking Fosters Generative Learning Strategies in Novices. *Journal of Educational Psychology,* 1989;*81*(2), 263–264. https://doi.org/10.1037/0022-0663.81.2.263

3. Carol A. Carrier, Amy Titus, "The Effects of Notetaking: A Review of Rtudies", *Contemporary Educational Psychology*, 1979;*4*(4), 299–314. https://doi.org/10.1016/0361-476X(79)90050-X. (http://www.sciencedirect.com/science/article/pii/0361476X7990050X)
4. Lieberman MD, Eisenberger NI, Crockett MJ, Tom SM, Pfeifer JH, Way BM. Putting Feelings into Words: Affect Labeling Disrupts Amygdala Activity in Response to Affective Stimuli. *Psychological Science,* 2007;*18*(5):421–428. doi: 10.1111/j.1467-9280.2007.01916.x. PMID: 17576282.
5. Matsuguma, Miyu, M Shirai, M Miyatani, and T Nakao. "Effects of Affective Ambiguity on Emotion Regulation Through Affect Labeling" The Society for the Improvement of Psychological Science, October 13, 2020.
6. Hillier M, Williams TL, Chidume T. Standardization of Standardized Patient Training in Medical Simulation. [Updated 2020 Sep 4]. In: StatPearls [Internet]. Treasure Island (FL): StatPearls Publishing; 2020 Jan. Available from: https://www.ncbi.nlm.nih.gov/books/NBK560864/

Chapter 19

Medical Accuracy on Set

Carrie Love

Contents

Cine-VR is proving to be a powerful training tool in healthcare education.[1] When done well, it is experiential, captivating, and increases empathy levels in participants.[2] While storytelling and production value are significant, the content's accuracy is arguably a healthcare project's most crucial task. This accuracy is only obtainable if the production partners with medical experts serving as consultants. Over the past four years, the GRID Lab has developed best practices to assure medical accuracy on a cine-VR set.

Getting Started: Build the team

From the outset, it is essential to invite the right medical personalities to join the project. These individuals need to be knowledgeable in the project's subject matter, reliable with deadlines, willing to seek answers from others in their organization, creative problem solvers, and aware of the time commitment required to produce a cine-VR project. Finding individuals excited to take on a new challenge and follow the proposed plan will be essential.

DOI: 10.4324/9781003168683-23

Photo 19.1   Dr. Elizabeth Beverly (left) stands next to director Carrie Love behind the VR camera for a doctor visit scene to watch for accuracy on the set of Lula Mae

Each department involved with the project will come to the table with unique project values and goals. It is the producer's responsibility to work as a cross-cultural translator between these potentially competing values and goals, seeking solutions to meet everyone's needs.

Pay attention when someone repeatedly uses different language for the same thing or sits with a blank stare after someone from another area proposes an idea. These are potential cues that this person is attempting to translate new concepts into their context and workflow. Adding background information for why a group has a particular request can help give traction to the problem-solving process.

This process is why building a great team is so important. Not everyone will be flexible and generous while trying to function within a new framework. Mutual respect and an openness to learn go a long way toward building a functioning collaboration.

We have identified at least six different perspectives commonly experienced on medical cine-VR projects. The more the producer can be an ally to these values, the smoother the production will be.

Medical professionals will be concerned with rapidly shifting best practices. The medical field is highly diversified and intricate. Individuals receive extensive training to be successful in a very narrowly defined segment of the industry. When creating educational content on a subject, expect your medical experts to verify all instructional points via consultation with several people. The doctors, nurses, technicians, psychiatrists, social workers, and support staff will have learned the same concepts on any given topic, but with a different language and slightly different expected behaviors. The expert should consult others to ensure that project content is appropriate. While time-consuming, if your expert is not seeking this verification level, you may need to check with another expert to ensure things are coming together appropriately. It is possible your expert is too shy to speak up or is not thinking through all of the audience groups.

Scriptwriters are concerned with creating emotionally engaging and challenging stories by developing narratives that organically embed teaching points within character needs, obstacles, and conflict. They understand that small, symbolic moments more effectively affect audiences than loads of facts presented at once. But scriptwriters are not experts in medical content and should rely heavily on the medical team to inform the scripts. Beware scriptwriters (and directors) are trained storytellers and will want a fair amount of autonomy to build out the narratives.

Professionals in cine-VR production have an entirely different set of concerns than scriptwriters. People in the film industry get hired based on the quality of their last project. As such, they will be committed to making the best-looking images and the cleanest audio. They will want visually compelling locations where they can control light and microphone placement. They will also want sufficient time to set up the gear. Shots matter most when they support the story, and the crew will attempt to translate the scripts into the best images and audio they can on a tight schedule and within budget.

Art departments, similarly, are hired for their next job based on the quality of their most recent body of work. They need an adequate budget, time to collect items, and time to dress the set and actors. Art departments are experts in world-building and can elevate your stories' messaging and drama in subtle yet meaningful ways. Ensure they have time (they begin many weeks before production starts), money, and a support team.

Post-production and web professionals (two entirely different fields) care deeply about putting all the pieces together into a finalized, meaningful unit. Unfortunately, these individuals rarely create the images but offer significant insights on which images provide the greatest flexibility in editing and web design. They need to be kept in the loop when it comes to key talking points in the material. They also need copies of all relevant logos and branding rules they will be required to follow.

Actors develop complex inner lives for their characters while also managing the mechanics of medical acting. These mechanics include blocking (e.g., washing hands each time they enter the room) and pronouncing complicated terminology (i.e., lisinopril or glipizide). Most actors do not have a medical background and need special rehearsals to look and sound convincing to the medical experts in the audience who will catch every mistake (see Photo 19.2).

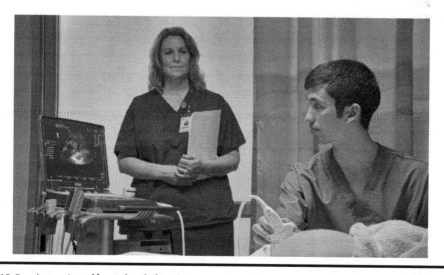

Photo 19.2   Actor Jennifer Inks (left) plays a prenatal nurse next to Zachary Taw, who was on set as an ultrasound consultant but agreed to make a cameo as an ultrasound technician in the *Destiny* project

Week 1: Develop a Plan

Set up an initial large meeting with all the various departments so key members can meet each other, share the vision and scope for the project, and discuss each group's values, strengths, and workflow requirements. Respecting individual workflow needs will give you a much better chance at success. If someone says they are rarely available on Thursday afternoons, try extremely hard to avoid scheduling events on Thursday afternoons. If a group needs the content to be accessible to a particular population, learn what that means and translate it into actionable priorities for the other groups.

Be honest about the workload required for each person and group when introducing the scope of the project. Describe the frequency of meetings, the outside work, and the timeline you expect to do the job well. This information will help individuals prepare for the tasks ahead. When preparing scripts with subject matter experts (SMEs) who don't have production backgrounds, let them know that scripts typically require between five to fifteen drafts to craft something accurate and compelling. The creative team will do the heavy lifting of making a narrative that brings content to life, but they in no way have the necessary medical knowledge to craft accurate content. The scriptwriters need experts to guide and correct the content's accuracy so that the resulting project can be a relevant, helpful tool. This process can only be accomplished in concert.

Week 2: Concept Development

Set up a series of regular meetings between the medical experts and the scriptwriters (every 1–2 weeks) where the narrative will be developed and turned into production-ready scripts. In the first meeting, discuss specifics about the goals of the project:

- Target audience
- Learning context *(e.g., university curriculum v. continuing education)*
- Format and timing *(e.g., live interaction v. online viewing at home)*
- Narrative specifics *(e.g., interactivity, length, supplemental materials)*

These meetings will be when scriptwriters and the producer set parameters to keep the project producible and on budget.

Once the project goals are defined, the medical experts need to prepare a list of information to start.

Subject matter: Which situations and patient groups are explored?

Desired learning outcomes: Examples include increased empathy, ability to identify obstacles a patient may face, ability to support a patient in their journey, or ability to encourage coworkers to be more supportive toward all patient groups.

Main character: Telling the story of one individual is more transformative than piling on statistics. Create an individual representing the group you want to explore and give them characteristics and background supported by research. Be sure to make the character likable. While they must carry the group's flaws, they also must offer the positives so viewers can identify with them as they struggle.

Worldbuilding: Paint a picture of the main character's world. What do this character's home and mode of transportation look like? Who is in their social circle? Give specifics that point to their economic situation.

Sample scenarios: Generate a list of scenarios that the character might have experienced in their lives that illustrate the key talking points of the educational outcomes, articulating what is notable about each scenario.

Week 3: Creating the Narrative

Once the medical team provides the first round of data, the scriptwriters will lock themselves in an office for hours to brainstorm and build out a world. They will flush out the main character, making them feel like a natural person with goals and obstacles to fight through. They will also invent supporting characters that add to both the drama and the story's educational aspects.

Week 4: Narrative Approval

After much discussion, planning, researching, and negotiating, the writers will outline the narrative journey to propose to the group. The scriptwriting team will want to present the story, or series of stories, to the medical professionals, highlighting the medical information organically embedded along the way.

The medical professionals need to identify any red flags that stand out. Because the writers are not likely to have a medical background, they may build out false plot points that do not exist in the real world. The producer should ask questions to see if the writers understand the concepts and to allow the medical professionals to offer information. The medical experts will likely have a list of questions to investigate to ensure the conversation is correct.

Please note, it is okay if the writers do not fully understand medical concepts or workflow; they just need to understand the basics to put the story pieces in the right place. Refining the accuracy can be sorted as the drafts begin.

Week 5: First Drafts

With an approved outline, the writers will go off and write the first draft of the scripts. At the same time, the medical professionals will seek answers to content questions. This round can take a couple of weeks, depending on the number of scripts needed.

Once the first drafts are complete, the experts and scriptwriters come together to review. I recommend reading drafts together aloud in the meeting instead of sending them out ahead of time. Hearing how a script sounds out loud is very helpful to see if the story is working. Before beginning the reading, assure the experts that first drafts of scripts are almost always terrible. The flow will feel false, and the medical content will be all wrong. Assure everyone that this is typical, and future drafts will correct this.

Read the drafts all the way through, as opposed to stopping to fix problems along the way. A functioning script should have a flow and build anticipation. Constant interruptions make it impossible to gauge if the flow and anticipation are working.

After the read, allow the experts to say what works and what does not work in the story. Common feedback on a first draft is, "This is really great, it's completely wrong, but it's great." Discuss if the concept is working for the goal of the project. Then have the experts articulate why they feel the story is "completely wrong" and see if they have suggestions on fixing the problem. Remember, there are two different aspects to address: the story itself and its medical accuracy.

At the end of this session, another round of drafts is written, and experts will have more questions to answer.

Week 6 and Onward: Finalizing Drafts

Continue having regular meetings to discuss and fix each draft. Be sure details work to assist in actor choices, costume design, location choices, and prop procurement. For future meetings, scripts can be sent out ahead of time or read within the meeting. We prefer to read the scripts within the meeting. Medical experts are often overloaded with other work, so any way to contain their obligation within our two-hour sessions made their lives easier.

Drafts need to continue until the scripts hit a point where both the writers and experts feel strong enough to move into production. At this point, the experts need to have a final signing-off, saying they think the script is ready to move forward. Hold off sharing scripts with your production team until this final approval, as old drafts will live forever, getting mixed in with newer drafts.

Utilizing Experts in Preproduction

The medical experts may or may not gauge precisely how little the cine-VR production team understands about the medical world. Even though the scripts go a long way to spelling out instructions, the creatives need medical questions answered.

Prediscussions on what to look for and final approvals should occur in most of the significant areas.

- **Locations:** the experts might help secure locations for the production
- **Set decorations:** pay extra attention to medical rooms and what is allowed
- **Medical props:** can room decorations, medications, and devices be borrowed?
- **Actor choices:** share audition tapes with the medical experts
- **Costumes:** experts may have access to authentic outfits
- **Makeup:** experts will have specific insights for make-up as it applies to particular injuries or ailments (see Photo 19.3).

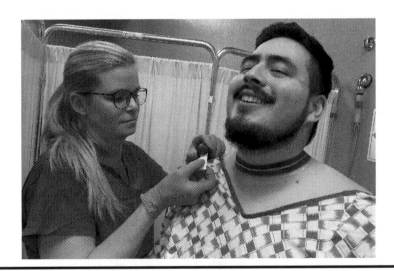

Photo 19.3 Surgeon Amanda Sammann applies injury makeup to actor Antonio Hernandez to assure the medical accuracy of a throat wound before recording at San Francisco General Hospital

Schedule a special rehearsal with the medical experts and the actors playing medical professionals or patients. In these rehearsals, the medical expert can give background information on the characters and answer any questions the actors might have about symptoms or patient-specific behaviors. Often, these characters will have recognizable ways of talking and carrying themselves that medical professionals in the audience will recognize immediately. The accuracy of character behavior is essential to the final product's effectiveness and its usefulness in training.

Start the session with a discussion between the experts and the actors. Then have the actors walk through their lines with crude blocking. Immediately the expert will have feedback like, "hold the stethoscope like this," or "don't turn away until you see the pills are swallowed." Rehearse until the experts and actors both feel comfortable.

Often, the actors playing medical professionals have complex vocabulary to memorize like "lisinopril" or "glipizide." In the session, record the expert pronouncing the complicated terminology. Then provide the recording to the actor for later review.

If it is possible, try to rehearse in a medical space similar to the one used during production. Medical professionals train for hours to function within spaces in specific ways. "Use hand sanitizer every time you enter or leave." "Check the vitals this way." If you cannot have this rehearsal ahead of time, schedule a time to rehearse on set before you record.

Expert on Set

Early on, let the experts know that you require an expert on set every day that includes medical content is recorded. Give them a heads up on which days you will be shooting, inform them that it will likely be all day (8–12 hours), with food provided, and that they can bring other work if needed. If they are unavailable, ask them to send other experts who can observe; otherwise, you will need to reschedule.

Having experts on set is essential. You are guaranteed to get something wrong if no one is there to catch it. Often, we use experts as extras in the background, which keeps them close to the action (to watch for problems) and gives them a fun cameo in the cine-VR experience.

You want to make sure your actors are doing their actions correctly because inaccurate content is unusable and a waste of everyone's time and money. If an expert is too agreeable (the camera, lights, and crew size can do that to an individual), press them to be more critical. Ask them specific questions such as: "Should the actor listen for a heartbeat-like this or like this?" "Is it better if they wash their hands or use hand sanitizer?" Hopefully, after a few questions, the expert will feel more comfortable providing suggestions.

Cine-VR is typically shot in long takes. Long takes mean your actor has to do everything perfectly for several minutes at a time while giving a compelling performance. This performance can be a more challenging goal to achieve for film actors than for stage actors. Film actors are accustomed to shooting their scenes in small takes edited together at a later time.

It is vital to watch your actors for details. Have a script supervisor note any errors in each take (no matter how small or large). These notes should include comments from the medical expert, as some mistakes are forgivable and some are not. Having professional notes from the set will remind you which is which when you are editing.

It is negotiable if an expert needs to be on the set for the entire production. Traditionally we ask the experts to be on set only for the medical scenes, then leave it up to them if they want to come the other days.

Photo 19.4 Maggie Guseman (left), daughter of Dr. Emily Guseman (center), and Dr. Elizabeth Beverly, play extras in a doctor's office lobby; Drs. Beverly and Guseman both consulted on Lula Mae's set and brought in their kids to play extras

Final Deliverable

As the project goes through the editing process, be sure to have the experts approve the chosen takes, logos used, and all other edits. Typically, they only need to be brought in toward the end to make sure the deliverable is lining up with the goals – although if there are questions about medical accuracy during the editing process, it is better to request input earlier rather than later.

If there is other supporting material (print work, website, graphics, etc.), again, be sure to get the experts' thumbs up. Of the whole project, these finalizing details are viewed the most often. Administration may not view the entire cine-VR piece, but they will see the supporting print and digital content. Do not let insignificant details taint a project well done.

Once the project receives the experts' final approval, you can close up the project and hand over the deliverables. Be sure to give ample praise to the experts in the credits and every other chance you can get. They are likely adding a lot of extra work to their schedule to help make this project work and deserve a great big thank you!

Viewing

To view and download cine-VR examples mentioned in this chapter, please visit: https://vimeo.com/channels/cinevr4healthcare/ (***password:*** *cineVR4health*).

Notes

1. Buchman, S., Miller, C., Henderson, D., Williams, E. & Ray, S. (2020). Interprofessional Students Learning to Save a Life through Cine-VR Simulation. EC Nursing and Healthcare, 2.11, 04–20. https://www.ecronicon.com/ecnh/pdf/ECNH-02-00120.pdf
2. Beverly, D. A., Love, C., Love, M. Williams, E. R. & Bowditch, J. (2021) Using Virtual Reality to Improve Healthcare Providers' Cultural Self-Efficacy and Diabetes Attitudes: A Pilot Study. *Journal of Medical Internet Research (JMIR)*. 23.1, 01–21.

Chapter 20

Advanced Cine-VR Production and Post-Production

Matt Love

Contents

Now that you're becoming more familiar with cine-VR content creation, let's take a look at some slightly more advanced production elements. In this chapter, we'll share some of what we've learned over the years about how to best leverage this medium for maximum effect, including a look at blocking, camera placement & movement, lighting, and working with plates. Be sure to look at the videos on our Vimeo Channel to see these techniques in action (see the end of the chapter for details).

Of course, production techniques could fill an entire book. There is such a book. If you'd like to read our book on narrative production techniques, please read *Virtual Reality Cinema: Narrative Tips and Techniques* by Eric R. Williams, Carrie Love, and Matt Love.

DOI: 10.4324/9781003168683-24

Blocking

The term blocking refers to where the actors position themselves and how they move throughout a scene. Blocking in cine-VR can call attention to a particular character, object, or event, which means it is beneficial when creating training content. The path a character takes as they move about the room, how close they are or aren't to the camera, and whether they sit or stand, and more can affect how a viewer experiences a cine-VR piece. With traditional forms of filmmaking, if we wanted to call attention to a patient monitor, we would simply cut to a close-up of the screen. With cine-VR, the viewer may be looking in the opposite direction, and cutting in for a close-up isn't an option. We can use blocking and audio cues to direct the viewers' attention. A glance from one of the characters, movement across the room, and audio cues can all focus attention where we want it. Be sure to consider the way your characters move throughout the space and react in your production.

Camera Placement

In addition to purposeful blocking, our work at the GRID Lab has shown us that camera placement in cine-VR requires careful consideration. Think about how a viewer will experience the space. Will their eyes be drawn to a particular part of the room? Is it rewarding to look around? How will the characters move about the space, interact with it? These are essential questions that inform the decision of where to place the camera.

Here is how we determined camera placement for a training series we completed for nurses who are learning to work with patients with Parkinson's Disease (see Chapter 10 for details on this project). To start, we followed the formula discussed in Chapter 2.

1. **We analyzed the script.** Who and what was significant in the scene? Should any actor or props be closer or farther away from the camera to emphasize their importance?
2. **We analyzed the space.** How would the characters move throughout the space, what options were available to alter those movements in ways which could help tell our story?
3. **We analyzed camera support options.** What options are available to securely mount the camera in a way that would allow us to achieve our desired goals and minimize work in post-production?

For our three scenes, the analysis informed where to place the camera, how to secure it, and some of our character's blocking. All three scenes occurred in various hospital rooms containing a bed, medical equipment, and carts. Given the need to keep the nurses' actions medically accurate, and our desire to place equal emphasis on the nurse and patient, we determined that optimum camera placement would be near the foot of the bed (see Figure 20.1).

The camera location allowed the viewer to be equidistant from the patient, the nurse, and any family members in the room. The nurse would need to cross from one side of the bed to the other, which would have them either passing close enough to the camera to be strange for the viewer or taking an awkward path to remain a comfortable distance away. To alleviate that issue, we placed the camera directly above the patient's shins, just under the nurse's eye height.

Having determined a location that would best serve the script, we had to consider how to rig the camera. Rigging to the bed would have risked the camera moving if the patient shifted their weight or bumped the bed. Having various methods to rig your camera in a given location is a

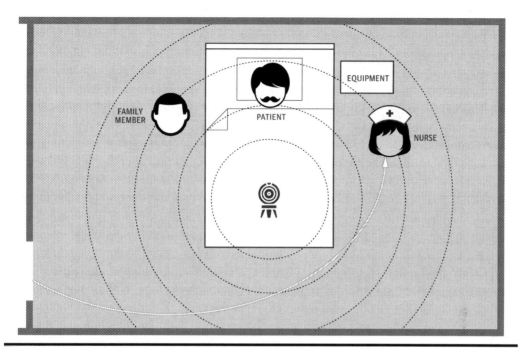

Figure 20.1   Camera placement for *The Parkinson's Series*

must for cine-VR work. In two of our scenarios, we used a scissor clip to suspend the camera from a drop ceiling, and in the third, we cantilevered the camera into place using a gobo arm attached to a c-stand which we removed in post (technique highlighted in Matt's cine-VR tutorials, see link at the end of the chapter).

When it comes to camera placement, think outside the box and experiment. We've suspended cameras from ceilings, attached them to shopping carts, mounted them to selfie sticks stuck in purses – all in the pursuit of sharing stories in compelling, engaging ways.

Camera Movement

Camera movement within cine-VR is a powerful tool but can be a bit tricky. On occasion, the viewer will suffer from a sensation of motion sickness or vertigo. This effect isn't to say that camera movement should be cine-VR taboo, but it does need careful consideration and used in moderation.

First and foremost, use a camera system with built-in stabilization. The results can be pretty surprising. If you cannot leverage a camera with stabilization, some stitching software can stabilize footage in post. With that said, stabilization has its limitations, and there are additional factors to take into consideration. For instance, this essentially eliminates low-frequency vibrations and handheld movements. Bobbing up and down or higher frequency vibrations are more complicated and can result in unusable footage.

Here are some suggestions.

1. **Smooth out the movement.** If you're attaching the camera to a person, have them practice moving in a way that flattens their gait. Suggest they keep their hips level and use the

articulation in their legs to absorb the up-and-down motion of their walk. Also, have them slow their movement by 20–30%. The slower speed feels more natural to the viewer and can make it easier for stabilization to do its job.

2. **Remove the source of unwanted vibration or movement**. Whether you're using a dolly, a wheelchair, or a car to move the camera, look for ways to make that movement as smooth as possible. For instance, choose carpeting or wood flooring over grouted tile. When recording in a moving car, we let some air out of the tires to smooth the ride.

3. **Secure the camera.** If you have the camera mounted to a selfie stick or gobo arm, attach other reinforcement points at various positions. Revisiting the shopping cart example, we initially attached a selfie stick to the cart's grated part, but that wasn't working well. By extending the selfie stick and connecting its base to the lower frame of the shopping cart while also attaching it higher near the top, we could produce a more usable shot. Having an assortment of mounting options can come in handy when looking for ways to reduce vibrations passing to the camera.

Introducing movement of the camera in cine-VR productions opens exciting opportunities to add emotion to our work. With time, audiences will grow more accustomed to these techniques, and they will become indispensable.

Lighting in cine-VR

While some filmmaking strategies (such as leveraging different focal lengths) are currently inapplicable in cine-VR now, others remain just as powerful. Lighting is a good example. If the scene is blocked to maximize the 360° space, and the camera is well placed, the audience can explore the environment effectively. Well-crafted lighting is one of the ways to encourage that exploration and call attention to essential story elements.

A question asked is if the viewer can see all around, where do we put the lights? Generally, the methods fall into the three categories covered in Chapter 2.

1. **Practicals.** The easiest way to hide a light is in plain sight. Using table lamps, floor lamps, and overheads are a beautiful way to light a scene. Dimming and color temperature shifting bulbs are available to control the quantity and quality of light. Also, diffusion or black wrap can modify the lighting.

2. **Hidden.** Another favorite is to leverage thin, flexible LED lights in creatively concealed ways. Stand where you plan to place the camera and observe the space. Cupboards, doors, and around corners are examples of spaces where lights can hide, allowing you to shape your environment.

3. **Removed.** Placing the light out in the open and then removing it in post can be a compelling way to light your scenes. Imagine you take an interior space and divide it in two. The action in the scene will take place on only one of those two sides for each take. On the other side, you can place the lights, the director, the sound recordist, etc. After recording the scene, you "flip" the two sides and record the other half of the scene, compositing the two images in post.

For lights you plan to remove in post, the concept is simple, but implementation can take practice and careful light metering. The trouble comes in where your two or more shots will meet and

Figure 20.2 **Removing lights in post: the concept is simple, but implementation requires practice**

be blended later on. Consider the following scenario: you're recording in a living room and have decided to split the scene into two halves for lighting purposes. One half of the room will contain the couch, while the other includes a chair and a plant. You start with half of the room, which consists of the sofa, and light it in such a way that it looks perfect. When it comes time to flip the room, you light it to look great (see Figure 20.2).

Everything seems perfect right up until you try to composite those two images together. The light shining toward the couch was spilling onto the floor and wall. However, in the shot focusing on the chair and the plant, that light isn't there at all. The more complicated your scene and the greater number of "slices" you want to merge, the trickier it becomes.

As you prepare your scene, map out the areas where you intend to blend your slices. At these places, carefully assess the way the light is falling in that area. An inexpensive light meter app on your phone would be a helpful tool. When it comes time to flip the room, try to get the same amount, color, and type of light hitting those areas, which will become your eventual seam. A little extra work while shooting will save hours of headache for your editor.

Working with "Plates"

Whenever there is action or actors in a shot, we call that a "take." When capturing imagery to conceal aspects of a take, we call that a "plate." Recall our earlier lighting example. We light one side of the room with lights on the other and record our scene. We then switch the lights to the side of the room we've already recorded and capture the other along with any action taking place on that side. We combine the two in post-production (editing), and voila, our viewer never knows the lights were there. Plates can remove the crew and other equipment as well. We can even use plates to replace things like overly bright windows or other image areas to make our final piece as compelling as possible.

As you explore cine-VR, you'll come to rely on plates and find yourself utilizing them often. For the magic to work, it is critical that the camera not shift or move in any way for each shot you plan to composite together in post. It is a sinking feeling to have had your actors nail a perfect take to then have someone accidentally kick or bump the camera before you've captured your plates. Once the director calls cut and says, "that's the one," the crew should calmly clear the room so that the director of photography and the camera crew can capture all of the plates needed for the scene. This set-up is also a good time for the audio team to gather room tone.

For an excellent example of how the GRID Lab combined all of these techniques into one startling scene, access the *Destiny – Motel* scene.

The Importance of Audio

Quality audio plays a significant role in cine-VR production. Given that the viewer will only see approximately one-fifth of the available visual content, the value of calling their attention with audio is quite powerful. We've discussed how lighting can help direct an audience's attention, but lighting can't call attention outside their field of view. Audio can.

We highly recommend cine-VR content that supports spatial (or Ambisonic) audio. Think of this as surround sound on steroids. By leveraging spatial audio formats, we can create an experience where sounds remain locked to a specific portion of the video, regardless of where the audience is looking. Imagine a scene where the action unfolds in the north direction, but you want to call your viewer's attention to the south. A lighting effect in the south is not apparent. A character could move from the north to the south, but that may not serve your story well. In this instance, spatial audio can come to the rescue because a sound can come from the south or any direction of our choosing. If the viewer is looking north, the sound comes from behind them; if they're looking east, it comes from their right, and if they're looking west, it comes from their left. Spatial audio experiences can be recorded on location using dedicated Ambisonic microphones. Additional sounds or entire soundscapes can also be created in post-production.

Immersive audio could also be the topic of its own book, but please see Chapter 12 for additional cine-VR audio information.

Post-Production - Overview

The most critical part of postproduction is ensuring that the content you've worked so hard to create is adequately protected, meaning backed up. There's a saying in filmmaking, "If you don't have it in three places, you don't have it." That means having the footage copied onto three independent hard drives, ideally spread across two physical locations. That way, any individual drive can fail, and you're safe. Even if your place is looted, flooded, or subjected to fire, your footage is secure.

With all our files safely backed up, our next step is to stitch our cine-VR footage. Regardless of the camera system, stitching is necessary. It is the process of taking the disparate images captured and combining them.

FRONT LENS ✚ BACK LENS ═ EQUIRECTANGULAR IMAGE

Figure 20.3 Side-by-side and stitched images from a dual-lens camera

The stitched result is either an equirectangular monoscopic image or a pair of stereoscopic images. Stereoscopic images leverage a separate image for each eye and require a camera system capable of capturing each image with two lenses. The handling of monoscopic and stereo-scopic images is similar, but we'll be referencing monoscopic imagery for the remainder of this section.

There are camera systems that perform the stitching process in-camera, but there are compelling reasons to handle the process in post. The first is quality. In most instances, in-camera stitching options reduce the resolution and file quality. This feature means that if you want maximum picture quality, you'll have to put the work in to stitch the footage. The second reason to consider stitching in post is control over image stitching. This consideration is crucial when utilizing set-ups using more than two lenses. Stitching the images in post allows you to fine-tune the areas where the images overlap and often make a final product more seamless.

Simpler, more consumer-centric cameras tend to offer proprietary software for stitching their files together. Some even provide plug-ins that allow the stitching to occur in real-time within your editor. In general, these approaches are straightforward and easy to use but offer limited customization. In the case of non-linear editor (NLE) plug-ins, performance can vary greatly depending on how powerful your computer is, and you may find that taking the time to stitch before editing is faster in the long run. To handle more complex stitching operations, it is likely that third-party software will be necessary.

Non-Linear Editor (NLE)

If you are accustomed to working with traditional video, you'll notice a few differences when you bring your stitched 360° footage into an NLE. The first is that your footage looks quite strange in its equirectangular format. To see the entirety of your clips and make editing manageable, your NLE takes the spherical video and flattens it, much in the same way that a globe looks different from a flat map (see Figure 20.4).

While working in an equirectangular format makes certain aspects of editing more manageable, it is also helpful to simulate what your viewer will experience, which is why NLEs such as Apple's Final Cut Pro and Adobe's Premiere Pro have dedicated viewers for 360° content. Once activated, they provide a simulated view that allows you to pan and tilt as if you were looking around in a headset. Some NLEs even permit attaching a headset for playback from the timeline. Within your viewer's settings, you will want to find the FOV setting and adjust that accordingly to

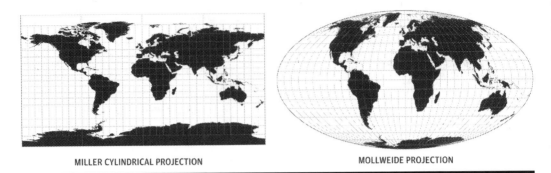

Figure 20.4   Miller and Mollweide projections

have an accurate representation of what your audience will see. For an Oculus GO, our preferred FOV setting is around 70°.

Orientation

A common refrain from directors new to cine-VR is "how do I know which way someone is looking?" Hopefully, as cine-VR storytellers, we'll give our audiences plenty of reasons to be looking around. While it is impossible to know which way a person will be looking at any moment, we can anticipate which direction they're likely to be looking. No matter which headset your audience is using, the opening frame will always look in the same direction. Let's call this north. As you put your first clip on the timeline, check your 360° viewer to see what appears. This direction will correspond to wherever the front of the camera was pointing when you recorded the shot.

If this isn't what you want your audience to see first, the solution is easy. Within your NLE, locate the controls for orientation, or apply the effect for reorienting your sphere. These controls will allow you to adjust which portion of the sphere is north. These are controls you'll use often. At edit points, analyze your outgoing clip carefully: which direction is the audience most likely to be looking? Now consider the incoming clip and what you want your audience to see. Reorient the incoming clip's sphere so that if the audience is looking the way you want them to on the outgoing clip, they'll know what you want them to on the incoming clip.

Another reason you may want to reorient your spheres is for aligning clips during the plating process. As a result of stitching, even if you didn't bump the camera during production, your shots may not line up perfectly. Here's a tip: apply a "difference blend mode" to the uppermost clip on your timeline. Aspects of the image that match the clip below will turn black, and different aspects will turn white. With this effect applied, you can reorient the sphere until the area you want to composite together is all black. Once that's done, return the blend mode to normal, apply your mask, and your two clips should be perfectly aligned.

Plates

Reorienting your clips so they align perfectly is something you'll get a lot of practice with once you start plating. You carefully mapped out your blocking and lit the scene. Hence, your overlapping areas had matching light quantity and quality, making sure the camera didn't move and that not a single piece of furniture near your stitch line got bumped. Now it's time to see if all your hard work has paid off!

In your NLE, you'll want to layer the clips you intend to comp together in the timeline. The most common approach is to place your main clip, the one with most of the action, on the timeline first. Then stack the other clips you want to use for plating above that and mask them so they cover what you're looking to hide on that main clip.

One way to wrap your head around how this works is to think of using different construction paper colors. All the pieces of paper start the same size, and if you lay them directly on top of each other, you only see the uppermost sheet, but if you cut away some of the top sheets and lay it back down, you know what is below. Imagine a bottom sheet that is a deep, dark blue color. Next, take a white sheet, cut a circle in it, and place it in the upper right corner. Take a yellow sheet and cut out a star, laying it in the upper middle of the sheet. The night sky is appearing where there was once just a pile of paper. Your base clip is the dark blue piece of paper, and each additional clip obscures a part of that base layer, adding something new to the image.

Within your NLE, you'll want to explore your options for masking. The particulars for masking can vary from NLE to NLE, but they all offer the ability to do what we want. Typically, there are shape masks or gradient masks, but the preferred method is a custom shape mask for our work. This type of mask allows you to click at various points around the area you're looking to mask and complete a custom shape. At each point along the way, you can use adjustment handles to curve the ends – allowing limitless options for masking. You can also try feathering the edges of your mask to help it blend.

What if, despite all your efforts, the two images don't appear the same? The most common culprit is differences in color or quantity of lighting. If that occurs, take away any feathering and focus on an area where the difference is most apparent. Then, using the color grading tools in your NLE, adjust the luminance and color values until the two parts of the image become seamless. You may have to adjust the shadows, mid-tones, and highlights separately, and it may take some back and forth, but with patience and persistence, you'll get there.

Eventually, you'll find yourself wanting to plate something or add some graphics on the portion of the image where it wraps within your NLE. This step can be especially problematic when attempting to mask something or placing a graphic in the correct position. Here's what we do at the GRID Lab. Our desired orientation is represented in the top image of Figure 20.5, but we want to come out the window, which falls on the part of the image where it wraps in our NLE. We reorient the image so that the window is easy to work on and comp away. As you look at the middle image of Figure 20.5, you see the window now has some beautiful snowfall outside. To regain our original orientation, we can render out this clip as is or reimport and reorient it, or if our NLE allows, we can create a compound clip and reorient that resulting in the finished bottom image. This technique works for plates, graphics, and more. You'll hear about it again in Chapter 9.

One last pro-tip. We've been discussing plates to remove elements such as lights from the set and to composite new window scenes in, but the usefulness for plates doesn't stop there. Imagine this. Two actors played out a scene in a living room. Both were on camera simultaneously, but the director likes Wash's performance in take two and prefers Zoë's in take five. Use what you've practiced with plates, and you're able to combine the performances from two different takes into one. It won't always work because of timing, but this is a technique that the acclaimed film director David Fincher uses regularly.

Figure 20.5   Reorientation

Audio

When it comes to audio, NLEs across the board have plenty of room for improvement at the time of this writing. While some are now gaining rudimentary support for Ambisonic audio, some have no support whatsoever. Most audio professionals rely on third-party plug-ins to use with their digital audio workstations for Ambisonic support. It seems that the landscape is shifting almost daily. Whether you end up working within Facebook Spatial Workstation, Reaper, Pro-Tools, or another avenue altogether, the important part is creating a rich spatial experience for your viewer. Not only will your content carry more polish, but you'll have an excellent slate of tools to direct the audience's attention as well.

For more detail about audio, please see Chapter 12.

Summary

When it comes to production and post-production, the common theme is to experiment, practice, and fine-tune your approach. Cine-VR is an evolving medium, and there is much to learn about how to best leverage it. Take what we have learned at the GRID Lab and build on it to add to the conversation. And be sure to share what you know with us!

Viewing

To view and download cine-VR examples mentioned in this chapter, please visit: https://vimeo.com/channels/cinevr4healthcare/ (***password:*** *cineVR4health).*

Chapter 21

Distribution Models

John Bowditch

Contents

This chapter provides guidelines for sharing cine-VR experiences with others. These approaches can work for both individual and multiuser experiences. Your content can be shared internally or with a global audience.

There are multiple factors to consider when picking a distribution platform, including cost, quality, audio requirements, and accessibility. We will focus on both individual headsets and streaming solutions that can synchronize multi-headset presentations (see Photo 21.1). While this overview will *not* cover every possible distribution method, we have found the following approaches practical for reaching both small and large audiences.

Cine-VR should ideally be played on VR headsets with headphones. While in a headset, most surrounding distractions are eliminated; little outside the experience can steal your attention, especially if you use quality headphones. In an era of continuous distractions, this sort of isolation creates a more engaging experience. For example, you are no longer distracted by your phone in VR because you cannot see or hear it.

If headsets are not available, playing cine-VR content on computer web browsers is an option. YouTube and Vimeo videos load similarly to traditional videos. Despite being viewed on a flat display, you can change the video's orientation to experience the full 360° by clicking and dragging the video itself with your mouse or trackpad. This approach is not nearly as immersive as

DOI: 10.4324/9781003168683-25

Photo 21.1 Cine-VR should ideally be played on a VR headset, blocking out surrounding distractions

headsets, and we find that audiences easily get distracted. Nevertheless, this is a good solution for mass distribution and sharing of basic content and ideas.

Smartphones and tablets are options as well. Similar to web browsers, you play the video back on your smartphone and tablet flat screen. These mobile devices have sensors on board that track your location and rotation while physically moving around. The movements are aligned with the location and rotation of the corresponding video. By sitting or standing with a mobile device held in front of you, the footage's direction will continually track and align with the device's motion (see Figure 21.1).

VR headsets and touchscreen devices like smartphones and tablets have similar hardware components. Both have built-in hardware sensors called gyroscopes and accelerometers. In fact, many VR displays are based on the same hardware architecture as popular smartphones. It's not farfetched to compare donning an HMD to strapping a smartphone to your face.

Gyroscopes track how much something is tilting and help to smooth the graphical playback to prevent videos from shaking. Accelerometers measure the actual movement in space. The combination of these two can track the device's position and orientation with remarkable precision. Gyroscopes and accelerometers, along with optical or infrared tracking, are integral parts of the VR headsets' tracking capabilities.

We bring iPads preloaded with our content to all highly attended demonstrations we give. Some people have preferred to not wear headsets but still want to participate. The reasons vary, but some elect not to wear a headset due to comfort or medical reasons, such as hearing and vision problems. Some have declined to wear headsets to protect their hair and makeup. Having a smartphone or tablet as a backup will help you avoid protentional accessibility accommodations.

There are more playback possibilities for cine-VR, including various projection systems. The projectors can cast to screens of all shapes and sizes, including curved, flat, or even dome-shaped surfaces. The dome-shaped projection screens are large, room-sized half-spheres, similar in shape to a contact lens. These domes are analogous to planetariums you see at science centers and museums. A computer with several graphics processors can stitch many projectors seamlessly together to make one continuous projected image. One notable limitation of the dome is that the field of view is usually 180–220°. Displaying the whole 360° cine-VR project is unachievable, but the limited image shown can be breathtaking, nonetheless. If the domes are large enough, you may

**Figure 21.1   A swivel chair allows the viewer to easily rotate in any direction to follow the 360°
action, whether using a headset or smartphone and tablet**

have dozens of participants viewing the content together. It is important to note that projection
systems require the most space and are often the most expensive solution.

Playback

Local Playback

Local playback means that media stored on a hard drive is accessible without network communication. The content is stored "locally" on your device's hard drive. Playing content locally on
a wireless headset or a computer will give you the highest quality experience. Another benefit of
local playback is that reliance on network speed and quality is not a factor. We have attempted to
download content on headsets in locations with poor network connections, and the process was
just too stressful. You should assume that network quality will be unreliable when traveling, so
plan to download and thoroughly test your content in advance.

Local cine-VR playback tends to consume a large amount of disk space which can be problematic. Disk requirements can be especially detrimental on some wireless headsets because they
may only have thirty-two gigabytes (GB) of storage in total. That could limit you to as little as
thirty minutes of cine-VR content per device. Hard drive sizes will undoubtedly increase with
new headset generations. We predict that wireless headsets will soon have storage space exceeding
a terabyte (1024 GB).

Our cine-VR production output file sizes are usually in the gigabyte range. Even short one-to-two-minute cine-VR films will exceed one GB with high render settings. Some higher-priced wireless headsets already have several hundred gigabytes of storage space. Media file sizes are only going to continue to increase in size as video and audio quality improves.

Content creators perpetually want to enhance the quality of the content. Coincidentally, digital media file sizes rise as hard drive sizes increase. All software and media files have a tendency to use as much free disk space as possible. For example, the popular *Call of Duty* video games series has continually required more hard drive space with each sequel. The first title, released in 2003, was simply *Call of Duty,* and it required 1.4 GB of hard drive space. In 2020, *Call of Duty Modern Warfare* was released, requiring 175+ GB (i.e., 125 times bigger). Ten years from now may put the storage requirements well into the terabyte range.

Always remember that the higher the quality of media productions, the more disk space you'll need. You may continually feel like your hard drives are never quite large enough for your needs. With appropriate media file compression settings and management, wireless headsets can still be effective for local playback.

Streaming

All wireless headsets support streaming content directly to headsets while maintaining decent quality. As mentioned previously, streaming is the easiest solution for mass distribution. Headsets, smartphones, tablets, and web browsers all support streaming natively.

Streaming content can reduce the need for hard drive space management because accessed files are not stored locally. Streaming platforms like YouTube and Vimeo are reasonably priced (and often free) depending on file upload sizes and quantity. If you need to stream 3D 360° content, YouTube and Vimeo support stereographic cine-VR as well. We use both services extensively. Uploading finished content to YouTube or Vimeo is suitable for archiving content as well. This book's supplemental cine-VR content is hosted on a password-protected Vimeo account.

Most of our student and research projects are uploaded to YouTube. YouTube allows us to upload unlisted or private videos, making them undiscoverable to anyone without a direct link. Some content may require restricted access. You may not be able to share projects widely because of funder limitations, HIPAA, or other requirements. Make sure you remind your teams of any restrictions to prevent accidental sharing violations. In addition to marking videos as private, you can also add password protection.

All Oculus headsets have an optional YouTube application that makes searching for cine-VR easier. As of this book's publication date, uploading 360° videos to YouTube requires an extra step to "inject" metadata into a video file to enable 360° navigation (known as the YouTube Metadata Injector). The metadata that is added to your video formats the directional playback controls. Adobe Premiere has included YouTube formatting for cine-VR since their 2019 version to help streamline the process. Other video editing software has followed suit.

Synchronizing Headsets

Network reliability may have a significant impact on your ability to stream content. Our teams always plan for network issues when visiting hospitals, conference centers, and other universities (see Photo 21.2). Hospital IT staff especially get anxious when bandwidth-hogging devices pop up on their networks. If your project requires networked headsets, make sure someone from your

Photo 21.2   Always bring a utility bag ready to address network and synchronization issues when visiting hospitals and conferences

team coordinates with the facility's IT staff in advance. If network access is not needed, our recommendation is to play your content locally on a headset.

Network access is essential for various reasons, including synchronization. For example, if your headsets must be networked to manage synchronous playback, bring your own Wi-Fi router for your headsets. We commonly deploy synchronized playback at conferences and workshops using our own router without much trouble.

Our synchronization approach uses VR Sync's software solution and their VR Sync Box, a turn-key Wi-Fi routing system. Turn-key means that all you really need to do is plug the system into an outlet and power it on. A computer (PC or Mac) is required to broadcast your selected content's playback commands to each headset. This computer will also connect to the same Wi-Fi router. The computer interface can also indicate which devices need troubleshooting.

Our synchronization solution relies heavily on content saved locally to each headset. We upload the cine-VR files to each device in advance to avoid streaming our content at the same time as our synchronization information. Streaming high-resolution content to each headset requires significantly more bandwidth. The only network traffic generated is simple play and stop commands because the VR content is downloaded on the headsets.

Photo 21.3   Large group presentations require synchronization of headsets to reduce user confusion and the chaos of different audio playing out of sync

VR Sync requires a monthly subscription per device, but many comparable solutions are available from other vendors. However, this may be a built-in feature on future headsets, eliminating the need for a third-party solution altogether. If VR is commonly used in future classrooms, offices, and large gatherings, we believe synchronization is vital and worthy of direct platform support (see Photo 21.3).

Kiosk Mode

There is software that can make your headset behave like a digital kiosk. Kiosks are designed to provide information without the assistance of a human. Think of a movie theater ticket kiosk. You walk up to the kiosk, select your movie and screening time, pay with a credit card, and your tickets print out. There is no need for an employee to assist you. Similarly, sometimes you just want someone to put on a headset and automatically play content without requiring assistance.

Let's say we have an exhibition booth at a conference or event. In this scenario, we may choose to put our Oculus headsets in an auto-play mode. We achieve this functionality by licensing an application called EZ360 (although there are many solutions to choose from). Some headsets, like those manufactured by Pico, support this feature natively. Instead of fumbling around with a controller or a computer to initiate playback, once in the headset, the user simply needs to stare at the video they want to watch. Their focused gaze triggers the content to load. An approach like this requires minimal tech support.

In our experience, kiosk mode is not optimal for large groups consuming the content simultaneously. We have had groups where each participant plays the headset content at their own pace. As a result, the process is overwhelmingly disruptive. If you don't use headphones and play sounds directly through the headset speakers, the noise coming from all non-synchronized headsets is chaotic at best. Imagine being in a room with dozens of speakers all playing content out of sync, and you begin to grasp the chaos. Similarly, if everyone's headsets are out of sync, everyone ends their experience at a different time. If your goal is to avoid having the audience waiting around for others to finish each experience, we recommend using a synchronized solution over kiosks.

We no longer hand out VR controllers with our headsets and try to limit user interaction with the device's operating system as much as possible. A user randomly hitting the wrong controller button can result in lengthy troubleshooting. Even if the solution only navigates back to the correct content, the delays can be stressful for both the presenter and the user. This problem amplifies as group sizes increase, requiring more tech support staff onsite.

Cine-VR as Supplementary Material

The workshops and conferences we host usually focus on a specific healthcare topic (i.e., diabetes, opioid abuse, Parkinson's disease, and so forth). In these workshops, the cine-VR content is actually just one of many educational tools used. A typical presentation starts with a slide deck presentation. Traditional videos are interspersed throughout the slides (no headsets at first). These videos help introduce the fictional characters and settings the audience will experience in the cine-VR experiences. Once the presentation is ready for the cine-VR content, everyone puts on a headset and synchronously watches the content together. Once concluded, a short group discussion about the experience occurs. The combination of presenting with slide decks, traditionally shot video, cine-VR, and group discussion makes an effective instructional environment for our audience. Synchronizing the headsets helps manage the presentation's pacing and gives the presenter a moment to prepare for the next section.

Accessibility

Planning for various accessibility needs was not something we fully addressed before hosting our first workshops. There may be audience members who cannot wear a headset due to physical limitations, or they just do not want to. We have had audience members terrified of VR due to a previous experience with the medium. Novice users may become easily disoriented, motion sick, or overwhelmed by the level of immersion. To help alleviate these feelings, those unfamiliar with VR should always begin seated. Once they become comfortable with the platform, you can let them stand up if your cine-VR experience calls for it.

As mentioned earlier, our best solution for those who do not wear a headset is to provide tablets (iPads). This solution is not as immersive as wearing a headset, but having the option can make the experiences meaningful nonetheless.

Audio Playback

Consider audio playback requirements as early as possible. For instance, YouTube currently supports Ambisonic audio in its playback, but Vimeo currently does not (see Chapter 12 for details). Most VR headsets have headphones or speakers built into them, but environmental sounds may interfere with the experience's overall quality. Especially if the project is shown in a highly trafficked area.

The best solution is to use earphones. Over-the-ear headphones have worked best for us, but they require cleaning between uses. We have given out disposable earbud headphones to limit the need for sanitizing. These cheap earbuds have poor sound quality and are wasteful if used once and discarded. We only use earbuds when overwhelmed by the number of users at a particular moment and struggle to sanitize devices quickly.

Sanitizing Headsets

Create a plan for sanitizing headsets and earphones between users. Fomites, like viruses and bacteria, can quickly become an issue with neglected care. It's easy to imagine how communal headsets are optimal breeding grounds for germs. Sweat, makeup, and other matter come off people so effortlessly that the risks of spreading germs are high.

There are two sanitization practices we use constantly and one we use occasionally. Our best practices:

1. The most straightforward procedure is to wipe down faceplate fabric and lenses with antiviral wet wipes. This solution is quick and affordable for removing most fomites. If you want to use spray-on cleaning solutions, do not spray the headset directly. Spray the solution on a clean microfiber cloth and then wipe the headset. The microfiber cloth can be laundered and reused.
2. The second solution uses ultraviolet (UV) light to kill off viruses and bacteria. We use a box-shaped device that functions as a miniature oven. Our particular hardware is manufactured by Cleanbox. Users simply hang the headset inside, run a cleaning cycle, and remove the disinfected device once complete. The entire process takes about a minute per headset and other devices like cleaning controllers, headphones, and other small electronics. We have deployed several of these boxes in our VR classroom and lab spaces.
3. The third solution is often wasteful, but using disposable face masks is an option. The masks cover the user's forehead, nose, and areas around their eyes. It does not obstruct the mouth or nostrils. Made from a light fabric material, it attaches to your ears and has two holes for your eyes. The solution is wasteful because each mask may only be used once and discarded. Still, you can limit the number of masks used and ask they be individually reused. One plan might be to communicate to your guests that they must use their covers for their entire day. A mask can be worn for multiple experiences by the same individual. If there are dozens of different VR stations to experience, reusing these masks can be a somewhat green, cost-effective solution.

Conclusion

One unfortunate side effect of cine-VR production is that the content you create will have a limited lifespan. Cine-VR content created for today's headsets will most likely look underwhelming on future devices. When you make your distribution plan, try to imagine your content's expected lifespan and strategize accordingly. We have found each cine-VR production may only be used two-to-three years before it needs to be outmoded or remastered. Suppose your initial cinematography was shot at a high enough resolution. In that case, you might be able to remaster your content for the newest headset generation and redistribute it. Remastering content may extend the shelf life by several years (see Chapter 7 for more details on high-resolution cinematography).

Whether you're producing content for an individual or an entire industry sector, keep in mind the importance of planning for distribution. Whether it's private or public, designed to last five years or one year, played on a headset or web browser, the overall approach differs little. Define your needs, choose a platform, address accessibility, clean devices frequently, and determine an expected lifespan for your cine-VR.

Glossary

360° split screen: A cine-VR editing technique to combine two or more shots from different times or locations into the same 360° experience.

360° video: Video representing an entire 360° sphere, allowing a viewer to look in every direction.

absolute orientation: Method by which metadata embedded within a cine-VR media file can instruct a media player to orient clips and graphical overlays.

accelerometer: An instrument for measuring acceleration.

Advanced Trauma Life Support (ATLS): Trauma training course.

agency: Extent to which an audience's choices influence an encounter or the outcome of an interactive experience.

aliasing: Jagged pixel edges. Commonly seen by zooming in on digital images.

Ambisonic audio: Audio that covers an entire 360° sphere.

Appalachia: A 205,000-square-mile region that encompasses 420 counties in thirteen states from Mississippi to New York. The Appalachian Mountains are the prominent geographic feature of this region.

Appalachian Ohio: In Ohio, the Appalachian region encompasses 32 counties, which are located in eastern Ohio, southeastern Ohio, and southern Ohio.

Arc of Engagement: Tracking a cine-VR story's emotional and intellectual development using the Christmas Carol Continuum.

Behavioral Intervention Team (BIT): Group of school officials who regularly meet to collect and review information about at-risk community members and develop intervention plans to assist them (NaBITA).

binocular FOV: Area where our left eyesight and our right eyesight overlap. *(also see: central vision)*

BIT: See: Behavioral Intervention Team

blind (or to blind): Prescribing a random identification code associated with a patient allowing you to track their data without knowing who the patient is.

blocking: Physical positions and movements of actors on a set.

bystanders: Someone who is physically at an event but does not do anything to interact.

C-stand: Stand designed for use on film sets and utilized for various tasks, generally for holding flags or other light modifiers.

cardboard VR: Inexpensive delivery system to view virtual reality with one's smartphone.

case mix: Type or combination of patients treated by a hospital or unit.

Christmas Carol continuum: Illustration of the fundamental balance between story fabrication to story comprehension in a cine-VR story.

cine-VR: 360° video professionally produced in a cinematic manner and ideally viewed in a head-mounted display to provide autonomy to the audience.

cinema camera: Camera with controls and capabilities which are well suited to filmmaking.

cinematography: Art of making moving pictures with a camera.

classroom management to threat assessment continuum: In higher education, a range of disruptive behaviors that gets progressively harmful requiring a response anywhere from a classroom instructor to a law enforcement professional, depending on the totality of the circumstance.

co-morbid: Diseases or medical conditions that are simultaneously present in a patient.

Cognitive Load Theory: States that an increased load on a learner's working memory can compromise the learner's acquisition of knowledge.

command center: Production staging area with access to electricity for charging and reliable Wi-Fi connections for device communications.

competence: State of having sufficient knowledge, judgment, skill, or strength.

compositing: Means by which to combine two or more elements into one final image by layering them on top of each other.

DAW: Combination of hardware and software used for recording, editing, and producing audio. *(also see: digital audio workstation)*

de-escalating: To decrease the potential for harm during a situation.

debrief: Predetermined way to investigate learning by asking specific questions; conversational sessions revolve around sharing and examining information after a particular event has occurred.

detective mode: When the audience disregards their emotional agency and instead focuses their attention on intellectual observation.

Dickens approach: A cine-VR storytelling method in which the narrator guides the audience didactically as if it is the narrator's story to tell (as opposed to the Scrooge approach).

digital audio workstation (DAW): Combination of hardware and software used for recording, editing, and producing audio. *(also see: DAW)*

directorial agency: When the creative curiosity of the audience strongly influences where they will look within cine-VR.

directorial control: When the creative decisions of the crew strongly influence where the audience will look within cine-VR.

emotional agency: When the audience chooses where they will look within cine-VR based on their empathic connection to specific characters or locations.

empathy: The ability to understand and share the feelings of another.

equirectangular: Means by which to display all elements of a sphere in a two-dimensional way by distorting the portions which appear near the poles.

evidence-based teaching: Approach to education based on the best available scientific evidence, rather than tradition, personal judgment, or other influences.

field of view (FOV): What a person can see without turning their head from side to side. *(also see: FOV)*

file naming protocol: An agreed-upon pattern for labeling digital information during production.

fisheye lens: Very wide-angle lens with a field of vision of which can be up to 180° or more.

foley: The art of post-production sound effects whereby foley artists (those who perform the foley) and producers/engineers (those who record and process the foley) make realistic facsimiles of sounds needed for the production.

FOV: What a person can see without turning their head from side to side. *(also see: field of view)*

gobo arm: Steel rod with a grip head permanently attached to one end. Used to hold items in place on a film set.

GRID Lab: The Game Research and Immersive Design Lab is a state-of-the-art production facility including 360° and Cine-VR video production, walkable VR, immersive sound design, VR interaction and animation, motion capture, and viewing/educational labs.

grip head: Clamping cylinder used to hold items in place on a film set.

guided simulation: A pre-recorded cine-VR face-to-face conversation with characters in the headset. Viewers are encouraged to speak pre-determined dialogue to a character in the headset and hear them respond.

gyroscope: A device consisting of a disk spinning that alters direction, maintaining a reference direction in navigation systems and stabilizers.

haptics: Using the sense of touch.

head-mounted display (HMD): Device worn over the eyes to replace what is naturally seen with some sort of digital (or digitally enhanced) visual. *(also see: HMD)*

high-fidelity: Simulation with mannequins or computer-based equipment that simulates real to life functions.

higher order Ambisonics (HOA): Any Ambisonic audio above first order (four channels) is considered "higher order Ambisonics" (HOA). The greater the number of channels, the greater the spatial accuracy of the reproduced soundfield and the higher the order.

HIPAA: Health Insurance Portability and Accountability Act.

hitboxes: Invisible regions layered on top of the video to detect when something is interacting with it. Common in video games, hitbox tracking is necessary for eye-tracking cine-VR.

HMD: Device worn over the eyes to replace what is naturally seen with some sort of digital (or digitally enhanced) visual. *(also see: head-mounted display)*

House Supervisor: Registered Nurse in charge of the healthcare facility during off-hours.

image stabilization: Method of reducing the effects of camera movement or vibration in the final image.

implicit bias: Represent unconscious attitudes, beliefs, or associations toward a social group. Implicit biases attributed to members of a particular group of people are known as stereotyping.

Integrated Clinical Education (ICE): A graduate educational process designed for students to become familiar with the clinical environment, integrate didactic knowledge, gain confidence with patient management skills, and enhance self-awareness of professional behaviors.

Kolb's Experiential Learning Theory (KELT): A continuous learning process where knowledge is created through experiences that change the way one thinks and acts in a situation.

lavalier microphone ("lav"): Small microphones generally used to record monophonic dialogue spoken by a single actor; often used with wireless transmitters and receivers.

layperson education: Education geared toward anyone regardless of their profession.

level of function: Evaluative findings intended to reflect how effectively an individual can perform in various personal, interpersonal, and community domains such as activities of daily living; social functioning; thinking, concentration and judgment; and adaptation to stress.

live capture: Recorded events in a hospital that use actual patients in real-time.

Lovrick montage: A 360° editing technique where crossfades are used to transition in or out portions of the 360° screen, resulting in a ghosting effect as an image enters or leaves the space.

low-CRIS production process: A low-cost rapid implementation strategy that uses 360° video to capture actual patient care in a healthcare setting expeditiously to minimize patient care interference and facilitate rapid implementation.

low-fidelity simulation: Simulation used to build knowledge with very low technical qualifications.

medical-surgical inpatient: Patients that stay overnight in an acute care hospital recovering from surgical or have medical conditions.

mental health crisis: Any situation in which a person's actions, feelings, and behaviors can lead to them hurting themselves or others, and put them at risk of being unable to care for themselves or function in the community in a healthy manner.

mic: Microphone.

MIDI: See: musical instrument digital interface.

monoscopic: Image presented from a single perspective as opposed to a stereoscopic image.

musical instrument digital interface (MIDI): Standardized method of communication between musical instruments and computers. MIDI is not musical notes or sounds in itself, but it carries data and signals that can be converted into myriad notes or sounds.

naloxone: Generic name for an opioid overdose antidote.

Narcan: Trade name for an opioid overdose antidote.

NAS/NAWS: Withdrawal syndrome that can occur in newborns exposed to certain substances, including opioids, during pregnancy.

National Council for State Boards of Nursing: Independent, national organization through which nursing regulatory bodies act and counsel together on matters of common interest and concern affecting public health, safety, and welfare, including the development of nursing licensure examinations.

never event: First used by Dr. Ken Kizer in 2001, the term refers to particularly shocking medical errors that should never occur (e.g., wrong-site surgery).

NLE: Software used to modify and arrange video clips. *(see also: non-linear editor)*

nodal point: Point in a lens where light rays cross and create a parallel emergent ray. The point in a lens where you can pan it left or right with no parallax effect.

non-linear editor (NLE): Software used to modify and arrange video clips. *(see also: NLE)*

opioid epidemic: Ever-growing number of overdose and deaths related to opioid misuse; also referred to as "opioid crisis."

opioids: Class of drugs that include the illegal drug heroin, synthetic opioids such as fentanyl, and pain relievers available legally by prescription, such as oxycodone (OxyContin®), hydrocodone (Vicodin®), codeine, morphine, and many others.

orientation points: Spatial markers that enable the viewer to situate oneself in a virtual space.

parallax: Resultant difference in two images as a result of variance in their nodal points.

Parkinson's disease: Progressive neurodegenerative disorder that predominantly affects dopamine-producing neurons, causing movement and non-motor symptoms.

part-practice approach: Technique used in learning a new skill or task that involves practicing the sub-components of the skill or task in preparation for the whole task or skill.

pixels per inch (PPI): The number of pixels in one square inch. More pixels mean higher display resolution.

plate: Image captured to utilize it to remove or replace elements in a scene through compositing – generally void of actors or moving elements.

point of interest: Specifically, where the audience is looking at any given moment.

post-production: Aspect of a media project after all images and sound have been recorded and are now being assembled to tell the story; the project is said to be "in post." This is typically when the project is edited, sound is mixed, graphics and credits are added.

practical: Light that appears naturally within a scene.

pre-brief: Information provided to assist the learner before undergoing a learning experience. Delivery of needed content to successfully be able to complete the experience.

pre-production: Duration of the project before images and sound are recorded; the project is said to be "in pre-production." This is typically when the project is scripted, locations are secured, actors or patients are recruited, and equipment is secured.

PREality: Portmanteau word combining "preparation" and "reality." PREality uses cine-VR to prepare the viewer for a reality that they will experience in the future.

primary emotions: Feelings that a character has in a story.

production professionalism: Expected behavior when producing media, including the hierarchy of roles, proper procedures, and workflow, as well as courtesy and accountability to the location, the equipment, and the cast and crew; also known as set etiquette.

production: Duration of the project when images and sound are recorded; the project is said to be "in production."

realism: Experiencing a real-world situation through the safety of a headset and feeling as if the experience was real.

room-scale: An open space that allows for free exploration within a defined area while wearing a VR headset.

Roger's Innovation Curve: A model attempting to explain how, why, and at what rate new technologies spread within society.

safe zone: Area on a spherical canvas where vertical distortion does not occur.

scissor clip: Device which allows lightweight filmmaking equipment to be temporarily suspended from a drop ceiling.

screen-door effect: Gaps in between pixels common on all digital displays. It creates the illusion of looking through a screened door.

Scrooge approach: A cine-VR storytelling method in which the audience constructs the story themselves based upon their observations (as opposed to the Dickens approach).

secondary emotions: Feelings that the audience has while enjoying the story.

selfie stick: Extendable pole, which is designed to be handheld to position a camera far enough away from one person to capture an image of the person holding it.

sidewards: Metaphorical movement that is neither up nor down, neither forwards nor back; often used to describe creative movement through time and space.

simulation: Artificial representation of a real-world process to achieve educational goals through experiential learning, allowing the acquisition of clinical skills through deliberate practice rather than an apprentice-style education.

slices: Individual images captured independently, which can later be combined into a 360° sphere.

Social Determinants of Health (SDoH): Conditions in the places where people are born, live, learn, work, and play that affect a wide range of health and quality of life outcomes, including diabetes.

spatial audio: Audio, which covers an entire 360° sphere-see spatial audio.

spherical grid: Square-shaped lattice laid upon a 360°-degree space to identify specific areas of the space.

staged capture: Recorded event in a hospital that does not use actual patients. Instead, they use actors to play the role of patients, and the event is repeated until adequately performed. Patients are sometimes asked to serve as actors; in such a case, the event is considered "staged."

stereoscopic: Image presented from two slightly different perspectives as opposed to a monoscopic image.

stitch line: Border where two disparate images are joined to create a complete 180°- or 360°-degree image.

story engagement matrix: Illustration of the fundamental balance between story fabrication to story comprehension on the X-axis, and the dichotomy of being able to absorb either the details or the emotions of a cine-VR story on the Y-axis.

Subject Matter Experts (SME): Individuals identified as experts of the content.

teaching strategy: Methods of instruction to deliver course materials to keep students engaged and practicing different skill sets.

threat assessment: Violence prevention strategy that involves: (a) identifying student threats to commit a violent act, (b) determining the seriousness of the threat, and (c) developing intervention plans that protect potential victims and address the underlying problem or conflict that stimulated the threatening behavior. (NASPA)

tone words: Specific words that help express an author's attitude about the subject matter. Words typically have a positive, negative, or neutral connotation. Tone words help authors show whether they feel positive, negative, or neutral about what they're writing about.

Transcultural Self-Efficacy Tool: Eighty-three-item scale that assesses changes in self-efficacy for cultural knowledge, cultural practical skills, and cultural awareness.

trauma care: Care of critically injured patients.

triptych: A set of three associated artistic works intended to be appreciated together.

virtual reality cinema: Telling a story through the use of cameras and microphones that capture their surroundings in 360°-degrees. Virtual reality cinema is ideally viewed through a head-mounted display and headphones.

visceral response: Emotional response to an event.

visuomotor sensitivity: Symptom that results from the conflict between vision and vestibular inputs and often results in nausea, dizziness, vertigo, and loss of equilibrium.

whole-practice approach: Technique used in learning a new skill or task that incorporates the entire skill or task's performance at one time.

word cloud: Image that illustrates word usage by highlighting specific words using various sizes according to how often they are used in the text that is being studied.

workplace violence: Hostile or violent situation at a place of employment.

workplace violence - Type I: Perpetrated by a group or individual with criminal intent and no relationship to the employees or facility.

workplace violence - Type II: Perpetrated by a customer, client, or patient while receiving care.

workplace violence - Type III: Employee-to-employee violence, also known as horizontal violence.

workplace violence - Type IV: Perpetrated by a group or individual with a personal relationship to the victim(s), often viewed as a domestic situation.

Index

Note: Locators in *italics* represent figures and photos in the text.

Printed in the United States
by Baker & Taylor Publisher Services